ANCIENT EPISTEMOLOGY

Ancient Epistemology explores ancient accounts of the nature of knowledge and belief from the Presocratics up to the Platonists of late antiquity. Professor Gerson argues that ancient philosophers generally held a naturalistic view of knowledge as well as of belief. Hence, knowledge was not viewed as a stipulated or semantically determined type of belief; it was a real or objectively determinable achievement. In fact, its attainment was identical with the highest possible cognitive achievement, namely wisdom. It was this naturalistic view of knowledge at which the ancient sceptics took aim. In the concluding chapter, the ancient naturalistic epistemology is compared with some contemporary versions.

In this, the first book in the new series *Key Themes in Ancient Philosophy*, Lloyd P. Gerson presents a lively and accessible contribution to a vibrant area of the discipline.

LLOYD P. GERSON is Professor of Philosophy at the University of Toronto. He has published widely on ancient philosophy including most recently *Aristotle and Other Platonists* (2005) and *Knowing Persons. A Study in Plato* (2004).

KEY THEMES IN ANCIENT PHILOSOPHY

SERIES EDITORS

Catherine Osborne

Reader in Philosophy, University of East Anglia

G. R. F. Ferrari

Professor of Classics, University of California, Berkeley

Each book in this new series offers a concise and accessible treatment by a single author of a topic of major philosophical importance in the ancient Greek and Roman world. The emphasis is on a discussion of those debates of real philosophical interest, placed within their historical context. Future volumes will consider topics such as virtue, knowledge, psychology, cosmology, society, love and friendship, cause and explanation and persuasion and argument. The books are designed for use in a teaching context, where they will bridge a gap between general introductions to individual philosophers or periods and specialist monographs. They will also appeal to anyone interested in the enduring influence and significance of ancient philosophy.

ANCIENT EPISTEMOLOGY

LLOYD P. GERSON

CAMBRIDGE
UNIVERSITY PRESS

CAMBRIDGE
UNIVERSITY PRESS

University Printing House, Cambridge CB2 8BS, United Kingdom

Cambridge University Press is part of the University of Cambridge.

It furthers the University's mission by disseminating knowledge in the pursuit of
education, learning and research at the highest international levels of excellence.

www.cambridge.org
Information on this title: www.cambridge.org/9780521691895

© Lloyd P. Gerson 2009

First published 2009

A catalogue record for this publication is available from the British Library

Library of Congress Cataloguing in Publication data
Gerson, Lloyd P.
Ancient epistemology / Lloyd P. Gerson.
p.   cm. – (Key themes in ancient philosophy)
Includes bibliographical references.
ISBN 978-0-521-87139-6 (hardback) – ISBN 978-0-521-69189-5 (pbk.)
1. Knowledge, Theory of – History.
I. Title. II. Series.
BD161.G47   2008
121.09–dc22
2008040774

ISBN 978-0-521-87139-6 Hardback
ISBN 978-0-521-69189-5 Paperback

For my sons and daughters
David
Elizabeth
Jonathan
Catherine
Veronica

Contents

Preface

The present book has its genesis in my reflecting on the millennium-long dialogue in antiquity concerning the nature of knowledge. Amidst the complex ongoing disputes, there was implicit agreement that the very possibility of philosophy stood or fell on the possibility of achieving wisdom, the highest or best type of knowledge. The particular structure of the book arises from my conviction that contemporary epistemology stands to benefit from bringing ancient views about knowledge into the discussion, and that this is so despite the vast scientific gulf that separates them from us.

I am deeply grateful to G. R. F. Ferrari and Catherine Osborne for their invitation to publish my book in the series of which they are the general editors. Their gracious support and criticism of earlier drafts have been enormously helpful. I have also benefited from the advice and criticism of Panayot Butchvarov, Franco Ferrari, Francesco Fronterrota, Christopher Gill, Brad Inwood, James Lesher, David Reeve and Alan Silverman, each of whom read all or part of the work with a critical eye. The errors from which they saved me will, I am relieved to say, never see the light of day. As for those errors from which they could not save me, try though they may, I can only say that it might afford these eminent scholars and philosophers some measure of satisfaction to correct them in public now that they are in print. As always, I am most grateful to my best critic, my wife Asli Gocer.

In chapter 4, translations are adapted with slight alterations from H. G. Apostle and Lloyd P. Gerson, *Aristotle. Selected Works* 3rd edn Grinnell, IA: Peripatetic Press, 1991); in chapters 5 and 6, from Brad Inwood and Lloyd P. Gerson, *Hellenistic Philosophy. Introductory Readings* 2nd edn, Indianapolis: Hackett Publishing Co., 1997); in chapter 7, from John Dillon and Lloyd P. Gerson, *Neoplatonic Philosophy* (Indianapolis: Hackett Publishing Co., 2004). All other translations are the author's alone.

CHAPTER ONE

Ancient and modern perspectives

A book on ancient epistemology is sure to face the suspicion that its subject is only of antiquarian interest. What, after all, could ancient epistemologists teach modern practitioners in the field? The prospects for a positive answer to this question might, to the untutored eye, seem to dim further when we realise that ancient epistemology is a form of naturalism, that is, an account of cognition in general rooted in an understanding of the natural world to which humans belong and also from which they somehow stand apart as observers or thinkers. Reasonably enough, one might suppose that an antiquated view of nature would inevitably produce a view of human knowledge destined to be antiquated as well. The viability of ancient epistemology will depend on how persuaded we are that epistemology ought to be assimilated to natural science. Modern philosophers are divided over this question. It would, however, be a mistake to try to make a case for the continuing relevance of ancient epistemology by treating it as a fore-runner of contemporary *non-naturalism*, roughly, the view that epistemology is largely a matter of logic and semantics and not a legitimate branch of natural science. In fact, ancient epistemology is not accurately represented either as an obsolete or inchoate version of modern naturalism or as a version of the non-natural 'criteriological' approach. It constitutes a third approach. Broadly speaking, from the beginning of ancient Greek philosophy up to Descartes, epistemology was viewed as both naturalistic in its shape and content and as irreducible to the enterprise that we would call empirical science. What this means is a large part of the story that I aim to tell. In this chapter, I shall sketch some basic differences between the ancient naturalistic approach to knowledge and the contemporary non-natural or criteriological approach. In the last chapter, and in the light of the discussion of the theories presented in the central chapters, I shall consider the contrast between ancient and contemporary naturalism.

An obvious preliminary objection to a plan to consider ancient episte-mology in general is that it is a mistake to speak of 'ancient epistemology' as if it were one thing and as if there were not in this period a plethora of divergent theories about what knowledge is. There were indeed numerous rival candidates for the correct account of the nature of knowledge. What makes it possible to speak generally about ancient epistemology is that all the philosophers with whom I shall be concerned shared the belief that knowledge is a natural state or a 'natural kind' and that it is possible to have incorrect or correct accounts of what that is. In this they set themselves apart from all those who think that knowledge is just a belief that meets certain criteria more or less arbitrarily determined. On the latter view, only the belief itself could be a natural kind. Additionally, their shared naturalism is characterised by their view of the anomalous status of knowledge as a feature of nature. Knowledge is as real as a fever or a pregnancy, but it is not an object of scientific investigation in the same way these are.

Epistemological questions are obviously central to a tradition that holds that wisdom is the supreme goal of life and that wisdom is either identical with knowledge or the highest form of it. Many of the issues raised in contemporary epistemology have their analogues in antiquity. It is not possible in one book to treat of all these. I have chosen to focus mainly on the accounts of knowledge and belief, touching on other issues only as needed. A central problem I have had to face is that the English word 'knowledge' is not an entirely helpful translation for any single Greek word. It is usually the word that translates *epistēmē*. For reasons that will emerge, one should not assume that *epistēmē* is related to *doxa* (the word which is usually translated as 'belief'), as knowledge is related to belief, or at least as they are typically related in contemporary epistemology. For example, in English it would certainly be odd to say, 'I know p, but I don't believe it' though one might perhaps say, 'I know p, I don't *just* believe it.' By contrast, Plato and Aristotle, to take two central figures, do not assume that the things of which one has *epistēmē* are the same as the things of which one has *doxa*. To counter that if one has *doxa* of p, surely in some sense one knows or at least *can* know p as well, is to use the word 'know' in a way that does not, generally speaking, correspond to the ancient use of *epistēmē* or its verbal forms. I shall be constantly alerting the reader to the pitfalls of understanding *epistēmē* and its contrast with *doxa* in terms of knowledge and belief.

The quickest way to reveal the divergence of assumptions between ancient and modern epistemologists – especially those whom one may term 'non-naturalists' – is to begin with the so-called Standard Analysis of knowledge that constitutes the starting point in countless contemporary books on epistemology. Here we learn that, a subject S knows p if and only if (1) p is true; (2) S believes p; and (3) S is justified in her belief. Despite endless discussions about the details of this analysis – especially how to satisfy the third condition – many philosophers still maintain that this is basically the correct analysis of the concept of knowledge.

The Standard Analysis is thought by some to have been first proposed by Plato; indeed, it has been suggested that it is implicit in even earlier discussions of knowledge. I shall argue, however, that Plato rejects the basis for this analysis on the grounds that knowledge is not a sort of belief; it is not belief – even *true* belief – 'plus' something else. The Standard Analysis might be thought to make another sort of indirect appearance in the writings of the Academic Sceptic Carneades, in an analysis of what we might call rational belief. As we shall see, however, Carneades is quite clear that this is not an analysis of knowledge. The real beginning of the Standard Analysis is in the seventeenth century amidst the philosophical analysis performed in support of the new science. Philosophers were then engaged in providing the epistemological foundations for science. The above three criteria – especially the third, justificatory or evidential condition – were obviously crafted with a view to the methods of empirical science. Accordingly, the determination of exactly what counts as a *justified* belief was in the hands of those who were engaged in refining scientific methodology. As a result, the criteria for scientific knowledge came to be accepted as the criteria for knowledge *tout court*. It was not surprising that David Hume would later aver that a 'science of man', including, of course, his cognitive powers, would treat man as a part of nature, not set over against it.[1] Thus were sown the seeds of subsequent attacks on the non-natural approach to epistemology from what could properly be called 'a naturalistic perspective'.

Before we attend to some of the details of the Standard Analysis, it is worth considering what 'the' concept of knowledge is supposed to be. Some concepts like 'fun' or 'adult' divide up or categorise the world with some practical purpose in mind. My concept of fun very likely picks out activities quite different from those picked out by yours. There is no suggestion in this case that I have misused the concept because I apply it to things that you would regard as anything but fun. The concept of fun is not in this case supposed to represent a 'natural kind', something 'out there in the world' with its own distinct nature. There are other concepts – like the concepts of marriage or terrorism or courage – where there is legitimate dispute over whether or not these do or do not represent real features of the world,

---

[1] See David Hume, *A Treatise of Human Nature*, ed. D. and M. Norton (2 vols., Oxford: Clarendon Press, 2007), vol. 1, Introduction.

whether, for example, marriage is what it is regardless of what anyone thinks or whether marriage is whatever anyone happens to conceive it to be or, more likely, what conception is expressed in a law. Still other concepts – like viviparous or gold – are supposed to demarcate real features or things in the world. Although some philosophers have argued that viviparous is no different from fun or adult in this regard, there does seem to be a much bigger problem with the (false) claim that insects are mainly viviparous than there is with the claim that you can be an adult in one country but a child in another.

Returning to the concept of knowledge, it is not difficult to discern a certain ambivalence among those who concern themselves with the ins and outs of the Standard Analysis. On the one hand, if knowledge is like fun, it hardly seems to make sense to argue about the concept of knowledge. Yet, many philosophers do think that argument here is perfectly appropriate and that it might be desirable to change one's concept of knowledge. If, though, we suppose that the concept of knowledge is like the concept of gold, representing a distinct sort of natural thing in the real world, the Standard Analysis itself gives us reason for pause. That analysis tells us that knowledge is nothing but a belief that is true and justified. A belief, though, is true because of some feature of the world, not of the belief itself; and a belief is justified because of something apart from the belief itself, namely, the evidence, that is supposed to justify it. So, if what turn a belief into knowledge are factors in the world independent of the belief itself, we might properly conclude that the only real or objective thing is the belief; the knowledge is just the belief considered in terms of these other factors. There is, in short, only a conceptual difference between a belief and that same belief considered as knowledge. If knowledge is just belief considered in a certain way, should we not agree that the concept of knowledge does not aim to represent a distinct kind of thing in the world as does the concept of gold?

Here is another way of looking at the underlying issue with the concept of knowledge. Scepticism about the possibility of knowledge is either a serious position or a trivial one depending entirely on what we think knowledge is. It is serious if knowledge is something that one really might have or claim to have, and especially if that knowledge is thought to be potentially consequential. It is trivial if knowledge is merely a concept, that is, a set of rules or criteria for the application of the word 'knowledge'. For in this case, whether one knows or not depends on meeting the stated criteria. Yet since these are changeable and even as arbitrary as we like, to be sceptical about whether one knows or not in this sense is rather pointless. For if you are prepared to count me as knowing owing to the fact that I have met the criteria you have decided to employ, it is to say the least obscure what scepticism in this case is supposed to amount to. Scepticism, which is expressed in the claim, 'well, I doubt whether you meet *my* criteria', is only going to bother one who aims to meet them. This sort of scepticism is not just trivial; it is unstable and transitory. The ancients took scepticism seriously because they believed that the sceptic was challenging the claim that real knowledge was possible for human beings to possess. The 'dissolution' as opposed to the refutation of the sceptics' claim is, in fact, relevant only to knowledge viewed as a concept and not as a real feature of the world.

Let us return to the problematic third condition of the Standard Analysis, the so-called justificatory or evidential condition. Insisting that justification is a necessary condition for knowledge pretty much guarantees that knowledge is going to be viewed in a way that is fundamentally different from the way it was viewed by the Greek philosophers. It is justification – however the details of this are worked out – that is supposed to transform a mere true belief into knowledge. Compare the use of the word 'justification' in a claim of justified homicide. When such a claim is successful it does not turn the homicide into something else; similarly, a justified belief that something is the case is in reality apparently no different from a mere belief that something is the case. In insisting on this condition, there is a further consequence that sets this modern conception of knowledge apart from the ancient. Although one can certainly claim to be justified in one's own belief, such claims are typically subject to contradiction by the judgment of others. We mark the difference by distinguishing someone's claim to know or be justified from the fact that others have determined that the relevant criteria have or have not been met. Of course, 'others' here can even include oneself, as in those cases when we look back at claims we made at a previous time. In short, people are not supposed to know merely because they claim to know.

This 'third-person' or social dimension of justification means that we do not typically acknowledge that someone knows unless we can imagine him having gone through the canonical justificatory process of arriving at his belief. We do not suppose him to possess knowledge unless either we ourselves possess it or we can imagine ourselves possessing it, as in the case when someone knows some fact that we simply do not happen to know at the moment. The consequence of this is that attributions of knowledge (as opposed to mere belief) are meted out in a fairly minimalist fashion. We do not acknowledge others as possessing knowledge in those cases in which we cannot even imagine how we could arrive at the same point. Nor do we acknowledge others as possessing knowledge in those cases in which we cannot even imagine how that knowledge (as opposed to the mere fact of belief) could be communicated to us by the putative knower. The ancients maintained that 'wisdom' was the name for the most important knowledge, extremely difficult to obtain and equally difficult to communicate, but ultimately life-enhancing in some way. If, again, knowledge is something with its own nature, the possibility of being able to communicate it or even being able to justify one's claim to it is secondary to the question of whether one actually possesses it or not. It is no accident that modern epistemology offers up as paradigm cases of knowledge the most mundane beliefs. By contrast, the massive amount of attention the ancients paid to the question of how significant knowledge was acquired originated in the conviction that knowledge was worth a lifetime to acquire.

One might at this point suppose that the two different conceptions of knowledge I am here sketching really amount to two different kinds of knowledge. So, we might guess that modern epistemology is focused on empirical knowledge, whereas the ancient Greek philosophers were focused on knowledge of non-empirical matters, like the soul, God, the ultimate nature of things, and so on. This is one of those half-truths about the history of philosophy that does a lot more harm than good. For though it is undoubtedly true that some philosophers focus exclusively or primarily on empirical matters whereas others turn their attention to non-empirical matters, the error here is in the assumption that this implies that there are two (or more) kinds of knowledge. More precisely, the error is in supposing that the assumption that there are two (or more) kinds of knowledge is itself not a feature of a view of knowledge fundamentally at odds with the ancient view. The fact that there may be different sorts of things that are knowable does not entail that there are different kinds of knowledge.

In order to answer the question of whether there are different kinds of knowledge, we might begin by asking what makes something knowable. From the perspective of the Standard Analysis, the answer is that whatever can be expressed in a proposition is theoretically knowable because, as this analysis holds, knowledge is *of* propositions. If we press a little further, however, we realise that on this analysis one can only know true propositions. As a result, the question of what is knowable amounts to the question of how we can tell the difference between a true proposition, on the one hand, and a false proposition or a meaningless string of words, on the other. More specifically, it amounts to the question of the criteria for determining the truth of propositions. On this approach, we could either say that unknowable propositions are those whose truth was indeterminable or, alternatively, we could say that we will only call propositions those sentences whose truth is determinable. In the latter case, we would have stipulated that all propositions are knowable. Yet, even if this is the case, to say that knowability pertains to all and only true propositions is hardly equivalent to telling us what knowledge is.

On the ancient view, along with the rejection of justification as a necessary condition for knowledge goes the idea that knowledge is of propositions. Consequently, the question of what is knowable is not a question of identifying those propositions whose truth can be determined, but of finding out what something must be like to be knowable, that is, to be able to put us in the real state of knowing. Here what is relevant is not semantics but rather something analogous to the question of what makes something edible. Just as we have to understand what eating and digestion are in order to answer this question, we have to understand what knowing is in order to answer the question about the knowable. And understanding what it is is no more a matter of deciding what we shall call knowledge than understanding what digestion is is a matter of deciding what we shall call 'digestion'. As it will turn out in fact, on the ancient view the question what is knowledge and the question what is it to be knowable cannot be answered separately. This is in stark contrast to the view that identifies knowability with true propositions at the same time as it leaves unanswered the question of what that knowledge is that is supposed to be somehow related to propositions.

The idea of non-propositional knowledge is a strange one, especially if one starts with the assumption that knowledge is a form of belief and beliefs are 'propositional attitudes', that is, mental states related to propositions. Propositional attitudes are generally thought to contain imbedded 'that' clauses, as in 'S believes that p' or 'S knows that p'. Certainly, ancient epistemologists recognised, sometimes implicitly and sometimes explicitly, that there are such propositional attitudes. The question is whether they held that knowledge was one of these. More precisely, we need to ask whether they held that the highest type of cognition – the *ne plus ultra* of thinking, so to speak – was a propositional attitude. If we discover that they in fact did, we might want to conclude that they had no really good reason for thinking that there is more than a conceptual distinction between knowledge and belief. If, on the other hand, we discover that they generally maintained that the highest form of cognition is non-propositional, we shall need to explore the reasons for this striking view.

Speaking in general terms, in ancient Greek philosophy the fundamental division within the genus cognition (*gnōsis*) is between perceiving (*to aisthanesthai*) and thinking (*to noein*). What differentiates perceiving from thinking are the objects of each: 'perceptibles' and 'intelligibles'. Roughly, the primary objects of perception are the immediate objects of the five senses. The primary objects of thinking, intelligibles, are usually identified by analogy with the primary objects of perception. Just as we can hear sounds, so we can think these objects. Our difficulties rapidly multiply when we begin to try to say more about these intelligibles and how they are related to perceptibles.

First, that which is perceptible is not necessarily *un*intelligible. We can smell cinnamon and cloves and also understand that they smell differently. The intelligibility of the difference seems to rest on some sort of intelligible difference in the smells themselves. Second, we do not just perceive perceptibles, we can perceive or grasp that such and such is the case. This fact would seem to indicate that perception itself can be a propositional attitude. Yet the propositional attitude 'perceive that' is *derived* from and therefore distinct from 'perceive'. For 'perceive that' indicates cognitive activity that goes beyond perception strictly speaking into the realm of belief without altogether leaving the realm of perception itself. The principal point in all this for our present purposes is that the basic division between perception and thinking is the division between primary non-propositional perception that can be worked up into a propositional attitude ('perceiving that') and primary non-propositional thinking that so, it is supposed, can also be worked up into a propositional attitude. The analogy is that just as 'perceiving that' is derived somehow from primary perceiving, so 'thinking that' is derived from primary thinking. In both cases, one should not be conflated with the other.

One might contest the analogy. Thinking, it might be held, is always propositional precisely because it is always derived, whether from perception or from some other physical interaction with the world. Settling this issue will depend on whether thinking is essentially derivative in this way. If we were to answer 'no' to this question, that would not mean that we were committed to the view that all thinking is non derivative, for, clearly, belief in those cases when 'believes that' is equivalent to 'perceives that' is derived. Nevertheless, the derivative nature of the type of thinking that is belief does not entail that thinking is essentially derivative or even that belief is exclusively derived from perception analogous to the way that asphalt is a byproduct of the production of crude oil.

Even if we choose to use the word 'knowledge' for the highest or most perfect type of cognition, and even if we allow that knowledge has a real nature independent of how we stipulate that the word 'knowledge' is to be used, still we might want to insist that knowledge has to be understood 'from the bottom up', that is, as a process or state or capacity arising somehow from a biological or chemical basis. Even to countenance the possibility that what thinking essentially is cannot be understood from the bottom up is to enter a world substantially different from our own. Even though there were philosophers in antiquity – like Atomists, Stoics and Epicureans – who were in principle receptive of a 'bottom-up' approach to explanation, they operated in a milieu in which the opposite approach dominated. As a result, some, like the Stoics, were apt to make claims about knowledge difficult to reconcile with a bottom-up analysis even if they were in principle open to the reconciliation.

We might think to make short work of a view of knowledge that is in some ways the antithesis of the modern view by charging it with an insupportable attachment to folk psychology. After all, it is perhaps the case that the assumption that thinking is not analysable into natural (i.e., physical, chemical or biological) terms is just a result of the inability to imagine how cognition is really at bottom explained by nothing but that to which those terms refer. One need not be an eliminative materialist to hold that all forms of cognition should be understood, broadly speaking, in a bottom-up way. Yet Plato and Aristotle, at any rate, and all their disciples in antiquity thought that cognition could not be thus understood. I would suggest that if they were wrong in maintaining this position, it was not because they were in thrall to folk psychology, for they did in fact have serious arguments to support their view. And unless one assumes that all such arguments must beg the question in favour of folk psychology, it will, I hope, be found illuminating to examine them.

Ancient epistemology differs from modern epistemology in maintaining that knowledge is a natural state that is in essence not reducible to the subject matter of empirical science. The key word here separating the ancient from the modern view is not 'reducible' but 'essence'. As I just noted, there are many contemporary epistemologists who would resist the reduction of epistemology to biology or to physics. For the most part, however, these are philosophers who also maintain that knowledge does not have an essence because they do not think that 'knowledge' names a real thing with its own nature. What one thinks about knowledge in this regard will inevitably affect what one thinks about belief.

The move from 'S believes p' to 'S knows p' invites us to consider knowledge as a type of belief, as I have already suggested. The hypothesis that knowledge has a distinct essence invites a rejection of this move. Consider that if S knows p, it is presumably not the case that S no longer believes p. The putative knowledge is just the belief plus whatever additional conditions we think have been met, specifically, that the belief be true and that it is justified. This is just another way of saying that knowledge does not have a distinct essence. By contrast, on the hypothesis that knowledge *does* have a distinct essence, that distinctness will be manifested in some way other than by meeting conditions external to the belief itself. It may, for example, be manifested in having objects or things knowable other than propositions, which are the objects of belief. Knowledge would then seem to be the sort of thing such that it is not possible to know that which is believed and it is not possible to believe that which is known.

One may, of course, maintain that we cannot know the things we believe for different reasons. The sceptic may do so in order to cast doubt on the rationality of belief. When the sceptic does this, she depends on an argument that knowledge like, say, immortality, has a real essence but that it is unattainable by us. The non-sceptic may insist that since knowledge does not have a real essence, it is not at all unreasonable just to call 'knowledge' beliefs that are well grounded or justified. From this perspective, the sceptic's stance looks to be nothing if not captious.

The ancient approach, however, insisting on the claim that knowledge has a distinct nature, surmises that we cannot know the things we believe because the only things that are knowable are different from the objects of belief. And yet an obvious objection immediately arises. If belief has propositions as objects, surely there can be propositions whose truth conditions pertain to the things that are supposed to be knowable. So, we can know the things about which we have beliefs just because we can have beliefs about the things we know. Making good on this claim will depend on what the requirements are for 'having a belief about' something.

We have already seen that 'perceiving that' is somewhere between 'perceiving' and 'believing that'. Perhaps it is the case that one cannot have a belief about something unless one perceives it. This is, however, obviously too narrow, for we often have beliefs about things we cannot perceive, including the unperceived causes of the things we do perceive. It is precisely here that some ancient philosophers would want to distinguish a mode of cognition distinct both from belief and from knowledge. Whether *this* mode of cognition is propositional and if so, whether it can be 'about' the same objects that are knowable, is a question requiring exploration.

The different views of knowledge I have been trying to characterise divide over whether or not knowledge has a distinct essence. The ancient view, which maintains that it does, conceptualises the various types of cognition differently from the modern view. Not only is belief really distinct from knowledge, but so is that mode of cognition that does not depend on perception even if it can be 'about' the objects of knowledge. The primary division between thinking and perceiving serves to establish the two foci: perception strictly speaking, what we sometimes call 'sensation', and thinking strictly speaking, which the ancients identify as the *ne plus ultra* of cognition. Sometimes, they use for this highest or primary type of cognition a term – *epistēmē* – that we usually translate as 'knowledge'. This is Plato's considered preference. Sometimes, they used a term – *noēsis*, obviously derived from the basic term *to noein* – that we tend to translate as 'understanding' or 'intellection'. This is Aristotle's preference; it frees him to use *epistēmē* for a mode of cognition derived from the primary mode but distinct from belief (*doxa*).[2]

The hypothesis that 'knowledge' stands for a distinct real nature is, it would seem, inevitably connected with the assumption that epistemology is rooted in metaphysics. On the ancient view, thinking is of the intelligible as perception is of the perceptible. Knowledge, as the highest form of thinking, cannot be grasped apart from grasping what it is to be knowable against the background of what it is to be intelligible. If knowledge were not held to have a distinct essence, as it is usually not on the modern view, it would be much easier to maintain both that the intelligible is continuous with the perceptible and that cognition generally can be defined operationally rather than on the basis of a metaphysical position. Thus, one can approach questions about how human beings interact with their environment in the special way that is denoted by cognitional language without taking any position on how the world must be structured for it to be knowable. Detaching epistemology from metaphysics makes it all the easier to reattach it to empirical psychology or biology or physics. Deciding whether the ancient view is 'ancient' in a pejorative sense depends on how we evaluate its insistence on keeping epistemology attached to metaphysics.

It is not too difficult to see – even from the perspective of the Standard Analysis – why the ancients were at least initially inspired to insist on this attachment. Knowledge is, after all, supposed to aim at the truth. There is no knowledge of anything but the truth. On the modern view, 'true' usually names a feature of propositions and 'aiming at the truth' is aiming at a belief that is justified and is in fact true. This would perhaps have been sufficient for the ancients if meeting the justification condition guaranteed the truth. But, alas, it does not. Philosophers have mostly come to agree that one can

---

[2] The reader needs to bear in mind that the word *doxa*, here and throughout the book translated as 'belief', has a range of connotations that do not match up precisely with those of the English word 'belief'. I begin to try to clarify these in the following chapters.

be justified in one's belief without knowing, for the simple and decisive reason that the justification does not guarantee the truth of what is believed. So, we either say that there are no guarantees in life, and we do the best we can, or else we say that achieving the truth is not a matter of belief, or at least that it is not primarily a matter of belief, even if there can be beliefs that are in fact true. To say the latter is to maintain that it does make sense to aspire to a cognitive state that does come with a guarantee or at least provides a better guarantee than does any belief. This, however, in turn only makes sense against the background of a view about the way the world is or the way it must be. 'Truth' here is not a property of propositions but a name for a property of reality itself; 'attaining' the truth is not equivalent to believing a true proposition. So, arguments about knowledge depend on arguments about reality. It will perhaps surprise some to learn that the realisation of the apparent circularity in basing our account of knowledge on a strategy of first coming to know the nature of reality is not foreign to the ancients. There is in fact more than one solution to this problem on offer, though they all share, again perhaps surprisingly, a naturalistic assumption. This is, though, a naturalism that rejects the claim that the natural sciences provide the foundation for epistemology.

In light of the above brief considerations regarding the differences between ancient and modern conceptions of knowledge, one might suspect that these conceptions are simply different and therefore not comparable. Perhaps the Greek word *epistēmē* and the English word 'knowledge' have non-overlapping semantic ranges. For example, if ancient philosophers treat knowledge as non-propositional and contemporary philosophers treat knowledge as propositional, one might suppose that these philosophers are not talking about the same thing. It is certainly also true that if one philosopher takes 'knowledge' to refer to a natural kind and another one denies this, there is some danger of their talking past each other. But it seems to me a mistake to draw from these facts the conclusion that ancient and contemporary views are utterly incommensurable. The basis for the comparability of ancient and contemporary views is that all parties take knowledge to be the supreme cognitive achievement, even if, or especially if, there are disputes regarding the criteria for recognising this. One who rejects the ancient account of this achievement in favour of another account – whether that account is naturalistic or criteriological – is assuming or implying some critical engagement with the reasoning behind the former. In addition, he is offering his account as a better response to the sceptical challenges regarding the possibility of knowledge and rational belief. Here at least are two grounds for comparison.

In the next chapter, we will start with the conception of nature among the Presocratic philosophers and the rise of epistemology. I aim to show why the ancient Greek philosophers (at a time when science and philosophy were not clearly distinguished) came to hold that understanding what it meant to have knowledge of nature was a philosophical and not a scientific enterprise.

CHAPTER TWO

The origin of epistemology

Despite the fragmentary nature of the evidence regarding the thought of the Presocratics, there is little doubt that recognisably epistemological claims and questions arise practically simultaneously with philosophy itself. In this chapter, I will try to explain why epistemology was inseparable from the enterprise of philosophy as the ancient Greeks understood it. Among other results, I hope to show why the Sceptic Sextus Empiricus, some eight hundred years later, looking back on the entire history of philosophy as he knew it, was correct in seeing that an attack on the possibility of knowledge was virtually an attack on philosophy itself. As Sextus realised, philosophers supposed that they were aiming at wisdom and wisdom was a sort of knowledge. If knowledge is not possible, the quest for wisdom as traditionally conceived is vain.

Philosophy begins in ancient Greece with a simple hypothesis: nature (*phusis*) is or has an order (*kosmos*) or structure. If nature has an order or is structured, that order is intelligible. It is subject to reasoning or argument or understanding, in short, to *logos*. The idea of a *kosmos* is closely related to the idea of a universe or world. The idea that nature is a *kosmos* appears to sit closely alongside the idea that there is a single or unique order to nature. In this sense, ancient *cosmological* speculation from its inception bears the hallmark of scientific reductionism, that is, the operating assumption that multiple explanations are themselves ultimately reducible to or derived from a single explanation. Thus, the understanding of one system or phenomenon is not, ultimately, unrelated to the understanding of any other, but rather, there must be minimal or even one single law or set of law-like facts underlying it which provide the basis for explanations of the discrete data. As we shall see, the assumption that the explanation of complex *explananda* will converge on one or a few irreducibly simple *explanans* goes to the heart of ancient epistemology.

Having begun with the hypothesis that nature is or has an order, one arrives quite unsurprisingly at the conclusion that this order is not evident to us. After all, it is the opposite assumption – that nature does *not* have an order – that underlies the pre-philosophical aetiological myths, that is, the attribution to the gods of the causes of things. We need not suppose that prior to the emergence of philosophy human beings had no expectations about the regularities of nature. It is just that these regularities were, generally, attributed to divine agency. And since divine agency was imagined along the lines of human agency, it was, ultimately, inscrutable or at least multifarious. The hypothesis that nature was a *kosmos* thus gradually allied the transparency of the order of nature with its necessity. But neither the ultimate unity nor the necessity were immediately evident to anyone.

So, the hypothesis that nature was a *kosmos* presented with utter clarity the question of how the order is to be discerned. If nature has an underlying order, but appears not to have one, still it is from the appearances (*phainomena*) that the order has to be inferred. The ancient Greeks must have realised very early on that we can distinguish two senses of 'appearance': what modern philosophers have called 'epistemic' and 'non-epistemic'. Epistemic appearances are those that putatively represent or reflect reality. They are the 'face' of reality presented to us. According to this sense, we say that such-and-such appears to be the case because it actually is the case. Non-epistemic appearances are those that do not accurately represent reality. In this sense, things appear other than as they really are. If all appearances were unambiguously epistemic, a philosophy of nature would be nothing more than a catalogue of nature's bounty. So, presumably, the appearances supposed to be that from which the explanation for the order of nature could be inferred are at least in some ways non-epistemic. If, for example, things appear qualitatively diverse and complex but are in reality nothing but atoms in the void, the appearances from which we started are non-epistemic. The obvious problem is, however, how to distinguish epistemic from non-epistemic appearances.

When the task of trying to determine how things really are from possibly non-epistemic appearances is recognised, epistemological problems seem inevitably to arise. These problems all converge on the fact that if appearances are non-epistemic, we do not possess anything like an obvious way of understanding what the order of nature is. Most of the Presocratics proposed hypotheses about the material basis of nature and supposed 'transformation laws' that would show how we got to here from there. Despite some remarkable intuitive leaps made with this approach, it is obvious that the sort of theorising that this engendered was open to sceptical challenges. For no single hypothesis decisively excluded any others; no array of data demanded a unique explanation.

Perhaps the earliest of the explicit Presocratic epistemological utterances is this seemingly sceptical fragment from the Ionian philosopher Xenophanes of Colophon (*ca* 570–478 BCE),

No man knows or will ever know the clear truth (*to saphes*) about the gods and about everything I speak of; for even if one happened to succeed completely in saying what has come to pass, he nevertheless does not know it; conjecture (*dokos*) is arrayed over all things (Fr. B34, DK).[1]

Three features of this passage stand out. First, Xenophanes seems to be contrasting truth with non-epistemic appearance. Second, the use of the word 'conjecture' (*dokos*) for the non-epistemic appearance is related to the word for belief (*doxa*). A belief is in this case generated by a non-epistemic appearance. Third, Xenophanes claims that even if we speak the truth, we do not know it, thereby suggesting that in order to know the truth some one or more criteria must be met beyond the truth criterion. One might suppose that it is the justification criterion that is here being alluded to. But just as there is a difference between saying what is true and knowing that what one says is true, so there is a difference between there being a justification or evidence for what one believes and knowing what that is. Yet we might reason that knowing what the justification is (i.e., what makes it a justification) without knowing that the justification entails the truth of what one believes is not possible. For on Xenophanes' account, if this were not so, I could presumably know that I am justified in believing something without knowing that it is true. So, the idea that justification is inseparable from truth in knowledge (as opposed to belief) emerges. It is, though, not difficult to see that any putative justificatory proposition I identify is itself in the same position as the original possibly true proposition that I utter but do not know is true. An infinite regress obviously threatens.

One response to this potential problem is scepticism: we can never know that what we are saying is true even if it is. Along these lines, we may consider the even more ominous possibility that not only can I not know what I am saying is true since I cannot know the justification for saying it, but also that if I do not *know* that I am justified, I in fact have no justification at all. In short, a justification that does entail what it justifies may well be no justification at all. And if this is so, what becomes of the putative justification that distinguishes a rational belief from an irrational one? Another fragment of Xenophanes suggests that he did not follow this

[1] DK = H. Diels (ed.), *Die Fragmente der Vorsokratiker*, 6th edn, rev. W. Kranz 9th edn (Berlin: Weidman, 1960).

approach: 'the gods have not revealed all things to men from the beginning; but in time, by seeking, they will find out better' (Fr. B18, DK). Whatever exactly 'better' means here, he appears to be suggesting that some beliefs are more likely than others to be true, namely, those that result from 'seeking'.[2] As we shall see, many sceptics will be unimpressed with this solution. And yet other sceptics – the so-called Academics – will appropriate its essential idea, namely, that we can be more or less justified in our beliefs so long as we follow a suitable procedure. One condition, though, for acceptance of this approach is that we do not call even our 'best' beliefs 'knowledge'.

As already suggested in the previous chapter, it would be foolish to cavil at a decision to call one class of beliefs 'knowledge', namely, those that meet our highest standards of justification whatever these might be. This was not, I think, what lay behind the sceptical strategy of acknowledging more or less justified beliefs while at the same time denying the possibility of knowledge. Rather, this denial sprang from the recognition that the cognitional states arising from non-epistemic appearances are fundamentally different from a possible cognitional state whose object is, instead of such appearance, reality itself. Apart from the sceptical response, one can maintain that knowledge of reality is possible for human beings, in which case one embraces 'dogmatism' of some variety. Or else, one can attempt to draw reality into the ambit of what was supposed to be non-epistemic appearance, essentially by attempting to efface the distinction between non-epistemic and epistemic appearance.

The earliest and most challenging of the 'dogmatic' responses came from the Eleatics – Parmenides (late sixth to mid fifth century BCE), and his disciples Zeno (*ca* 490–?) and Melissus (fifth century) – who resisted the very idea of explaining non-epistemic appearances by an intelligible order. The issue separating the Eleatics and virtually all the other Presocratics was whether the admittedly non-epistemic appearances possessed any measure of intelligibility themselves. If they did, these might be somehow understood as effects of their intelligible causes. If we decided that they did not, this was but another way of rejecting the hypothesis that nature was a *kosmos*.

Remarkably, this approach did not amount to a reversion to the pre-philosophical aetiological myths. The Eleatics retained the idea of the intelligibility of reality without identifying reality in any way with nature. Parmenides' cryptic claim that 'it is the identical thing that can be thought and can be' (Fr. B2, DK) at once separates thought and sense-perception, denies that what is unintelligible in some sense cannot be, and asserts that

---

[2] Cf. his claim, presumably, consequent upon his enunciation of some cosmological theory, 'let these things be believed as being like (*eoikota*) the things that are real (*tois etumoisi*)' (Fr. B35, DK).

being is intelligible. No reason for this is to be found in the extant fragments, though both Plato and Aristotle will pay close attention to the claim, ultimately endorsing it in some sense. The logical passage from 'being must be thus and so in order to be intelligible' to 'being is intelligible' must pause to explain why 'being must be thus and so'. When Plato and Aristotle each finish making this stop, they find themselves leaving behind Parmenides' denial of the intelligibility of nature. That is, they arrived at conclusions about the intelligibility of being that did not entail that nature had to be unintelligible.

Parmenides' single work, a hexameter poem, survives in bits that scholars have struggled mightily to reassemble. The poem falls into two parts, the first of which explores 'the way of truth' (*alētheia*); this is followed by the second, 'the way of belief' (*doxa*). The burden of the argument is that the latter has nothing to do with the former or at least that following this way will lead you away from the truth. The way of belief, pursued by ordinary mortals, including, presumably, Parmenides' predecessors, is the way that starts out with the phenomena of nature and aims to understand their order or structure arising from the way things really are. The way of belief is thus inseparable from our sense-experience. And though Parmenides insists that this way is not the way to truth and brings no 'true conviction' (*pistis*), yet one might learn why ordinary beliefs are believable, in short, why what are in fact non-epistemic appearances are supposed to be epistemic.[3] One might wonder, though, why an explanation for the non-epistemic bent appearance of the stick in water is fundamentally different from any other sort of explanation, including those on the 'way of truth'. Evidently, Parmenides is attempting to make a somewhat deeper point, namely, that the deliverances of our senses are in principle inexplicable and that therefore, insofar as we aim to understand reality, we had better turn our backs on them. This is surely a discomforting if not exactly paradoxical result. We start out by trying to understand the order of nature – the reality behind appearances – and we end up having to turn our back on appearances altogether. This result is perhaps inevitable if we are forced to concede that all appearances are non-epistemic.[4]

---

[3] The crux of Parmenides' complaint against the beliefs of mortals regarding appearances is that they assume that appearances possess properties that being cannot in fact possess, in particular the property of changing or becoming.

[4] Parmenides' goddess, the source of his revelation of the way of truth, assures him that she will tell him how beliefs came to be believable (Fr. B1, 31–2, DK) and the 'likely arrangement of things' (*diakosmon eoikota*) (Fr. B8, 60, DK). Parmenides, perhaps quite intentionally setting himself in opposition to Xenophanes, refrains from saying that the account of the way of belief or of non-epistemic appearances is like the *truth*.

The great proponent of the strategy of attempting to efface the distinction between epistemic and non-epistemic appearances was Protagoras of Abdera (*ca* 490–421) who wrote a book provocatively titled *Truth* (*Alētheia*) that is, unfortunately, not extant. We are therefore mostly reduced to understanding his contribution to epistemology through the filter of his disciples and detractors. Sextus Empiricus (second century CE), however, tells us that the book began, 'Man is the measure (*metron*) of all things; of the things that are, that they are, and of the things that are not, that they are not' (Sextus *M* 7.60; cf. Plato, *Tht.* 161C3).[5] Sextus tells us:

Some, too, have reckoned Protagoras of Abdera in the ranks of those who eliminate the criterion (*kritērion*), since he says that all the impressions and beliefs that there are are true and that truth is among the things that are relative (*pros ti*) because everything that appears or is a belief for someone exists at once for that person (*M* 7.60).

Sextus seems to be using the word 'criterion' as synonymous with the word 'measure'. How, we may ask, is man the 'measure' if Protagoras has 'eliminated the criterion'? As Sextus has previously explained in a chapter on the various senses of 'criterion' (*M* 7.29–30), the sense in which the sceptic denies that there is a criterion is the sense in which a criterion is a means for justifying our truth claims. Protagoras, in Sextus' account, could be thought to have eliminated the criterion of truth where truth is supposed to be *non-relative* or 'absolute' (*kath' hauton*, *M* 7.64). He does this by making truth relative to the one who has the belief or the one to whom something appears.

The contrast between relative and absolute here can be understood in two ways: as the contrast between the subjective and the objective or the contrast between the relational and the non-relational. A claim regarding the existence of a relation is not necessarily a denial of its objectivity; on the contrary, it is equivalent to an assertion of it. What Protagoras might be arguing is that truth is subjective because it is relational. The only way a truth arises is by my believing it. So, water cannot be hot except in the sense that it is hot for someone, that is, one believes that it feels hot to him. It cannot be objectively hot. To argue thus is to threaten to eliminate the distinction between epistemic and non-epistemic appearances.

There were in antiquity at least two sorts of objection to this line of reasoning. Let us start with the Sceptic's own. Sextus claims that Protagoras

---

[5] Sextus has the title of this book as *Kataballontes* (*Adversative [Arguments]*), but it seems clear that this is the same book that Plato repeatedly refers to as *Truth* (cf. *Tht.* 152C, 161C, 162A, 170E; *Crat.* 386C, 391C). Diogenes Laertius (*ca* 200 CE) does not list the work among those extant at the time of writing his history of philosophy.

recognises that things appear relative to someone or other owing both to their internal capacities for appearing variously and to the internal capacities of those to whom things appear (*PH* 1.218). Sextus complains that neither of these internal capacities are themselves appearances and so Protagoras is committed to insisting on non-apparent truths, that is, objective truths about the internal capacities of things and people.

The second sort of objection is this: suppose (1) A believes, 'the water appears hot to me' and (2) B believes, 'the water appears hot to A'. It would seem that if (1) is true, what B believes in (2) is true as well. Then (2) contains an objective truth which is not equivalent to (3), B's additional subjective belief that B believes that A believes the water appears hot to him. So, one might conclude that there are at least some truths that are not subjective.

Plato in his *Theaetetus* (170D4–171C7) employs the central strategy of this argument against Protagoras. He gets his interlocutor Theodorus (representing Protagoras' position) to agree that people generally do often believe that others have false beliefs. If, for example, one were to believe that Protagoras' belief that man is the measure of what is true is false, Protagoras would either have to agree that that belief is true, in which case Protagoras' belief is false, or he would have to claim that that belief is false, in which case he would again have to acknowledge that his own belief that man is the measure of what is true is in fact false. The belief that human beings are the measure of truth is not like my subjective belief that the water is hot for me. It is like my objective belief that the water is hot for you. If this were not so, Protagoras could not maintain that his belief is objectively true whether or not anyone else believes it. If, however, he cannot maintain this, he must allow that when someone else believes that Protagoras' belief is false, his belief amounts to nothing more than the true belief for him that Protagoras' belief is false.

Protagoras' own formulation of his doctrine seems to expose him to such an objection. For he claims that a human being is not just the measure of what is, but also the measure of what is not. Immediate judgments about what I feel now seem to be different from and prior to mediate judgments about what is not the case on the basis of what I feel now. To put it crudely, I do not have immediate experiences of negation. If such mediate judgments are intelligible, I seem committed to objectivity of some sort, namely, the objective truth that something is not the case because of something else that I feel. The intelligibility of inference presumes objectivity in a way that the mere expression of a subjective state does not.

The connection between cognition and objectivity is made in the passage above from which Plato's argument is summarised. To suppose that someone knows something that someone else does not, or that someone is a more reliable judge than someone else is to suppose a comparison whose criterion is reality itself. According to the testimony of Sextus, Protagoras does not avail himself of the option of claiming that epistemic and non-epistemic appearances can be conflated by the simple expedient of denying that we have any access to objective reality. One does not know how he would respond to the implication of Plato's argument that belief is not the sort of thing about which one could sensibly say that it cannot be false. To maintain that there cannot be false beliefs is to maintain that if someone believes p, it is necessarily the case that p is true. It is, in effect, to maintain that there is no real difference between belief and knowledge. It seems pointless, though, to insist on the infallibility of belief precisely because we believe what we do *because* we believe that what we believe is true and we divest ourselves immediately and involuntarily of a belief when we come to believe that that belief is false.

The idea of belief is rooted in the distinction between epistemic and non-epistemic appearances. Yet, just as epistemic and non-epistemic appearances may be indistinguishable 'from the inside', so the truth or falsity of one's own beliefs may be indeterminable, based on the awareness one has of these. If this were not so, given the fact that we do divest ourselves of false beliefs as soon as we believe them to be false, we could not have any beliefs that are in fact false. Much to our misfortune, this is manifestly not the case. Whether the ancient view of philosophy is considered to be a quest for the elimination of all false beliefs or for the achievement of something other than belief, namely, knowledge, it is difficult to see how the Protagorean position, shorn of its concession that some knowledge of the 'non-evident' is possible, is not a prelude to the abandonment of the entire philosophical project. Plato's pejorative term 'sophist' for Protagoras and those of his ilk, indicates the battle-line. A sophist (*sophistēs*) is a counterfeit of a wise person (*sophos*), one who aims to know.

In antiquity, the epistemological views of Democritus (*ca* 460–350) were generally associated with those of Protagoras. This was evidently not simply because they were both from Abdera. Again, according to Sextus' testimony, Democritus criticised Protagoras on grounds similar to those of Plato (Sextus, *M* 7.389–90). The extant fragments of his vast output display the full array of epistemological issues gradually being revealed throughout the period. Perhaps the most famous fragment combines the basic statement of the Atomists' position with its primary epistemological consequences:

By convention (*nomos*) sweet and by convention bitter, by convention hot, by convention cold, by convention colour; but in reality (*eteē*) atoms and void (Sextus, *M* 7.135 = Fr. B9 DK/D16 Taylor).

Generally, when Presocratic philosophers contrast convention and reality, the usual term for the latter is 'nature' (*phusis*). The term *eteē* is evidently Democritus' coinage. 'Convention' seems here to represent what I have termed non-epistemic appearance, though the term can also indicate that which is stipulated as such-and-such rather than what appears to be such-and-such.[6] The latter is employed without any implicit assumption about how by contrast things are in reality. For example, it would be exceedingly odd to say that the convention of driving on the right side of the road in North America and on the left side in Britain is in contrast to the way things really are. Democritus' claim, however, pretty clearly insists on the contrast between the way things appear to us and the way they really are.[7] It may be that his reluctance to use the word 'nature' for the latter rests upon his conviction that the way things really are is radically different from the referent of the word 'nature' in the vocabulary of his times. In any case, Democritus seems to be making an anti-Protagorean claim in suggesting that the way things appear to each of us ('by convention') is *not* the way they really are. Protagoras, as we have already seen, appears to Plato and Aristotle at least to commit himself to non-evident truths that are supposed somehow to explain the epistemic appearances. Is Democritus just being more consistent than Protagoras in inferring that objective reality – atoms in motion in the void – guarantees that all appearances will be non-epistemic?

One would probably conclude so, were it not for Aristotle's repeated insistence that Democritus maintained that all appearances are true, that is, the Protagorean position.[8] Perhaps we were too quick to assume that 'sweet by convention' indicates non-epistemic appearance. After all, it might well both be the case that what is truly atoms and void does truly appear sweet to one and bitter to another *and* that people mistakenly suppose that the way things appear to us is the way they truly are. According to this suggestion, non-epistemic appearances get promoted to the equivalent of epistemic appearances so long as they do not take themselves to be indistinguishable from objective reality. Speaking on behalf of this Pyrrhic victory of non-epistemic appearances, another fragment of Democritus has the senses say

---

[6] *Nomos* comes from the verb *nomizein*, 'to practice', 'to believe in', 'to acknowledge', 'to consider'. A convention is an objectified belief. There is often little difference in the ancient texts between 'it appears to me so' and 'I believe it so.'

[7] Cf. what is perhaps a similar thought in Heraclitus (late sixth to fifth century), Fr. B123 DK, 'Nature loves to hide itself'.

[8] See *GC* 1.2.315a34–b2, 1.2.315b6–15; *Met.* 4.5.1009b7–17. Cf. John Philoponus, *Commentary on Aristotle's De Anima* 71.19–34 Hayduck; Alexander of Aphrodisias, *Commentary on Aristotle's Metaphysics* 271.38–272.2 Hayduck.

to the mind, 'Wretched mind, you get your evidence from us, and yet you overthrow us? The overthrow is a fall for you' (Galen, *On Medical Experience* 15.7 = B125 DK/D23 Taylor). In other words, even if all appearances are true, if they are not strictly epistemic, in what sense can they be said to be evidence for that which is non-evident? If, on the other hand, they are evidence, what grounds do they provide for a theory that has reality constructed in a way other than the way it appears?

It will be noticed that we have come round to the potential problems with the Standard Analysis by means of the employment of the distinction between epistemic and non-epistemic appearances. In particular, if the truth condition and the justificatory condition are allowed to be independently met, it is difficult on the one hand to see what justification amounts to and, on the other, why we should suppose that the way things appear to us is really the way they are. To insist that all appearances are true sounds like a stipulation that we are justified in believing what we do owing to our appearances. Yet, to insist as well on the *contrast* between 'convention' and 'reality' is to take back what was given.

Sextus argues that both Democritus and Plato held that only intelligibles are real and that therefore they 'rejected the senses', which in the context of this passage means that they rejected them as evidence for their views about intelligibles (Sextus, *M* 8.6ff.; 56). This rejection of the senses as evidence, however, does not amount to the Eleatic claim that that of which we have belief has no part in the truth. It does, though, suggest that the mode of cognition appropriate for reality is different from the mode of cognition appropriate for appearances. This difference is an explicit theme in Plato as we shall see, as it is not in Democritus, so far as we know. If the end point of our investigation is knowledge of reality, the beliefs that arises from our sense-perceptions are not evidence for our knowledge claims. Further, if beliefs are only the consequence of sense-perception, if reality is non-sensible or intelligible, cognition of reality will not be belief. If reality is not intelligible, the sceptic prevails.

This is an odd conclusion. Did not Democritus believe that in reality there was nothing but atoms and void? Our inclination to answer this question 'of course he did' indicates the pull of the Standard Analysis, according to which knowledge is belief, albeit the ideal sort. To the extent that we are willing to see this analysis as other than inevitable, we may perhaps more readily appreciate Democritus' distinction between two forms of 'judgment' (*gnōmē*), one genuine and one 'bastard' (Sextus, *M* 7.139 = B11 DK/D22 Taylor). The latter is concerned with the deliverances of sense-perception; the former is, by contrast, 'separate from this' (*apokekrimenē*). Belief or judgment about sense-perceptions can no more be transformed into knowledge than can a bastard be transformed into a genuine offspring.

As Sextus goes on to tell us, what Democritus did in distinguishing knowledge from belief is to deny that the latter is 'inerrant' (*aplanes*). We have, though, already been informed that Democritus maintained that 'all appearances are true'. So, if I claim that the honey is sweet to me, in what sense am I 'errant' in that claim? Assuming that Sextus is correctly representing Democritus' view, inerrancy is evidently connected to cognition of reality as opposed to cognition of appearances. Even a true belief is errant in this sense if it is not 'about' reality. If, though, a true belief is about reality, for example, if the belief is that there is nothing in reality besides atoms and the void, what is the difference between true belief and knowledge? Presumably, the answer to this question – along the lines of the Standard Analysis – is that true belief becomes knowledge when evidence or sufficient evidence or a justificatory story is added to it. It is just that the deliverances of the senses cannot count as evidence. Hence, the 'rebuke' of the mind by the senses. If, however, the senses cannot provide evidence for our beliefs about the non-evident, it is entirely obscure what sort of evidence is available. Yet, if there is no evidence, and though we will agree that there is a difference between a true belief and a false belief in regard to reality, how are we supposed to tell the difference? How is one belief supposed to earn the label 'inerrant' thereby making it knowledge?

Democritus' assertion that knowledge is of intelligible reality and is separate from belief undermines the Standard Analysis because on that analysis, knowledge is a type of belief and there must be justifying evidence for the knowledge. We believe the evidence when and only when it appears to us as evidence, that is, it appears to us to be true. If, however, knowledge is not a type of belief, and belief in the evidence is belief in appearances, there is no way to distinguish knowledge from belief – or even true belief – merely by attributing evidence to the former. From a Democritean perspective, the only way to stay within the confines of the Standard Analysis is to reject the identification of reality with what is intelligible as opposed to what is sensible. This would amount to the denial of the distinction between epistemic and non-epistemic appearances. Such a denial, as we have already seen, seems to self-destruct in its inability to distinguish between true and false belief.

If this interpretation is correct, we are left with the puzzle as to why Democritus is supposed to have praised the words of his senior contemporary Anaxagoras of Clazomenae (*ca* 500–428), who is reported to have argued that appearances constitute a 'glimpse of the non-evident' even though things in reality are different from the way they appear (Sextus, *M* 7.140). He evidently maintained this despite his acknowledgment that the senses are 'weak'. Accordingly, he held that reason (*logos*) alone is the criterion (Sextus, *M* 7.90). Perhaps Anaxagoras means to maintain something like this: the evidence for the non-evident is constituted not by sense-perception itself, but by a critical reflection on sense-perception. This critical reflection or analysis would be the refined basis for our knowledge of reality. It is not too difficult to see why Democritus in a general way might have commended this approach. Thus construed, epistemic appearances would be refined non-epistemic appearances. If this is so, there is a natural constraint on the construction of reality. Reality, or what is intelligible, is not in principle unavailable to the senses; rather, it is simply in fact beyond the range of the senses. Thus, the atoms (and, indeed, the void) and Anaxagoras' notorious *homoiomereiai* or 'seeds' (infinitesimally small portions of every natural substance) are intelligible in the sense that we can understand that what we actually see must be explained by something like what these real things are thought to be. The non-evident here is just what is non-evident to us with our limited sense powers.

Aristotle seems to think that this identification of the intelligible with the theoretically sensible though practically non-sensible is the mistake that Democritus and most of his other predecessors habitually made:

Generally speaking, it is owing to supposing that understanding (*phronēsis*) is sense-perception, and that this is a physical alteration, that they [Democritus and others] say that what appears to our senses is necessarily true (*Met.* 4.5.1009 b12–13; cf. *DA* 3.3.427a17–29).

Aristotle's complaint is not based on the assumption that reality (as opposed to appearances) must be non-sensible in principle. It is based on the assumption – one which we shall explore in chapter 4 – that the mode of cognition related to sensibles is fundamentally different from the mode of cognition that constitutes the understanding of sensibles or of anything else. Aristotle (following Plato) will argue that it is not possible to understand what we sense, though it is possible to understand the intelligible structure of what we sense. To adduce theoretically sensible, albeit practically non-sensible, things as constituting the explanations for the order in nature is to abandon the possibility of explanation or understanding altogether.

With Aristotle's criticism of Democritus and Anaxagoras and others, we return to the epistemological problems underlying the enterprise of philosophy as the Presocratics conceived of it. If philosophy aims at understanding the order underlying nature, we need to account for appearances that can help us explain that order and appearances that cannot. This accounting will not be itself another appearance; it will require a mode of cognition quite different from the one that exclaims, 'I am appeared to thus and so.' Yet, if we are going to understand that which appears to us and the difference between epistemic and non-epistemic appearances, what we understand and what appears to us must somehow be related. The exploration of *this* relation is ineluctably a task for metaphysics.

CHAPTER THREE

Plato

I INTRODUCTION

In Plato's dialogues and according to Aristotle's testimony regarding his philosophical development, Plato's engagement with his predecessors' thinking about epistemological and metaphysical issues is nothing less than pervasive. At virtually every turn, we see him wrestling with the distinction between knowledge and belief, appearance and reality, epistemic and non-epistemic appearances and so on. He no doubt started with the universal Presocratic assumptions that knowledge is a real, not merely notional achievement, that it is more than merely belief, and that its desirability is manifest. As we shall see, however, he is prepared to scrutinise these assumptions from various points of view. His conclusions about the nature of knowledge are inseparable from his conclusions about what is knowable. Plato's successors in antiquity, despite revisiting the storehouse of Presocratic wisdom, are constantly grappling with these conclusions.[1]

The value of knowledge over belief underlies the so-called early or Socratic dialogues in a straightforward way. Socrates' interlocutors, such as the preternaturally obtuse Euthyphro, typically believe that they know what a pious or just or temperate deed or person is. Euthyphro is confident that in prosecuting his father for the negligent homicide of a slave, he is engaging in a pious action. Socrates seems to assume that if one does not know what piety is, one is hardly in a position to persist in this confidence.[2]

---

[1] I am going to assume without argument that the views expressed generally by Socrates in the dialogues are Plato's own. There is a very long and contentious debate in the scholarly literature about this assumption. I believe this assumption is warranted, but it is worth bearing in mind that Plato the author does distance himself from the words of the speakers in his dialogues. I shall below suggest a reason for Plato doing this based upon his account of knowledge or, if one insists, based upon the account of knowledge found in the dialogues.

[2] Cf. *Eu.* 6E3–6: 'Teach me what this self-identical character (*idea*) is so that by looking to it and using it as a paradigm I can say that if what you or someone else does is something of this sort, it is pious, but if not, I can say it is not.'

Conversely, if one does possess this knowledge, one is in a powerful, if not invincible, position to acquire true beliefs about putative cases of piety. The point is easily generalised. Unless we know what some nature or essence is, we are in no position to be confident that our belief that *this* is or has an instance of it. A belief in which we had *no* reason to be confident, would hardly be one that is sustainable, given that we maintain our beliefs because we think they are true.

Let us for the moment leave unexamined the further assumption that there really are such essences as piety or temperance or justice. If, though, we do go along with this assumption for the time being, Socrates' point seems to be a fair one. And yet here is where our problems really begin. One might want to insist that knowing piety is nothing more than knowing how to apply the word 'piety'. This 'know how' amounts to having a concept of piety, that is, having internalised a rule or rules for the application of the word. So, Euthyphro might argue, he knows perfectly well what piety is: it is, for example, what he is presently doing in prosecuting his father. Socrates' ready reply to this gambit, namely, that we could not know that *this* is an example of piety unless we know what piety is, is not obviously effective. For, we might ask, how else could one know what piety is but by learning how to use the word or apply the concept? To put the question in epistemological terms, why is knowing what piety is something different from having true beliefs about what things are called 'pious'? Reflecting on this question takes us back to the assumption we left unquestioned. Knowing what piety is is assumed to be something different from knowing how to use the word 'piety'. Yet even if we grant this, we might well still wonder why knowing piety is supposed to be something different from having beliefs about putative instances of it.

One obvious way of responding to this puzzlement without allowing that knowing piety is something quite apart from having beliefs about pious deeds is to take refuge in the so-called Standard Analysis (see chapter 1). So, we might suppose that knowing piety is nothing other than having true justified beliefs about things having the property of being pious. Euthyphro himself is completely unable to provide such justification, but that is neither here nor there. The fact that one might reasonably construe the knowledge of piety in this way, however, might seem sufficient to undercut the claim that knowing piety is fundamentally different from having true beliefs about pious things.

In Plato's dialogue *Meno* (97Aff.; cf. 85C–D), there is a passage that could be taken to endorse this approach. In this passage, Socrates distinguishes between one who knows the road to Larissa because he has actually travelled it and one who merely possesses true belief about the road. As he goes on to claim (98A), what differentiates the former from the latter is that a knower has 'bound' his belief with a 'figuring out of the explanation' (*aitias logismos*). When and only when this binding has occurred, the stabilisation of wavering belief (even a true one) will be realised. There are two principal problems in this passage. First, it is not clear what 'figuring out the explanation' has to do with the personal acquaintance that the traveller has with the road, as opposed to the one who merely truly believes what the road to take is. Second, it is not clear what this explanation has to do with 'recollection' (*anamnēsis*), with which it is identified.

The first problem has typically elicited the response that one who knows the road, that is, one who has travelled it, is in a position to explain why, say, taking one path will eventually lead to Larissa, whereas taking another will not. Even if this is approximately correct, the ability to give such an explanation is a *result* of the supposed knowledge, not the knowledge itself. We can see the importance of this point if we consider that whether or not someone can give the explanation or cause of something's being the case, there is presumably one to be had. So, the fact that there is an explanation or cause is beside the point; what is relevant is that one knows that it is the right one. Presumably, the true belief that the explanation is the right one would not be enough, since we were supposing that the way one is related to the explanation is what differentiated knowledge from true belief.[3] One who binds the true belief by figuring out the explanation is a knower. She understands why the true belief is true. In Platonic terms, the explanation for the truth of a true belief is to be found in the nature or essence (*ousia*) owing to which something is correctly said to be or to possess an instance of that essence.

The puzzle about the identification of recollection with binding of the true belief by figuring out the explanation is solved, at least in part, if we suppose that the knowledge of the essence is here not simply the acquaintance with it, but the acquaintance with it as the source of the explanation.

---

[3] A similar issue surrounds all of Socrates' requests to his interlocutors to give accounts (*logoi*) of those entities supposedly responsible for things being correctly said to have certain properties, like piety, justice and so on. Knowing what piety is must be distinct from the ability to give an account of piety, even if one who knows what piety is uniquely able to give that account. If this were not so, one who is able to give a true account could transmit it to someone else as easily as he could transmit any other bits of information. This is not possible, since no one who does not already know that of which the account is true is in a position to know the account to be true. And yet, as the *Meno* passage tells us, true belief is as good as knowledge for practical purposes. One who, for whatever reason, unknowingly applied the account given by one who knows would always arrive at a true belief about questionable cases. So, if knowledge is supposed to be really different from and superior to true belief, knowledge is neither the ability to give an account nor even the ability to apply it.

One who recollects can 'see' why a true belief is true. I shall return to this point in the next section.

On the one hand, the tendency to identify what is known with what is truly believed is natural if, as in the example of the road to Larissa, the knowledge or belief could be expressed in a single true proposition. On the other hand, the doctrine of recollection introduced in *Meno* (and developed further in *Phaedo*) does not assume that what we knew prior to the act of recollecting is identical to what it is we aim to have a true belief about, even if what we recollect does explain why our belief is true. Some contemporary scholars have claimed that it is a fallacy for Socrates to assume that knowing what F is is necessary for having confidence in one's beliefs about instances of F. It would indeed seem so if the knowledge of F had as its 'content' the identical proposition that one had when one had a true belief about an instance of F. That which some scholars take to be a fallacy, Plato apparently took to be a paradox resolvable by the doctrine of recollection. So, 'having' the explanation for the truth of a true belief can be entailed by having knowledge without that knowledge being of what the true belief is true of.[4] Nor does it follow that if the true belief is justified on the basis of the knowledge, then the justified true belief is itself knowledge.

2 REPUBLIC

In *Republic* Book Five, Plato provides his most sustained argument for the conclusion that knowledge and belief have mutually exclusive objects.[5] He does this in the context of his discussion of philosopher-kings and why their rule is necessary for the establishment of the ideal state. This discussion of these philosopher-kings is carried through to the end of Book Six, where Socrates introduces the Idea of the Good, and the analogy of the Divided Line. At the beginning of Book Seven, he adds the famous allegory of the

---

[4] *Meno* 98A5–6 says: 'when they [true beliefs] are tied down, first they will become pieces of knowledge (*epistēmai*); next, they will become stable'. There are several things that are unclear in this line, especially what a 'piece of knowledge' is and why stability follows upon the conversion of a true belief into a piece of knowledge. The line leaves open the possibility that one who has knowledge through recollection is in a different position with respect to his true belief from one who does not have the same knowledge is with respect to his true belief. If this is the case, it does not follow that the knowledge of the former is of the same object as his true belief.

[5] The argument is made in three stages: (A) 476A9–D6; (B) 476D7–478E5; (C) 478E7–480A13. In (A), Plato seeks to distinguish lovers of sights and sounds from philosophers by the objects of their love; in (B), he tries to establish the difference between the modes of cognition belonging to each, belief and knowledge; in (C), he seeks to explain in greater detail the sorts of objects distinguished in (A).

Cave.[6] The rest of this book is taken up with the education of the philosopher-kings. The characterisation of the philosopher (and his counterfeits) is thus the fulcrum of the entire work, for it is he alone who is capable both of transforming the state and of the true happiness that coincides with the perfectly just life. The distinction between the philosopher and his counterfeits rests upon the distinction between knowledge and belief. In the pursuit of these is the *métier* of each to be found. This does not of course mean that the way that the Standard Analysis distinguishes knowledge and belief cannot be endorsed by Plato. It does, though, strongly suggest that the distinction between a philosopher and these counterfeits – 'lovers of sights and sounds' – is going to be a deep one, not plausibly characterised as one of degree or of relative success in engaging in the identical endeavour.

In the first stage of the argument for the distinction between philosophers and lovers of sights and sounds (A), it is simply asserted without argument that whereas the latter are concerned with beautiful sights and sounds, the former are concerned with Beauty itself. The counterfeits believe in (*nomizein*) beautiful things but not in Beauty itself. They identify beautiful things, which are in fact merely likenesses of Beauty, with Beauty itself. Philosophers, believing in Beauty itself, are able to distinguish it from its participants or instances. Evidently, 'Beauty' is here a stand-in for the entire intelligible realm since it seems highly doubtful that Plato means to make the preserve of the philosopher a single Form only. After all, it is not as if the lovers of sights and sounds can be plausibly supposed to reject a Form of Beauty, but affirm the existence of a Form of, say, Justice.

This passage has been taken to imply that if philosophers can believe in the Form of Beauty, they can have beliefs about this Form. And since what they aim to do is have knowledge about the Forms, it follows straightforwardly that they can have beliefs and knowledge about the same object. If this is so, we might be encouraged to think that just as there can be both belief and knowledge about Forms, so there can be belief and knowledge about the things that primarily concern the lovers of sights and sounds.

The evidence in stage (B), however, contradicts this line of reasoning. The argument contends that knowledge and belief have different objects: knowledge has 'that which is completely' and belief has 'that which is and is not', midway between the first and 'that which is not' (477A6–7). We do not get further information about how to understand the vague expressions 'that which is' and 'that which is not' until stage (C). Yet, even before this, we get a

---

[6] The Idea of the Good (504B–509C); the Divided Line (509C–511E); the Cave (514A–521D).

claim that knowledge and belief are not identical powers (*dunameis*) because knowledge is inerrant (*anamartēton*), while belief is not (477E6–7).[7]

We might express the inerrancy of knowledge in this way. If S knows p, p; by contrast, if S believes p, there is no entailment of p. That is, there is nothing about the nature of the belief, even from S's point of view, that indicates whether p is true or not. Even if S believes p with all his might, this does not guarantee that p is true. By contrast, if S knows p, and p therefore follows, there must be some property of the 'power' of knowledge itself that distinguishes it from belief apart from the truth of what is believed or known. And yet we would not find it odd to hear someone say, 'I cannot tell whether I know p or I just believe it.' This application of the ordinary words 'knowledge' and 'belief' should alert us that Plato is assigning a technical meaning to the word *epistēmē*. The claim that knowledge, as opposed to belief, is inerrant is a crucial feature of that technical meaning.

The inerrancy of knowledge evidently has something to do with the fact that its object is 'that which is completely'. In stage (C), the object is identified with Forms, like the Form of Beauty (479E1–5). By contrast, lovers of sights and sounds have as objects the many beautiful things that also appear to be ugly (479A5–B7). There is no suggestion here at all that these beliefs cannot be true, that is, that one cannot in regard to a beautiful thing believe truly that it is beautiful. What is wrong with the belief is that nothing that appears to the believer to be beautiful does not also or cannot also appear to be ugly. One way to deal with such awkward situations is, as we have seen in the last chapter, to say, following Democritus, 'beautiful to me, ugly to you, in itself neither beautiful nor ugly'. This, however, is most definitely not Plato's way. He argues in general that if something is correctly called 'f', this is because Fness exists and the thing partakes in it.[8] Unlike Democritus, Plato does not have to explain how that which is not really so can appear so; he has to explain how that which is in fact beautiful can also appear ugly.

A belief for Plato is derived from an appearance and appearances are, primarily, sensible. The belief that Helen is beautiful is derived from a sense-experience of Helen. The belief itself is the internal application of the word 'beautiful' to Helen based upon rules for the application of terms

---

[7] This claim might be taken to suggest that the fundamental contrast here is not knowledge vs. belief, but true belief vs. false belief; after all, true beliefs are always true and in that sense they are never errant. To proceed in this way depends on assuming that although lovers of sights and sounds aim for true belief, they fail, whereas philosophers succeed. But it is belief itself (not true or false belief) that is the power distinguished from knowledge in this passage. There is nothing to suggest that true belief is a power distinct from false belief.

[8] Cf. *Eu.* 6D10–11; *Phd.* 100D–E; *Hip. Maj.* 287C on the instrumentality causality of the Forms.

previously acquired. The rules could only be rules for correlating certain sense-experiences with the application of the term. Thus, a belief is rooted in sense-experience. But to sense a shape or colour is not, according to Plato, to sense anything that is exclusively related to one Form rather than another, in this case, a Form of Beauty. That shape or colour could just as well be the basis of a belief that Helen is ugly. This is not just a point about relative properties. Any belief about any sensible thing has to be based on sense-perception of properties the account of which must in principle be different from the account of the Form in which the thing is supposed to partake. How could it be otherwise, since Forms are non-sensible? The account of Helen's beauty is not just different from the account of the Form of Beauty; it is an account whose elements (shapes, colours, etc.) also belong to the account of ugliness.

The claim that sensibles or the 'many beauties' careen around between being and non-being or 'real reality' and 'nothing' is based on the prior claim that essence (*ousia*) by itself (*kath' hauto*) is distinct from whatever partakes in essence by means of the sensible properties that constitute it. For instance, something partakes of the Form of Largeness by being constituted of a certain amount of material. Because of this, sensibles are not 'that which is completely'; because they do partake in essences, they are not nothing either. As per stage (B), knowledge has that which is completely as its objects; belief has 'that which both is and is not at the same time'.[9] The inerrancy of knowledge is then it seems related to the fact that, unlike the objects of belief, the objects of knowledge are non-sensible. There is something about these non-sensible objects that makes them knowable, that is, makes them apt for a mode of cognition different from belief. This mode of cognition is essentially inerrant. Knowledge is, for example, of the essence of Beauty which accounts for things being beautiful or not and for the possibility of the *true* (and false) beliefs that they are so.

The triptych consisting of the Sun, the Divided Line and the Cave is, minimally, supposed to provide an elaboration of the basic distinction between the lovers of sights and sounds and philosophers. Perhaps most startlingly, the Idea of the Good, analogous to the sun in our sensible world, has attributed to it an extraordinary role:

Therefore, you should say that not only do the objects of cognition owe their being cognised (*gignōskesthai*) to the Good, but their existence (*to einai*) and essence

---

[9] The word *hama* ('at the same time') (478D5) makes it clear that 'that which both is and is not' cannot indicate a proposition that can be true or false at different times. Nor can the phrase be plausibly taken to indicate a class of propositions.

(*ousia*) are present to them owing to it, although the Good is not essence, but something above essence, exceeding it in rank and power (509B5–9).

Whatever else we are to make of this famous text, an account of Plato's epistemology cannot hope to ignore it. A host of questions immediately comes to the fore, perhaps the principal one of which is why knowable things need a cause or explanation for their knowability? Anticipating a bit, the Good turns up again in the Divided Line, where it is by grasping (*hapsamenos*) this first principle of everything as cause of the knowability, and the existence, and essence of the knowable that one is able to achieve the highest type of cognition, knowledge (511B6).

In the passage differentiating philosophers and lovers of sights and sounds, Plato speaks broadly of belief and knowledge as distinct powers. When we get to the Divided Line (509D–511E), he implies that there are two modes of *epistēmē* or knowledge, the primary type of which is intellection (*noēsis*) and the secondary type understanding or thought (*dianoia*).[10] However, Plato will later specify that the primary mode of cognition alone is to be called *epistēmē* and that both primary and secondary modes together are to be called *noēsis* (533E4–534A2).[11] I am henceforth going to follow Plato's clarification and use 'knowledge' only for that primary mode of cognition. Regarding the fundamental distinction between knowledge and belief, the question is now whether inerrancy is a property only of the primary mode of cognition or whether it is a property of the secondary mode as well. Since understanding is now taken to be neither belief nor knowledge, we cannot be sure if its having intelligible objects like knowledge makes it more like knowledge than belief or its not being knowledge makes it more like belief than knowledge. If what makes knowledge inerrant is that it has 'what is completely' as its object, this would presumably also be

---

[10] The translation is, I am afraid, not entirely adequate. The word *dianoia* covers both the thought process that occurs on the way to a result, and the result itself, namely, understanding. Both senses need to be kept in mind. The word seems to imply discursiveness (the prefix *dia* implies some sort of connectedness or relation) in contrast to the word *noēsis*, which indicates a direct or unmediated type of cognition.

[11] See below for discussion of *Tim.* 51D3–E6 where this new usage seems to be confirmed. Cf. Plato's *Seventh Letter* (342B–E), which might count as further evidence of terminological flexibility. I accept the authenticity of this letter, though many scholars do not. I do not believe, however, that this obscure passage can be taken to indicate a change in Plato's thinking about epistemological matters from what we find in *Republic*. The primary mode of cognition, which is in the letter called *nous* (and which may or may not be used synonymously with *epistēmē*) is said (510D1–3) to be the 'closest' in nature to the intelligible object, the Form. The 'sameness' of intellect and Form is for Plato a fundamental condition for the possibility of knowledge. Among other things, this fact tells us something about the mental state that knowledge must be. If knowledge were a representational state, there is no apparent reason why things that are not the same as intelligible objects could not have knowledge.

true of understanding; if, alternatively, understanding is like belief in that it is at least mediated by propositions, it would be no less 'errant' than belief. What happens, for example, if you think you have understanding and you are mistaken? Do you then merely have (false) belief? And in that case, do you have a belief about the intelligible world, something that the distinction between philosophers and lovers of sights and sounds seems to reject?

The fundamental contrast made between knowledge and understanding or thought in the Divided Line is this. Understanding hypothesises entities like odd and even, various types of figures and angles and seeks to derive conclusions about these. It is noteworthy that Plato here uses only mathematical examples. This is a point to which we shall return. These seekers after understanding are not interested in the visible shapes or figures or numbers they draw in their proofs, but about the square or the diagonal itself, for example. One might say they think about the visual images, but they are after understanding of the intelligible mathematical objects (510E–511A).[12] By contrast, seekers after knowledge use the hypotheses of the others as starting-points for an ascent to a first unhypothetical principle, the Good (511B–C). And just as there is a distinction between the practice of mathematicians and the understanding they seek, so there is a distinction between the practice of philosophers, called 'dialectic', and the knowledge they seek. It is only when the first principle is grasped that knowledge is attainable. This claim coheres exactly with the previous one that it is the Idea of the Good that provides knowability to Forms.

A host of questions and problems arise immediately from this account, only some of which can be treated here. What differentiates the knowledge of the Form of Square, apparently possible only when seen in relation to the Good, from the understanding of the 'square itself' that the mathematician seeks? How does the interposition of understanding between knowledge and belief shed any light on this latter distinction? Finally, why is the grasp of the Good necessary for knowing Forms themselves?

Let us start with the first question the answer to which turns on a narrow point. Are the 'square itself' and the 'diagonal itself' (510D8–9) the same as the Form of Square and the Form of Diagonal? It might appear so at first reading, but the text tells us that after going through their proof, the mathematicians arrive at agreement about their conclusions (510D1–3). This agreement presumably amounts to collective understanding of some properties of, say, the square and the diagonal as expressed in theorems. But it is not knowledge (cf. 533C3–5). So, we might speculate that knowledge is

---

[12] Hence the studied ambiguity of the word *dianoia*.

of the Forms of the Square and of the Diagonal, which is not possible
without connecting these somehow with the Good, and understanding is of
their properties. On this reading, when mathematicians hypothesise definitions of the square and the diagonal for use in their demonstrations, they
do not have knowledge. They do not have knowledge of the proposition 'a
square is an equilateral rectangle', though this is true, and understanding
that it is true is the basis for the understanding of the properties of a square.

The reason understanding of the square itself is not knowledge of the
Form of the Square is not likely to be that for knowledge one would have to
analyse the definition of the square into its components, 'equilateral' and
'rectangle' and then analyse these into their components, 'equal' and 'angle'
and 'right', etc. For the mathematician also hypothesises things like 'odd'
and 'even' which themselves are not analysable. Further, if we could reach
ultimate definitions of the 'elements' of geometrical figures, there seems to
be no reason why the cognition of these would not count as understanding,
too. That is, the difference between understanding and knowledge, insisted
upon by Plato, would be effaced. It seems rather to be the case that he takes
understanding and knowledge to be fundamentally different mental states,
not a single mental state with more or less simple conceptual objects. So, I
suggest that understanding the square itself, that is, understanding some of
its properties, is not equivalent to having knowledge of the Form of the
Square, something which is only possible when the Good is reached.

In order to answer our second question, it is necessary to say something
further about understanding. To understand a mathematical proposition or
formula is to cognise the identities behind samenesses we perceive. We
understand that things that are numerically many are in fact in some way
the same, and that the only way this can be explained is if a self-identical
essence exists 'over and above' the many but is also somehow present in
them. This is the mode of cognition manifested when we see the various
instantiations of, say, a single pure function or mathematical rule. The
'seeing' is mental seeing, but it is also 'seeing that' which means that what
we see is the truth of a proposition or the fact that something is the case.

Yet this understanding is distinct from belief, which arises from sense-
perception and refers directly or indirectly to the objects of sense-perception,
not to intelligibles.[13] To expand a bit on Plato's mathematical examples,
understanding that a Chihuahua and a Great Dane are both dogs is not

---

[13] Many scholars have noted that Plato's Divided Line requires that its two middle sections (for *dianoia*
and *doxa*) must be equal, though they represent distinct modes of cognition and distinct objects. The
meaning of this equality is disputable, or even that there is an intentional meaning. I interpret Plato to

equivalent to having the belief that this animal before me is a dog. And though in English we find no difficulty in sometimes substituting 'believe' for 'understand' when expressing our grasp of a 'one over many', we miss something if we ignore Plato's sharp distinction and just assume that belief and understanding are interchangeable. We can, after all, believe all sorts of things that we do not understand, at least on ordinary criteria of what constitute belief. It is easy to appreciate that the class of persons who believe that e = mc^2 is not identical with the class of persons who understand this equation. The understanding however, is not, according to Plato, equivalent to knowledge.

Plato describes the highest type of cognition, knowledge, as analogous to sense-perception (532A; 533A). Moreover, it is the exact opposite of imagining, the mode of cognition of the lowest type of cognition of the bottom portion of the Divided Line. Here, one cognises images of sensibles, shadows, images, in short, non-epistemic appearances. Knowledge is analogous to the sense-perception of these non-epistemic appearances. And, as Plato adds in an important passage in *Timaeus*:

If intellection (*noēsis*) and true belief are two kinds, these Forms that are imperceptible by us and intelligible only definitely exist by themselves. If, though, as it appears to some, true belief does not differ at all from intellection, all that we perceive through the body should be taken as the things that are most stable. Now we should assert that they [true belief and intellection] are two different things, for they are distinct in origin and they are not the same. The one is produced through instruction, the other by persuasion; the one is always accompanied by true *logos*, the other is without *logos*; the one is immovable by persuasion, the other is able to be controverted; and, it should be said, true belief is shared in by all men, whereas intellect belongs to the gods and a small class of human beings (51D3–E6; cf. *Rep.* 534A2).

Intellection in general, which we recall includes understanding as well as knowledge, depends on the existence of Forms that are knowable only insofar as they are cognised in the light of the first principle. Intellection is always accompanied by true *logos*, but neither of its types are equivalent to a *logos*. Understanding includes mentally seeing that a *logos* is true, but this is not the same thing as believing that it is true. This passage indicates that even a true belief is equivalent neither to understanding nor to knowledge; indeed, it is 'without *logos*', that is, without an explanation of why the true belief is true. Such an explanation does not turn the true belief into

be indicating the strong connection between having a belief regarding things in the sensible world and understanding what it is one believes, despite the fact that these modes of cognition are different and sensibles are different from what is understood.

knowledge or even understanding of the object of belief, though the explanation is equivalent to understanding or knowledge of that which makes the true belief true. We thus have a confirmation of the above interpretation of the *Republic* passage in which philosophers are radically separated from lovers of sights and sounds by their separate objects, intelligibles and sensibles.

This brings us to the difficult question of how the Good makes the Forms knowable or why they cannot be known without our 'ascent' to the Good. One natural interpretation of this claim takes it to be saying that we cannot know what, say, Justice is without knowing why Justice is good or why it is good to be just. This seems highly unlikely, however, since it is a constant principle of Plato's various accounts of definition that we cannot know whether or not a Form has a property without first knowing what that Form is. If this is so, then whether or not we need to know why Justice is good, we cannot answer this question until we know what Justice is. But the text seems to insist that we cannot know this without 'grasping' that which makes Forms knowable and gives them their being, namely, the Idea of the Good (511B–C). Grasping this must mean at least having some sort of cognition of how it and the Forms are related.

The allegory of the Sun employs the metaphor of light to express the relation between the Good and the Forms. Just as the Sun shines light on the objects of sight, so the Good shines its 'light' – truth – on the objects of the intellect. We can press this metaphor a bit further, noting that the Sun is for the ancients generally the paradigmatic source of light as fire is the paradigmatic source of heat. Everything that is hot is either fire itself or caused to be hot by the presence of fire in it. Fire is also hot in the highest degree. So, the Good is the paradigmatic source of intelligible being. But as we saw in the passage on the Good quoted above, it is 'above essence'. According to my interpretation of this most contentious claim, the Good is virtually all of the Forms and is analogous to the way that 'white' light is virtually the spectrum, or a function is virtually its domain and range. As with light or heat, that which is good is either the Good itself or anything to which the Good is present. To be intelligible is to be an expression of the unique first principle of all. Such intelligibility as the sensible world has is owing to Forms and the objects of understanding – the so-called mathematical objects – whether these be Forms or not. The intelligibility and hence knowability of the Forms themselves is owing to the first superordinate principle of everything, the Idea of the Good.

We can begin to answer the further puzzling questions of why this principle is called 'the Good' and what this has to do with the mathematical objects of understanding if we take into account Aristotle's testimony regarding Plato's philosophy. Aristotle tells us that for Plato the Good is also called 'the One'.[14] More generally, Aristotle reports that Plato analysed the intelligibility of the intelligible realm in terms of number.[15] This is a hugely contentious and obscure matter. A fair evaluation of Aristotle's testimony requires an examination of passages in *Republic*, *Parmenides*, *Timaeus*, *Philebus* and elsewhere. It also requires making a judgment on whether Aristotle's testimony does or does not accurately represent Platonic teachings that are not found in the dialogues, the so-called oral doctrines. I am inclined to the view that Aristotle's testimony is basically accurate and that the dialogues confirm this testimony more than many have thought. But consideration of these complex issues is beyond the scope of this book. Nevertheless, a few remarks will perhaps be useful.

First, a general reductivist tendency is, as we have already seen, endemic to Presocratic philosophy. To assume nature to be a *kosmos* is already to set oneself on a path the endpoint of which is intellection of the one or very few principles unifying everything. In this, Plato does seem to be following the Presocratics lead by explicitly declaring that the first principle of all is that which makes everything intelligible. Second, as I have interpreted Plato's account of intellection in general, intellection is essentially a reductivist enterprise. Intellection amounts to cognising a 'many' as essentially one. Intellection as reduction is evident most conspicuously in mathematics where every equation of the form $A = B$ amounts to a claim that two 'things' are the same owing to a self-identical underlying one. It is also evident in, for example, the reduction of geometry to arithmetic. In this regard, it should be noted that for Plato, as for all the Greeks, one is not a number but the principle of number. According to Aristotle's testimony, in addition to the One, which is the first principle of everything, there is a first principle of multiplicity, variously called the Indefinite Dyad or the Great and Small. Thus, the smallest number, two, is constructed out of, that is, it is to be understood as an expression of the One and the Indefinite Dyad (i.e., indefinite plurality), which is virtually what twoness is.

---

[14] Aristotle explicitly identifies the One with the Good at *Met.* 13.4.1091b13–14, though he does not here refer specifically to Plato. Cf. *EE* 1.8.1218a19–21; *Met.* 1.6.987b18–22. The term *to hen* ('the One') can be used as a name or a definite description. Since the first principle is 'beyond *ousia*', however, a 'definite description' of it is not, strictly speaking, available. Still, 'that which is one' would be the best way to refer to that which is the identifying unity beneath the multiplicity of Forms.

[15] There is an abundance of material regarding this in Aristotle's *Metaphysics*, especially Book 1 chapters 6 and 9 and Books 13 and 14.

For the Greeks generally, number (*arithmos*) is not primarily a way of counting. Number is primarily an orderly array or plurality of units of a certain sort and it is these that are at issue in the question of whether Forms are Numbers.[16] If Aristotle is correct in his report that Plato maintained that Forms are Numbers, they are not numbers in the sense of what we count with. They are rather the ideal paradigms of ratios of pluralities of units of a certain kind of material, as for example, in musical harmonics or in the elements of a body.[17] The numbers that mathematicians deal with (and the relationships among these) are repeatable instances of Ideal Numbers. Accordingly, ratios and their mathematical properties apart from those that are ideal would be within the purview of the mathematical sciences, specifically subordinated by Plato to philosophy. By contrast, philosophy aims to know the ideal or paradigmatic ratios; this is just what seeing them 'in the light of the Good' entails. To see or pick out an ideal ratio amidst the infinite array of non-ideal ratios is to see it as an expression of the Good. The Good is virtually all of these because it is the One, the unique first principle of all, the first principle of number.

Intellection is, as we have seen, either understanding or knowledge. On Aristotle's recounting of Plato's philosophy according to which the Good is the One and Forms are Numbers, understanding is intellection of the ratios that underlie various cases of sameness in difference. For example, to understand what it is that makes two shades of red the same or two different shades of red both red would be to have intellection of the ratio of elements going to make up that colour. Knowledge would be the mental seeing of the ideal ratios, where 'ideal' indicates the entire divinely produced order of nature.[18] This mental seeing includes or depends upon cognition of the unity of all Forms, that is, of the fact that they are various expressions of that first principle which is virtually all of them.

On this interpretation, there is clearly no room for the possibility that there is knowledge of the sensible world, though it does seem to open up the possibility that there might be belief about that of which there is knowledge. Could one not have belief about Form-Numbers, if there be such, short of knowledge? For example, could one not believe falsely that a tangent touching a circle touches it at infinitely many points? Presumably, one

---

[16] Cf. Aristotle, who at *Phys.* 4.11.219b6–7, distinguishes between number as 'that by which we count' and number as 'that which is being counted'.

[17] Cf. e.g., *Rep.* 531C and the construction of the World Soul at *Tim.* 35B–C.

[18] Cf. *Tim.* 53B where the Demiurge – Plato's god – produces order in the disordered chaos of 'material' by introducing 'shapes (*eidesi*) and numbers' into it. These shapes are geometrical quantities and the numbers are ratios.

could have such a belief, but it would not be a belief about the Form of Circularity. To believe a proposition about something is for Plato paradigmatically to refer to that something and to claim that it partakes of some essence.[19] The only way to refer to the Form of Circularity is to cognise it, either hypothetically (in understanding) or along with the unhypothetical first principle (in knowledge). One may understand or fail to understand; one may know or fail to know. In neither case does this amount to belief about the objects of knowledge. The false belief about the tangent and the circle must be a universal belief about some class of images of Forms, in this case particular drawn circles and tangents.

The difficulty in grasping the above arises principally from operating within the framework of the Standard Analysis. In this analysis, knowledge is a form of belief and belief is some sort of representational state, wherein the proposition believed is the representation. Believing and knowing are both the having of 'propositional attitudes' in relation to these representations. By contrast, for Plato if knowledge is the inerrant or infallible mental seeing of Forms or essences, it is not a representational state. It is not of propositions. When representations do occur, belief, including false belief, is possible. A non-representational cognitive state like knowledge is one in which (1) what is known is present to the knower and (2) the knower is aware of that presence. It is analogous to a non-cognitive, non-representational state like, say, having a pain, though in the case of knowing there is intelligible content.[20] The content can be represented or expressed to oneself and to others, but the knowing itself is not the representation or expression. The awareness of the presence of intelligible content cannot itself be a representation either if there is no such thing as false knowledge or understanding. Therefore, such representations as there are must arise subsequent to the presence of intelligible content and the awareness of that presence in the identical subject. For if the subject of the awareness differed from the subject of the content, the content of the awareness would be by definition a representation of the original content.

The presence of essence to an intellect capable of being aware of that presence is first proposed by Plato in *Meno* and *Phaedo* where he argues that

---

[19] Cf. *Soph.* 262E–263B which tells us that a true *logos* refers to a subject and 'says something about it'. At 264A1–2 *doxa* is said to be just the *logos* 'in the mind'. Cf. 261C6.

[20] 'Intelligible content' refers to the one nature or essence shared by a many. Understanding, in contrast to knowledge, has that many as a constituent. It is cognition of the one that is manifested as a many. Because the many is constitutive of the cognition, it is close to belief which is always derived from sense-perception of the many. Knowledge is cognition of the intelligible content apart from a many to which that content is potentially related.

there are certain cognitive acts we perform that we could not perform if we did not have knowledge of essence. In *Meno* (82B–86B) the slave boy arrives at true belief about a geometrical problem and in *Phaedo* (72E–78B) the interlocutors arrive at the belief that equal sticks and stones, though they be equal, are deficient in their equality in relation to the essence or Form of Equality. In both cases, those who have beliefs could not have them unless they already had knowledge. Yet they are both as yet unable to access that knowledge. They do not cognise what is already in their intellects.

One naturally supposes that the putative knowledge was thought by Plato to be acquired prenatally or discarnately roughly in the way that we normally suppose that we acquire knowledge, which is by sense-perception or, in general, by experience of some sort. Many scholars have noted the obvious point that the explanation for acquiring knowledge of Forms in this way will run into the same problems that Meno ran into when he proposed his paradox of learning to Socrates. Plato, though, need not be burdened with this elementary error. For he may well have come to realise that to be a subject capable of knowledge is already to be identical with that which is intelligible. Thus, essence is not acquired; actual, fully fledged knowing consists in the self-reflexive awareness of what one already is. Being capable of knowledge is to be not merely intelligent but to be intelligible. The illusion of a *tabula rasa* depends on mistaking the awareness for an acquisition. This mistake originates in the obvious fact that on any account, what Plato takes to be the awareness of the presence of essence is a process necessarily involving sense-experience of some kind. This sense-experience is indeed an acquisition, but it is not an acquisition of essence, for as Plato argues, without the presence of essence in us already, the acquisition of beliefs or of intellection would not be possible.

Further evidence for this interpretation resides in texts that are among the most controverted in Plato's works. In the *Sophist*, the Eleatic Stranger confronts the 'Friends of the Forms', those who identify what is completely real with Forms alone. The Stranger says:

Are we really going to be so easily persuaded that motion, life, soul and thought have no place in that which is completely real; that it has neither life nor intellection, but stands immovable, holy and solemn, devoid of intellect (248E6–249A2)?

It is possible to take this passage as arguing that Plato wants to allow that things other than what he has hitherto identified as really real are to be recognised as so, namely, things in the sensible realm that are in motion, including things engaged in psychic motion such as that of thought. It is also possible to take this passage as arguing that he wants to add to the realm of the really real another category, namely, that of a particular type of psychic activity or motion that is intellection. Neither interpretation, however, is compelling. Regarding the first, it is not clear what allowing sensibles into the really real – as opposed to just admitting that they are real – would accomplish other than to destroy the basis for the distinction between the stable objects of intellection vs. the unstable objects of belief that the Eleatic Stranger himself reaffirms. Regarding the second, if admitting psychic motion into the realm of the really real just amounts to allowing that intellection of Forms is possible, the Friends already acknowledge, indeed, insist on this. To allow the sort of motion that Plato typically associated with the realm of becoming into the realm of the intelligible is to concede that the fundamental division that Plato makes in his metaphysics between being and becoming or intelligible and sensible is mistaken. Yet there is no textual basis for thinking that Plato ever made such a concession.

In the light of the discussion of *Republic* and the passages from *Meno* and *Phaedo* another possibility – originating in the Platonic tradition – suggests itself. The 'place' of intellectual life in the really real refers to the inseparability of essence and intellect.[21] This inseparability is indicated in the case of the Demiurge in *Timaeus* who is implicitly cognitively identified with the Forms that he employs in putting order into the disorderly sensible world.[22] Thus, in knowing the Forms, and in being aware of their presence, he is identified with them. It seems reasonable to suppose that the Demiurge's intellect or *nous* is a paradigm of our own, not one whose operations are completely alien to ours. If we are to assume that the Demiurge is also a paradigmatic knower, the things present to his intellect are not representations of Forms. Nor, of course, can the Forms be reduced to concepts or representations, as is explained in *Parmenides* (132C–D). So, if we are intellects, we should conclude that we are not 'empty' ones waiting to be filled any more than is the Demiurge's intellect. It is worth mentioning here in passing, though I shall return to the matter at length in the next chapter, that Aristotle – no friend of the Forms – is in complete agreement with Plato

---

[21] Cf. *Phd.* 76E2–7 for the argument that the existence of Forms and the pre-existence of souls stand or fall together. The connection between this argument and the *Sophist* passage is not clear. Specifically, it is hard to see how the individual soul or intellect (that comes to birth knowing Forms in some sense) is related to the intellect that is (on the traditional interpretation) everlastingly inseparable from Forms.

[22] See *Tim.* 29E3, 30C2. In the first passage, the Demiurge is said to desire that the world he is about to make should be as much like himself as possible. In the second passage, the Demiurge is said to make the world in the likeness of the intelligible Living Being that contains within itself all Living Beings as parts. The 'shapes and numbers' delivered into the pre-existent chaos are copies of the parts of this Living Being.

on the inseparability of what he calls 'primary essence' and knowledge, whether this be in the Prime Unmoved Mover or in us. The Unmoved Mover, who *is* primary essence, is nothing but the living activity of knowing. This is exactly the case for us, when our intellects are separated from our bodies.

The inseparability of intelligibles from the divine intellect must not be taken to indicate the voluntarism of the Demiurge, as if, like Descartes' God, he is supposed to have the power to alter eternal reality. This inseparability does not imply that triangularity might be other than what it is if only the Demiurge had wished it so. The intelligibles are 'external' to the Demiurge only in the sense that their nature is not dependent on the one who thinks them. Their nature *is* dependent on the Good, as Plato specifically claims. In addition, we must be wary of identifying the Demiurge's eternal act of intellection with representation or conceptualisation, both of which for Plato seem to require embodiment.

Although some scholars will allow that the above picture is creditable at least as an extension of Plato's account of knowledge and belief in *Republic*, they will insist that the picture is shattered in *Theaetetus* where Plato more or less comes to his senses and joins the ranks of the adherents of the Standard Analysis. Accordingly, I turn to that dialogue in order to examine the question of whether this is so. As it will turn out, Plato in fact does not merely maintain the position he held in *Republic*, he also shows why knowledge cannot be as the Standard Analysis has it.

3 THEAETETUS

Plato's *Theaetetus* is, but for a crucial so-called digression, entirely taken up with the question 'what is knowledge?' Three answers are supplied by Socrates' interlocutor Theaetetus: (1) knowledge is sense-perception (*aisthēsis*) (151D–186E); (2) knowledge is true belief (187A–201C); (3) knowledge is true belief plus an account (*logos*) (201C–210A). All three definitions are rejected. The dialogue, like many of the so-called Socratic dialogues, ends in a roadblock (*aporia*). So much seems uncontentious. And yet if one supposes, as many scholars do, that a correct definition of knowledge must be found within the ambit of the Standard Analysis, one is going to understand this roadblock in a particular way. For even if it is the case that knowledge is not true belief and not even true belief plus a *logos*, since the standard account takes knowledge as true belief plus *something*, the apparent roadblock is really something else. It is a breakthrough (*euporia*), pointing to the right direction in which to pursue an answer to the question posed by the dialogue. At this point, one may adopt one of two alternatives: (a) Plato did not himself understand what this *something* is, though he realised that knowledge is true belief, or else (b) Plato did understand what this *something* is, though for reasons having to do with his view of how philosophical truth is to be communicated or how it cannot be communicated he did not wish to say what this is in the dialogue.

To take the position that the apparent *aporia* is really a *euporia* pretty clearly requires one to maintain that Plato has changed his mind about what knowledge is since writing *Republic*. Some scholars have indeed tried to retrofit *Republic* to put it in line with an interpretation of *Theaetetus* that has that dialogue proposing the Standard Analysis as the framework for defining knowledge. I have argued not only that this interpretation is mistaken but that it distorts the central argument of *Republic* as well. In this section, I focus on *Theaetetus* itself and will not assume a particular interpretation of *Republic*. I will try to show that the argument in this dialogue provides no comfort whatsoever to those who wish to recruit Plato into the ranks of contemporary epistemologists.

The definition of knowledge as sense-perception is to be examined according to whether or not it meets two criteria for knowledge: it must always be of what is (*tou ontos*) and it must be inerrant (*apseudes*) (152C5–6). These criteria appear also to be those on the basis of which the other two proposed definitions of knowledge will be rejected. It would hardly make sense to employ different criteria to reject these other definitions unless, of course, the definition of knowledge is a moving target and the criteria are adventitious in the sense that different criteria might be employed in different circumstances depending on how we propose to use the word 'knowledge'.

The first point needing emphasis here is that these criteria do not come out of nowhere. In fact, they are easily gleaned from *Republic* where knowledge is said to be of what is and is inerrant, though in this dialogue the word used is *anamartēton*. I will in a moment suggest a reason for this change in vocabulary. In any case, we seem justified in the initial assumption that the subject of *Theaetetus* is exactly what it is that differentiates philosophers from lovers of sights and sounds. But whereas *Republic* was primarily concerned with what sorts of objects are knowable, *Theaetetus* focuses on the nature of knowledge itself.

The second point is that if these criteria are necessary and sufficient ones, it would seem that we already have an answer to our question 'what is knowledge?' Thus, knowledge is whatever type of cognition has as its object 'what is' and is also inerrant. Of course, a moment's reflection suggests that it is far from clear what the words 'what is' and 'inerrant' refer to in this passage. More particularly, it is unclear why sense-perception and *true* belief would ever be thought *not* to meet at least the criterion of inerrancy. So, the possibility arises that although they might meet one criterion, they do not meet the other as they must if they are to be identified with knowledge. Here, though, while it is not too difficult to see why sense-perception might not meet the criterion that it be of 'what is' (since sensibles, as we learn from *Republic*, 'are and are not'), it is far from obvious why true belief does not, unless of course we are also going to assume that 'what is' is stipulated to be the preserve of knowledge and not belief. If indeed this is being assumed, one is at least entitled to some argument in this regard.

Finally, the possibility that sense-perception and true belief might meet at least one of the criteria of knowledge while not meeting the other suggests that the criteria are being treated not as criteria for a real definition but as stipulative. Compare the criteria for citizenship in a country. Normally, it is easy to discover here a disjunctive set of individually sufficient criteria for citizenship; it is not necessary to meet any one criterion or all of them. The criteria can and usually do change over time, as, for example, they did in ancient Athens. This is hardly surprising, since the concept of citizenship is not thought to consist in rules for applying the word 'citizenship' to a natural kind. Of course, we can lay down necessary and sufficient conditions for the application of a word, but here again there is no expectation that we shall be able to say why these and only these criteria are necessary and sufficient. That is, we shall not be expected to show any necessary connection among them.

It is quite otherwise with knowledge, at least on Plato's view. It is frankly unbelievable that Plato should have thought that what I shall henceforth call the reality criterion and the inerrancy criterion are unconnected, such that the decision to call something that meets both 'knowledge' and the decision to call something that meets only one by another name is an arbitrary one. The discovery of the nature of knowledge, like the discovery of the nature of piety, is presumably, on Plato's view, the discovery of something objectively real. The criteria that define it are the boundaries of that reality. To claim that something could meet one criterion without meeting another would imply that the latter has nothing to do with what it is. If knowledge alone meets both, surely that is because these criteria are necessarily connected in some way. That is, because knowledge meets one of them, it must also meet the other. If, however, this is so, and if it turns out that sense-perception and true belief are not knowledge, contrary to our original assumption, neither one of these meets either of the two criteria. This amounts to saying that if sense-perception and true belief are inerrant, they are inerrant in a sense different from that according to which knowledge is inerrant. Further, it amounts to saying that if true belief does not meet the inerrancy criterion in the appropriate sense, it does not, again contrary to what we assumed to be a reasonable supposition, meet the reality criterion.

One might go along with the above reasoning as it is applied to the two failed definitions of knowledge as sense-perception and true belief because one is convinced that things are otherwise with the third failed definition, true belief plus a *logos*. So, one might argue, true belief plus a *logos* does, according to *some* meaning of *logos*, meet both criteria. I shall have more to say about this below, but for the moment it is worth pointing out that if the elusive sense of *logos* is going to be anything like what the Standard Analysis has it as being, knowledge is still going to be a true belief, just one with bells and whistles. That is, it will have all the characteristics of a true belief. If this is so, it will have to be the case that the incapacity of true belief to meet either of the two criteria of knowledge does not in any way infect true belief plus a *logos*. It is difficult to see how this could work. For if the two criteria are necessarily connected, and true belief fails to meet the inerrancy criterion in the appropriate sense, it also fails to meet the reality criterion. If true belief plus a *logos* is still that same true belief, its object is the same and it, too, fails to meet the reality criterion.

We have already encountered one of the arguments against the identification of knowledge with sense-perception in the previous chapter. This is an argument against Protagoras to the effect that his doctrine that 'man is the measure of all things' is self-refuting. Scholars have frequently wondered why the definition of knowledge as sense-perception is supposed by Socrates to be identical with the doctrine of Protagoras (*Tht.* 152B). As it turns out, the Protagorean doctrine provides the best chance for the definition of knowledge as sense-perception to meet the two criteria. This is so, however, only if the Protagorean doctrine is given a 'secret' supplement, namely, the Heraclitean doctrine that all things are in motion (152C–E). This doctrine, as expressed here, maintains that all the things that we say are real are in fact in the process of becoming. So, combined with the Protagorean doctrine, 'man is the measure of all things' by being the measure of 'becoming', that is, the 'becoming for a perceiver'. With the Heraclitean supplement, it becomes even clearer that Plato is trying to give sense-perception the best possible run at meeting the criteria of knowledge. For if the reality criterion is met by arguing that reality is always and only reality for a perceiver, and if the inerrancy criterion is met by arguing that one who perceives is an inerrant judge of what he perceives, it would seem that we have established that sense-perception is knowledge.

We cannot explore the details of the treatment of the doctrines of Protagoras and Heraclitus. The actual refutation of the definition of knowledge as sense-perception tries to show that the reality criterion is not met in sense-perception, that one who can maintain that his sense-perceptions are 'true for him' does not therefore attain truth (184B–186E). However, the denial that what is 'true for me' is true is not a denial that my sense-perceptions are, nevertheless, true for me. What these words mean is, as the argument shows, that I am an incorrigible judge of how things appear to my senses. I can, like Protagoras, conflate epistemic and non-epistemic appearances so long as I am prepared to admit that in doing so I have no connection with reality. 'Incorrigibility' is a perfectly good translation for *apseudes*, so long as we do not suppose that incorrigible mental states meet the inerrancy criterion. This is so because inerrancy is with respect to reality, and incorrigibility ('true for me whatever anyone says') does not attain truth, that is, reality.

One might reply that so blithely to identify truth with reality is to miss the point. One who says 'true for me' about his sense-perceptions attains truth in the only way possible, that is, he believes a true proposition about his own (real) self. If we take this approach, though, we are turning the definition of knowledge as sense-perception into the second and hitherto unexplored definition of knowledge as true belief. This will hardly do. In fact, the sense in which sense-perception does not attain truth must refer to 'ontological' truth, that is, reality, rather than to a property of propositions.[23] This is so because – quite independent of the different definition of knowledge as true belief – the first definition is supposed to meet both criteria. The putative manner of meeting the reality criterion is by taking the Heraclitean line that since reality is in constant flux, reality is identical with what becomes for me in sense-perception. The meeting of the inerrancy criterion is the other side of this coin, that is, I am an incorrigible judge of what becomes for me, that is, what is true. My incorrigible sense-perceptions are the substance of reality, we might say. So, it would seem, in this case, meeting or failing to meet one criterion means meeting or failing to meet the other.

The specific refutation of the claim that sense-perception meets the reality criterion is that in order to meet this criterion one must attain to things common (*ta koina*), for example, being and non-being, sameness and difference, identity and otherness, one and numbers, odd and even, and so

---

[23] On ontological truth see *Rep.* 510A9–10; 511E3–5 and 585C13–D2, where truth, along with being or essence (*ousia*) admits of 'more or less'.

on (185C–D). To this list Socrates adds beautiful and ugly, good and bad. The claim is that sense-perception does not attain to these. Specifically, if one does not attain to essence (*ousia*), one does not attain truth; one who does not attain truth does not have knowledge. The words 'things common' are probably not a reference to concepts or universals, as many have thought, but stand in contrast to *ta idia* ('things private', 166C4), the sense-perceptions of the one who claims 'true for me'. That is, things common are the objective features of reality or ontological truth. Attaining truth consists in attaining essence.

The obvious objection to this way of proceeding is that with respect to essence, one is no better off than one is with respect to putative epistemic appearances. Is not one's judgment about the real nothing more than a representation of it, one that may or may not be propositionally true? If that is so, since there is no entailment from a proposition to the reality suppos-edly represented by the proposition, attaining truth or knowledge cannot be infallible. Then either we have to say that knowledge, when it attains reality meets one criterion, though it does not meet the other, and it is false that both criteria have to be met at once, or else we have to say that knowledge only attains reality in the way that true belief does, that is, knowledge is nothing but true belief.

If we take this approach, we shall see the refutation of the identification of knowledge with sense-perception as leading us precisely in this direction. There are, however, several considerations that should make us hesitate. First, the manner in which true belief, because it is true, supposedly meets the two criteria does not impel Socrates to conclude that it is knowledge. If true belief plus some additional factor nevertheless remains true belief, and it is because it is true belief that it so fails, we ought to conclude that this is not the direction in which we should be going. Second, in the previous section we have seen that Plato has already provided the tools for explaining the attainment of truth as consisting of something other than the repre-sentation of it; one attains truth by attaining essence, which is to have essence immediately present to one and to be aware of that presence.

The matter of 'truth attainment' is explicitly engaged in the argument regarding the definition of knowledge as true belief. The strategy employed in this argument is simple. If true belief is knowledge, false belief is impossible. But false belief *is* possible. Therefore, true belief is not knowl-edge. Our task is to understand why the major premise of this argument is thought by Plato to be true. Let us begin by noting that the argument itself provides conclusive support for the contention that Plato is assuming that knowledge is a real mental state distinct from belief. For if knowledge were merely conceptually distinct from belief – just another way of referring to a belief – the attempt to show that false belief is impossible if true belief is knowledge would be pointless.

Those who suppose that the definition of knowledge as true belief is at least on the right track, must suppose either that the argument that shows that false belief is impossible if true belief is knowledge is either a failure or else that the argument is intended to show that false belief is not possible just in the case when there is a true belief. In other words, the impossibility of false belief is like the impossibility of sitting when one is standing. It is, however, implausible that the lengthy and complex argument is intended to make this simple point. Moreover, if this *were* Plato's intention, the third definition of knowledge as true belief with a *logos* would not alter the fact that, in the above sense, false belief would not be possible.

Three attempts are made to describe how false belief is possible if true belief is knowledge: (1) 187E–188C; (2) 188C–189B; (3) 189B–190E. According to (1), false belief is a case where what one knows are things one doesn't know or where things one doesn't know are things one knows. According to (2), false belief is believing things that are not. According to (3), false belief is mistaking (*allodoxein*) one thing for another. Each of these failed accounts actually tells us about knowledge and not false belief. Simply put, it is not possible for one not to know what one knows. Of course, it is also not possible to believe falsely what one believes truly. It is in fact possible to have false belief about *something*, as Plato will show in his *Sophist*. The reason why true belief is not knowledge is *not* that false belief is impossible. Rather, the reason is that knowledge is the infallible awareness of the knowable or intelligible. True belief is not knowledge because there is no such thing as false knowledge, though there can be false belief. When and only when true belief is recognised not to be infallible knowledge is false belief seen to be possible.

At 196D–199C, the metaphor of an aviary is introduced to explain what is manifestly possible, namely, that though we have acquired bits of 'knowledge' (birds for our mental aviary), we sometimes fail to access that knowledge and, accordingly, we may arrive at false beliefs about things we already know. For example, though we seem to know that 7 + 5 = 12, we sometimes get hold of 11 instead of 12, when adding up this sum, even though we also know that 11 is not 12. This metaphor is adduced as a hypothesis about how, if true belief is knowledge, we can nevertheless have false beliefs.

As it turns out, though, true belief – if it is to be knowledge – must not be the mere possessing (*kektēsthai*) of the bit 7 + 5; rather, it must be the having (*echein*) of it (197B–D), that is, the awareness or direct cognition of what is known.[24] Possessing what is supposed to be knowable is distinct from having it occurrently, as we might say. If true belief were knowledge in this sense, it would not be possible to believe falsely that $7 + 5 = 11$, for this would amount to mistaking the sum of 7 and 5 as 11 at the moment that one is believing (or knowing) that it is 12 and, presumably, that one is believing that 11 is not 12. If true belief is knowledge, like Protagoras, one must believe to be false what one believes to be true. Once we see that true belief is not knowledge, we can proceed to try to explain what no one doubts for one moment to be the case, namely, that false beliefs do, alas, constantly clutter our minds.

In the distinction between possessing and having, it is easy to miss the crucial qualification that if S has what is known, S is *also* the possessor of what is known. That is, the one who has must be identical with the one who possesses. If this were not the case, possessing would amount to no more than the presence of the knowable *somewhere* or anywhere else but in the one who knows. But then there would be no difference between possessing and not possessing. If the one who has what is known is identical with the one who possesses what is known, knowing – the awareness of what is present to oneself – is a self-reflexive activity.

As we saw in the previous section, the self-reflexivity of knowledge is analogous to the self-reflexivity of perceptual states like feeling a pain. The analogy between perception and knowledge, however, reveals a problem. Must we say that whenever one thinks, one knows, analogous to the fact that whenever one acquires a belief about one's occurrent pains, one must be in pain? The correct answer to this question depends on seeing a crucial *disanalogy* between perceiving and knowing. For one cannot have a pain without being aware of it, whereas essence can be present to one ('one possesses the knowable') without one being aware of it. There seems to be no difference between being in pain and appearing to oneself to be in pain, regardless of the beliefs that these generate. By contrast, 'having' the essence is not a necessary step between 'possessing' it and representing that which we possess when we think. Our representation of it is, though, by means of images.[25] In the Platonic universe, an image of an essence is so called because it partakes in that essence. So, in acquiring a propositional attitude to a representation of an essence we do, in a way, have what we possess. Our understanding of, say, the truths of mathematics is not knowledge, but that

---

[24] Aristotle will employ the technical term 'actualisation (*energeia*)' for this, or, more particularly, 'second actuality' where the 'possessing' is designated as 'first actuality'.

[25] In *Rep.* 510B4, thinkers use as images the sensible objects which themselves are imaged at the bottom half of the Divided Line. I take it that this brief remark constitutes Plato's admission of the point that Aristotle will repeatedly make, namely, that there is no thinking without images.

understanding would not be possible for those not capable of knowing in the sense of possessing the knowable.

The conclusion of the passage in which true belief is shown not to be knowledge offers as examples of knowledge and true belief an eyewitness to an event and a member of a jury who has a true belief about the occurrence of the event (201A–C). It appears obvious that what the eyewitness has is not knowledge if what he has is characterised as sense-perception or as a mode of cognition dependent upon sense-perception. Evidently, what he in fact has is true belief plus something else. We are thus encouraged to pursue a definition of knowledge as true belief plus whatever it is that is supposedly present in the eyewitness. We have already seen, though, that if turning true belief into knowledge means adding something to true belief, at least we shall have to show that adding the right thing does not leave the result open to the objections already marshalled against true belief. Among other things, we shall have to show that 'true belief plus', if it is to be knowledge, leaves open the possibility of false belief. We shall also have to show that 'true belief plus' simultaneously meets the reality and inerrancy criteria.

Theaetetus reports the following view about knowledge: it is true belief with an account (*logos*); the things of which there is an account are knowable and the things of which there is no account are not knowable (201C–D). It is unclear exactly what an account here is supposed to be. One might guess that it is what the eyewitness has but the jury member does not. This is, however, difficult to maintain. The jury member has the right answer, we might say, but the eyewitness *knows* that it is the right answer. His putative account might then consist in his statement of this fact. Surely, it does not consist in his being able to give other reasons, that is, other evidence, why someone is guilty, since the jury could have these as well.

Socrates interprets the view expressed by Theaetetus in his 'dream', representing yet another view (201D–202C). According to this view, elements are simple components of all things. These elements can only be perceived and named; we can say nothing further about them in any way. Thus, there is no account of them. By contrast, things composed of elements can have an account. The account of these is just the nexus (*sumplokē*) of names. So, elements are not knowable and have no account although they are perceivable. Things composed of elements are knowable because there is an account of them.

The difficulty with the proposal is plain, as Socrates' following analysis shows (202D10–206B). Either the complex is the sum of its simple parts or it is not. If it is the sum of these parts, knowing the sum is just a matter of knowing each part. But the parts are themselves unknowable. Therefore, the sum cannot be knowable. If, however, the complex is not a sum of parts, but itself something simple – a whole – then, again, it is no more knowable than the putatively unknowable simple parts. The two horns of the dilemma are not making exactly the same point. In the first, it is concluded that the sum is not knowable. Socrates does not say that it does not have an account. In the second, he says that the complex considered as simple whole is both unknowable and has no account (205E). The apparent remedy is to deny that simples are unknowable, which would either allow the complex as a simple to be knowable or else would allow the complex as a sum to be knowable because its parts are knowable. If simples are knowable, knowledge cannot include an account insofar as that account precludes simplicity. Further, the supposedly knowable simples will be *perceived*, in which case we are back to the definition of knowledge as sense-perception. Even if it is thought that both complexes and simples or elements are knowable, the definition of knowledge cannot include an account if that account implies that only complexes are knowable.

The failure to explain the account that turns true belief into knowledge as an analysis of the simple parts of a complex is followed by three successive attempts to give an account of an account: (1) an account is the expression of a thought in speech (206C–E); (2) an account is the enumeration of elementary parts (206E–208B); (3) an account is a statement of a sign (*sēmeion*) that indicates the difference of what is known from everything else (208C–210B).

The first sense of 'account' does not distinguish true belief from knowledge because anyone who expresses his true belief would then know. The second sense of 'account' ignores the qualification of Socrates' dream theory that the elements are unknowable though the complex is knowable. In effect, it concedes the possibility excluded by the dilemma of the dream theory, namely, that the complex can indeed be knowable when the elements are not. Nevertheless, a mere list of the parts or elements of the complex does not yield knowledge. The reason for this appears to be that knowing the elements of a complex requires that one know how the same elements might comprise any other complex of which they are part. The point is not that it is not possible to be able to enumerate the elements of one complex without being able to enumerate overlapping elements of another. It is rather that if one knew the elements, one could not mistake them when they are found elsewhere. The very possibility that one should be able to give the right answer in one case without being able to give it in another indicates that the account in this sense adds nothing to true belief.

The final effort to define 'account' has from time to time been taken as an improvement over its predecessors, indeed as something rather close to the truth. The claim is that an account gives a sign of how something differs from everything else.[26] So, if knowledge is true belief plus an account in this sense, one has true belief about something plus the account of how that object of belief differs from everything else.

There are two rather obvious difficulties with this view, as Socrates shows. First, to have true belief about something already implies the ability to pick that thing out as a subject of belief (209D; cf. above). But that is what the account was supposed to do. Second, 'having' an account can mean nothing but knowing the differences. That is, knowledge becomes true belief plus the knowledge of the differences (209E–210A).

The principal complaint made about Socrates' first objection is that he falsely assumes that in order to have a belief about something one must already have the sign or distinguishing mark, in which case what is supposed to turn true belief into knowledge is superfluous. As we have already seen, belief requires reference to a subject. One cannot have a belief about a subject without referring to it. Note that the object of belief here is evidently that to which a proposition refers, not the proposition itself. If the sign or distinguishing mark is going to turn true belief about something into knowledge about it, the reference to that something in both the true belief and knowledge must be the same. That is, of course, what those who take Plato to be arguing that it is possible to have knowledge and belief about the same thing think is the case. On their view, Socrates is offering a weak argument for a conclusion that they accept. If, by contrast, true belief about something were to be transformed by a distinguishing mark into knowledge about *something else*, the patent fallacy of equivocation would undercut the proffered definition of knowledge. Plato's point I take it is that if the addition of a distinguishing mark produces knowledge, true belief will already be knowledge. And that possibility has already been rejected in the dialogue. If true belief cannot be knowledge, true belief cannot be transformed into knowledge of the same thing by the addition of a distinguishing mark. Knowledge of the distinguishing mark does not add anything to the true belief that requires a distinguishing mark. If, though, it should turn out that one who knows can give a distinguishing mark, that

---

[26] The 'sign' is probably equivalent to the 'property' (*pathos*) of a Form that in early dialogues such as *Euthyphro* and *Meno* would, if it could be found, serve as evidence for a Form's presence. But in these dialogues it is also evident that one could only 'have' a property if one knew it, and one could not know it unless one knew that of which it was a property.

ability is not constitutive of what knowledge is nor is it entailed by the possession of knowledge. For the ability to give or have a distinguishing mark or sign is a function of knowledge in the first place.

The view that *Theaetetus* ends in *euporia* rather than in *aporia* is not only not encouraged by anything in the text, it is a view that assumes that Plato is pointing to another sense of *logos* for some reason not here canvassed. That sense will amount to something like the evidential condition in the Standard Analysis. No one, however, has explained how meeting that condition would transform belief into what this dialogue takes knowledge to be. On the other hand, if Plato has come to hold that the word 'knowledge' is just a name for the *ne plus ultra* type of belief, most of the argument in this dialogue spectacularly misses the mark. The search for the definition of knowledge should have actually been a discourse on the conditions for arriving at a belief in regard to a proposition that is maximally justified or at least better justified than any other. Then, Plato should have explained why the honorific 'knowledge' is appropriately used for such a belief. This interpretation of the dialogue's message – whatever its merit as an independent philosophical view – seems to me quite remote from Plato's fundamental approach to philosophy. Plato no doubt appears differently to different readers. In any case, it is certain that he appeared to others in antiquity – both disciples and attackers – as the prince among proponents of knowledge, not of justified true belief.

The principal lesson of *Theaetetus*, as I have argued, is support for the conclusions of *Republic* via a series of *reductio* arguments. Knowledge is neither sense-perception nor the true beliefs arising from sense-perception nor sense-perception 'plus' anything, including a justifying story. The dialogue itself would be pointless if the question 'What is knowledge?' were merely aimed at discovering a perspicuous way to talk about a certain class of beliefs. If, by contrast, this question is understood as being concerned with an account of a distinct natural or real state to which human beings may actually aspire, there will be no motive for maintaining that Plato is here saying anything different from what he says in the dialogues discussed above.

4 KNOWLEDGE VERSUS BELIEF

Plato's account of knowledge and belief is complex, subtle and spread over a number of dialogues. Owing to this and to the considerable significance of these views for later philosophers treated in this book, I hope it will be useful to bring together in a summary fashion the elements of the interpretation I have offered and to say a bit more about some of its features.

Plato tells us in *Republic* that knowledge or intellection generally is of the intelligible world or the world of being; there is no knowledge of the sensible world, the world of becoming. Later in the dialogue he clarifies his terminology, specifically limiting knowledge to the top section of the top half of the Divided Line. So, there remains another mode of cognition, understanding (*dianoia*) of the intelligible world. The two modes of cognition together are called intellection (*noēsis*).[27] What distinguishes knowledge from any other type of cognition is that it is infallible. The property of infallibility is not equivalent to the semantic property of being true. A belief (*doxa*) may be true, but because it is a belief it cannot be knowledge and so cannot possess the properties of knowledge, including infallibility. Nor is infallibility equivalent to incorrigibility. The latter is a property of perceptual states, which, owing to their transience, cannot in principle be corrected. It would, however, be accurate to say that incorrigibility is analogous to infallibility; the first a property of sense-perception and the second a property of knowledge.

The infallibility of knowledge is sometimes characterised by philosophers in terms of the so-called K-K Thesis. This is the thesis that if someone knows, she knows that she knows. Sometimes, this iteration is glossed as someone being in a state such that what is known is self-evident to that person. The problem with characterising Plato's view of infallibility in this way is that the objects of knowledge in the K-K Thesis are propositions, whereas the objects of knowledge for Plato are Forms. One might well think to reply that for Plato surely the objects of knowledge are propositions about Forms. I believe this would be a mistake. For Plato, though he would agree that propositions or statements are representations of reality, would deny that knowledge is a relation of a subject to a representation. He would deny this for the same reason that other philosophers have denied that knowledge is infallible, namely, that there is no entailment from being in a representational state of any sort to the world being as it is represented to be in that state. So, *if* knowledge is infallible, it is not a state of a subject in relation to a representation. Why, then, insist on infallibility?

As Plato indicates in *Theaetetus*, knowledge requires one to 'attain' reality, that is, 'ontological' truth or *ousia*. Plato's view is that there is no other way of attaining the truth than by infallibly knowing it. Because the truth is contained in the intelligible world, there is no question of perceiving Forms and, say, making claims about them, some of which may be true and some of which may be false. To 'perceive' a Form is to cognise it infallibly,

---

[27] Hence, *Rep.* 534A2 is an explicit revision of 511D8 where *noēsis* is the name of the top section.

analogous (but only analogous) to the way in which one literally perceives one's own perceptual state. This cognition is what Plato called 'having' the object of knowledge (as opposed to merely possessing it). The 'having' is not the sort of having that consists in, say, exercising ownership of a physical object. It is more like the 'having' that occurs when one has a fever. It is a state in which one finds oneself, and just as we can distinguish between one's being in a feverish state and one's awareness of that state, so we can distinguish between one's 'possessing' knowledge and one's 'having' it. The self-reflexivity of awareness or the having of knowledge should be carefully distinguished from what someone else might have in regard to the subject's states. When A believes that B has a fever or is in some cognitive state, A's belief is not awareness of this in the way that B can be aware of it or have it. Hence, knowledge is irrevocably 'first-person'. A could never know that B knows, because only B can have a self-reflexive cognitive state in relation to what B possesses. This fact does not of course prevent A from knowing *what* B knows. But it does show in another way why for Plato knowledge is non-propositional.

If infallibility or the impossibility of error is a property of knowledge, one might well say so much the worse for knowledge, because there is no infallibility in this world. Plato does not believe that knowledge (the 'having' of it) is impossible, though he does seem to be dubious about the prospects for embodied individuals of attaining knowledge. He does, however, seem to want to insist that the fact that we 'possess' knowledge is inferable from our embodied capacity for other modes of cognition. This is the doctrine of recollection. In any case, if knowledge is possible, one infallibly 'attains' the truth in knowing. This attainment does not consist in representing anything, though representation of the attainment may follow.

If knowledge for Plato is non-representational because it is infallible, it might seem that Plato has thereby deprived knowledge of all content, presumably on the grounds that all content is representational. The idea that there could be a non-representational content that is infallibly 'given' to us is what the contemporary philosopher Wilfred Sellars famously called 'the myth of the given' (see *Further reading* below). But Sellars's point concerns an alleged perceptual content, whereas the possessing of knowledge for Plato is the presence of intelligible content in the intellect. In sense-perception, we can distinguish (a) the physical event in the perceiver caused by the perceptual object and (b) the cognition of the results of that event by means of some conceptual apparatus. In intellection generally and in knowledge in particular, what is analogous to (a) is the possession of the object of knowledge. But in this case, the possession is the possession of content, the intelligible Form that is cognised.

One might incautiously suppose that what is analogous to (b) is the awareness or the having knowledge of that content. This, however, could not be the case because (b) is a representation of (a) and knowledge is non-representational.[28] Analogous to (b) for Plato are the concepts and *logoi* used to express one's knowledge or to apply that knowledge to the world of samenesses and differences that reflect or instantiate Forms. The propositions purportedly representing truths about Forms that many scholars are inclined to identify as the objects of Platonic knowledge are, in fact, representations of images of Forms, whether these be the eternal images of Forms that are contained in mathematics or the images found in the sensible world that are the objects of belief. The proposition 'equals taken from equals are equal' is neither the content of a Form nor is knowledge the attitude one has to that proposition. There is only one Form of Equality. And yet, because one possesses knowledge of that Form, one can have understanding of this proposition. It is the Form that makes the proposition true and it is the knowledge of that Form that makes it possible for us to understand that it is true.

As for the propositions representing the world of becoming, there is neither knowledge nor understanding, but only belief. There is no knowledge because there is no entailment from S believes 'p', to p. In those cases in which S believes 'p' *and* p is true, there is still no knowledge because p being true might have nothing to do with S believing that it is true. Even if p's being true has *something* to do with S's believing 'p', or even if p's being true had everything to do with S's believing 'p', there is in principle no way to tell the difference between a p that made S believe 'p' and a q that made S believe that 'p' is false or that 'not-p' is true. And this is the case for a reason very much like the reason that Sellars offered for rejecting the myth of the given, namely, the gap between the physical events that constitute our perceptual experience and our beliefs about these. For Plato, these physical events bring us in touch with things that have a compromised intelligibility owing to their physical constitution. Sensibles cannot force us to believe some 'p' because, to put it roughly, these sensibles are capable of leading us to believe the opposite. That some propositions can nevertheless be intelligible and true is, for Plato, owing ultimately to the Forms which account for the samenesses and differences that our propositions affirm and deny. The

---

[28] Even if it is true that knowledge is of propositions, this hardly explains what knowledge is. It is equally unilluminating to insist that knowledge is a successful sort of representation.

mode of cognition of sensibles is as different from the mode of cognition of Forms as the sensibles are themselves from these Forms. To suppose that the belief that 'p' could be 'worked up' into the knowledge that 'p' is as wrongheaded as supposing, like the lovers of sights and sounds in *Republic*, that in experiencing multiple beautiful sights and sounds one has experienced the unique Form of Beauty.

There is also no understanding of the propositions that are subject to belief, even true belief. As the *Timaeus* says, whereas true belief is without *logos*, intellection (which includes understanding) is always accompanied by true *logos*. It seems on first considering this that it is a little excessive to say that *true* belief is without *logos*. But the hope of the defender of the Standard Analysis to turn the third definition of knowledge in *Theaetetus* into an expression of that position really seems vain if the argument made in *Timaeus* is taken seriously. Since true belief is without *logos*, there is no sense of *logos* that is going to turn it into knowledge because the objects of knowledge are different from the objects of belief. True belief has no *logos* because it reports or records a fact about the sensible world without any explanation of that fact. A putative explanation of the belief comprised of the sense-perception that caused it would only be the object of another belief. The sorts of explanations that are the objects of understanding or knowledge are provided by intelligibles, not sensibles. To understand why an ordinary proposition about the sensible world is true it is necessary to turn from the sensible world to the intelligible world, to the being that accounts for the samenesses and differences among things that become.

Plato's insistence that understanding is different both from knowledge and from belief must be kept in the foreground if we are to grasp the fundamental difference between the latter two. Just as one might think that it is easy to have beliefs about Forms – especially false beliefs – so one might think that it is easy to understand propositions that others just believe to be true. And so if understanding, which has as its objects propositions about intelligibles, can also be of the propositions that can be believed, the opposite must be true, namely, that we can have beliefs about intelligibles or at least about propositions referring to intelligibles. So, if there can be beliefs about that which we can understand, surely it must be possible to have beliefs about that which we can know. In reply to this line of reasoning, Plato in his account of the Divided Line in *Republic* carefully distinguishes the employment of images and *logoi* by those seeking understanding from the objects of understanding themselves. The former are indeed apt for belief, but there is no understanding of them. There is understanding only of the things which their images are like. But just as Plato distinguishes the

images used in understanding from the understanding itself, he also distinguishes the process of dialectic from the resultant knowledge. Knowledge
is possible only when one, using dialectic, sees the Forms in relation to their
first unhypothetical principle, the Good. Dialectic of course occurs with
words and concepts. So, one might argue in turn that propositions that one
might formulate with these words and concepts could refer to Forms
(including the Idea of the Good) and be potentially objects of belief as
well as knowledge or understanding.

There is a fairly obvious problem here. One cannot have a belief or assent
to a proposition that one does not understand, for example, a proposition
expressed in a foreign language. I am speaking here of the ordinary sense of
'understand', not the Platonic one. Nor can one believe a proposition the
subject of which has a completely indeterminate reference. But the only way
to refer to a Form or to understand what a proposition about a Form means
is to intellectually see that Form, that is, to know it. All of the supposed
beliefs about Forms are actually beliefs about their images.

If understanding in regard to, say, 'the triangle' is not equivalent to
knowledge of the Form of Triangularity, how does understanding differ
from knowledge? Two obvious differences are that knowledge is infallible
whereas understanding is not and knowledge requires cognition of the
Forms in relation to the first principle, the Good.[29] Because of this second
difference, understanding is in principle limited in its scope in relation to
knowledge. One way of expressing this difference is to say that one who
understands has cognition of the fact that there is a self-identical nature
that explains a particular case of sameness in difference. Understanding of
triangularity amounts to cognising a *logos* of the self-identical nature underlying the different types of triangle. Knowledge of the Form of Triangularity
would be the infallible cognition of the unity of Triangularity and all the
other Forms provided by the Good or the One; that is, cognition of what
the Good or the One is virtually. Let us recall that the Good or the One is
what explains the knowability of Forms. Forms are not knowable just by
themselves independently of the Good or the One. They are knowable
owing to the superordinate principle that is virtually all Forms. Without this
principle, there would be no ideal Forms standing apart from intelligible
structure in general. I strongly suspect that if this interpretation is basically
on the right track, we are going to have to take seriously Aristotle's testimony
that Plato viewed or came to view the intelligibility of the intelligible world in

---

[29] Here we need to keep in mind that *dianoia* ('understanding') includes the process of thinking as well
as the result. Accordingly, it is possible to engage in *dianoia* and then fail to achieve the desired result.

a mathematical way. That is, we are going to have to see the objects of knowledge as mathematical expressions of a first principle of number (the One) and a first principle of magnitude (the Indefinite Dyad, the Unlimited, or the Great and the Small).[30] The intelligible diversity of our universe is the expression of what the One is virtually; as object of desire for all things in the universe, it is called 'the Good'. This good is achieved by manifesting ideal mathematical structures or ratios of elements.

Paradoxically, Plato seems to want to maintain both that 'only a few men and the gods have knowledge' and that every human being possesses it. The possession of knowledge is what makes possible more mundane modes of cognition including understanding and belief. Insofar as attaining knowledge is a recollection of the cognitive state that actually identifies us, this attainment is a process of self-discovery. It is only on this interpretation of Plato's account of knowledge, I believe, that his extraordinary view of the indispensability of philosophy makes any sense.

---

[30] These are the terms Aristotle uses in Books 13 and 14 of his *Metaphysics* to describe the principle coordinate with the One. It was left to later Platonists to speculate on how the Indefinite Dyad was related to the One, for example, whether or not it itself was derived from it.

CHAPTER FOUR

Aristotle

I INTRODUCTION

Discussions of Aristotle's epistemology typically begin with the explicit or implicit assumption that, owing to his rejection of Plato's theory of Forms, Aristotle's thinking about knowledge and the objects of knowledge must be fundamentally different from Plato's. Indeed, if Forms do not exist, and if the motivation for radically separating knowledge and belief is just that cognising Forms is entirely different from cognising sensibles, that motivation is evidently not going to be shared by Aristotle. And yet Aristotle does repeatedly say, for example, that there is no knowledge of the objects of belief.[1] He even maintains that there is no knowledge 'by means of sense-perception'. So, one may well wonder whether Plato's point about the separation of knowledge and belief is a point that depends on a theory about Forms as opposed to a theory about the difference between what is intelligible and what is sensible generally. In the latter event, it is all the more interesting if it turns out that Aristotle – despite his substantial disagreements with Plato – agrees with his master's basic epistemological doctrines.

A terminological note is in order. In *Republic* as we have seen, Plato initially uses the term *epistēmē* for the two modes of cognition – *noēsis* and *dianoia* – in the top part of the Divided Line. He corrects this later on and limits the use of *epistēmē* to the highest portion, reserving the term *noēsis* for both. Aristotle adopts Plato's initial use of *epistēmē* for the two highest types of cognition, which he calls 'demonstrative' and 'non-demonstrative' knowledge. The latter is usually referred to as *nous* or *noēsis* (*Post. An.* 1.33.88b36). I translate it either as intellect or intellection, as appropriate. This is the highest type of cognition, equivalent to what Plato decided to call *epistēmē*. Aristotle uses the general term *to noein* ('thinking') for cognition

---

[1] He does allow that there is a sense in which there can be belief about an object of knowledge. See below, 70.

set over against sense-perception. Yet, whereas Plato sees no generic unity in *epistēmē* and *doxa*, Aristotle groups *epistēmē*, *nous*, belief (*doxa*) and practical wisdom (*phronēsis*) together as types of judgment (*hupolēpsis*) and makes these species of thinking.[2] In effect, Aristotle sees belief as closer to knowledge than to sense-perception and expresses this closeness in terms of their generic unity. Nevertheless, he will sharply distinguish between *epistēmē* and *doxa*. Plato uses 'belief' somewhat more narrowly such that it is always tied to sense-perception. We shall examine Aristotle's reasons for shifting terminology more closely below.

There is one further terminological issue deserving of note. When talking about *epistēmē* in Aristotle's *Posterior Analytics*, scholars not unreasonably sometimes translate that term as 'scientific knowledge' or even sometimes as 'science', in the sense of a body of knowledge (*Post. An.* 1.10.76a37ff.; cf. *EN* 6.3.1139b25).[3] This term is certainly the central one in Aristotle's construction of a philosophy of science. The typical translations seem to leave open the possibility that in Aristotle's epistemology there is another type of *epistēmē* – non-scientific – available for exploration. This is not the case. It is certainly not the case that *doxa* or belief is where non-scientific knowledge is to be sought. The above distinction between demonstrative and non-demonstrative knowledge is not the putative distinction between scientific and non-scientific knowledge, for non-demonstrative knowledge is an essential part of scientific knowledge.

2 POSTERIOR ANALYTICS

The work known as *Posterior Analytics* is almost unintelligible outside the framework of *Organon*, the collection of works wherein Aristotle outlines the conceptual tools whereby knowledge may be obtained. These works include

---

[2] The other species would seem to be imagination (*phantasia*). See *DA* 3.3.427b28. But Aristotle is doubtful about this, because animals have imagination but no thought. See 3.3.428a24; 3.10.433a10. It is more likely that the other species of thought is discursive thinking (*dianoia*) which typically leads to judgment. Cf. *EN* 6.3.1139b15–17 where craft (*technē*) and theoretical wisdom (*sophia*) *are* grouped together with knowledge, intellection and practical wisdom as faculties by which the soul attains the truth. Belief, which may be false, is therefore omitted. The grouping of the five faculties does not constitute a generic unity.

[3] Some scholars render *epistēmē* as 'understanding', which is how I have translated *dianoia* in Plato. There is much to be said for the implication that Aristotle's *epistēmē* and Plato's *dianoia* cover roughly the same territory. However, whereas Aristotle says that the primary mode of *epistēmē* is *nous* or *noēsis*, Plato in effect says the reverse, namely, that the primary mode of *noēsis* is *epistēmē*. Plato's remark at *Rep.* 533E that we should not quibble over terminology might be of some comfort here, yet both he and Aristotle are engaged in the making of numerous complex and subtle distinctions, a fact that I hope justifies some terminological fussiness in my exposition.

in order: *Categories, On Interpretation, Prior Analytics, Posterior Analytics, Topics* and *Sophistical Refutations*. The overall task of these works is to provide an account of the structure of the knowable such that we can understand how knowledge is acquired. Very briefly that structure is as follows.

The fundamental items of nature are substances (*ousiai*), for example, this man or this horse. These substances, of course, have parts, which are themselves capable of scientific investigation both as parts of substances and in their own right as 'elements' of nature. Individual substances have so-called accidental attributes. An accidental attribute is, roughly, that which a substance could lose or gain and still be the identical substance. That accidental attributes are gained or lost indicates that they are particular, always located in a completely specifiable space/time framework, e.g., 'this shape now' or 'this spatial location now'. In addition to the accidental attributes that substances possess, they also have essential attributes. These are attributes that substances could *not* lose and continue to be the identical substances they are. The essential attributes of a substance are, basically, those attributes which fix substances within species and genera. Thus, Socrates is essentially a human being, though his height and weight are accidental attributes. The accidental attributes of a substance themselves are instances of their own species and genera. Thus, this particular colour is an instance of a general colour that is itself an instance of colour. So, in a sense, the species and genera of particular accidental attributes do also belong to the substances to which the accidental attributes belong, that is, they belong to them indirectly.

A further crucial feature of this structure is that individual substances are actualisations of the species to which they belong as the species are actualisations of the genera. So, this man here is an actualisation or realisation of what humanity itself is; he is one realisation of humanity, which is itself one realisation of animality. Further, the accidental attributes of an individual substance are themselves actualisations of that substance. Socrates actualises himself in his accidental attributes. His identity is realised in his particular accidental attributes that are, of course, being continuously lost and gained. Thus, paradoxically, there is a lot more to Socrates than what he is actually now; a lot of what Socrates is is gone and a lot of what he is is 'not yet'.

One who aims to possess knowledge of the things that exist by nature aims to cognise the relation between the species and genera of particular accidental attributes and the species and genera of individual substances.[4]

---

[4] At *Post. An.* 1.2.71b9–12, Aristotle says that we know unqualifiedly when we think we have cognised the cause owing to which the thing is, as the cause of it, and that it cannot be otherwise. This is a

She aims to understand why substances of this sort have the kinds of accidental attributes they have. The particular accidental attributes are actualisations of their species and genera which are themselves knowable as belonging necessarily to the species and genera of substances. The knowledge will be of the relation between, say, a species and its commensurately universal properties, those properties that belong necessarily to a species as such. A property is an attribute that all and only members of a species possess. A commensurately universal property is one that belongs to the species owing to what the species is, not owing to what the genus is to which the species belongs. This qualification is crucial. For example, if we aimed to know why human beings are mortal, we must not suppose that mortality is a commensurately universal property of humanity; in fact, it is a commensurately universal property of animality. Human beings are, indeed, mortal, but it is owing to the fact that humanity is a species of animal and mortality belongs to animality that this is so, not to the fact that mortality attaches to humanity as such.

Suppose we are trying to make sense of the data regarding rat behaviour in a laboratory. Our goal is to understand what it is about rats that yields these data. If the questions we are asking are indeed about rats and not, say, about rodents in general or even about animals, success consists in our knowing why these data have occurred. That knowing is of the commensurately universal properties of this species of animal. To understand why a property belongs to a species is, for Aristotle, to have knowledge of a 'middle term'. The middle term is what supposedly 'links' the species and the properties such that we can see that they must be connected because the species is connected to the middle term and the middle term is connected to the property.

The middle term explains, which is to say in Aristotelian jargon, that it is a cause. Different sorts of explanation provide different sorts of causes.[5] The most straightforward cause, and, indeed, ultimately the focus of the entire framework of causal explanation, is an essential or formal cause. An explanation that proceeds by formal cause provides a definition of the species or statement of its nature. It is this definition that is the middle term. So, ideally, if we know what this species is, we can know why individual members of this species have the particular accidental attributes

definition of knowledge only in the loose sense that it tells us something of the whatness of knowledge (a type of cognition) and the *object* of knowledge, namely, the cause of that which cannot be otherwise. It is not a proper definition of knowledge because 'knowledge of the cause and of the fact that it cannot be otherwise' is, quite obviously, not the differentia of knowledge. Thus, it tells us nothing to say 'knowledge of p is having a demonstration of it'.

[5] For Aristotle's fourfold schema of causal explanation see *Phys.* 2.3.

they do (why, say, their behaviour yields the data it does), that is, why the properties of the species belong necessarily to it. Since the accidental attributes are instances of or cases of kinds of properties, if the properties belong necessarily to the species through the middle term, we will have explained why these individual substances have these accidental attributes. Knowing what the species is means knowing the species's essence. Knowing its identity means knowing *both* the essence *and* the properties of the species. That is, the properties belong to its identity; they are constitutive of it. For this reason, to ask for some further explanation as to why things with a certain essence have the properties they have amounts to asking why things have the identity they have. This is not for Aristotle an intelligible question.

This claim about identity and properties seems suspiciously strong, for it seems to imply that if you know the definition of a species, you must know all of its properties. This is clearly not the case. Rather, Aristotle's point is that it is not possible to know the definition and to know the properties and still wonder why the property necessarily belongs to the species. Knowing (as opposed to merely believing) that B is a property of A is inseparable from knowing the definition of A.

The difference between demonstrative and non-demonstrative knowledge or intellection is the difference between identifying the essence in the definition as that which is manifested in all its properties and identifying the essence in the definition as that which is manifested in each and every individual substance that has that essence. To come to know that, for example, mammals are viviparous owing to their mammalian nature is to acquire *demonstrative* knowledge; to come to know that all mammals are things with this nature is to acquire *non-demonstrative* knowledge of the essence.[6]

In both cases, knowing is an act of identifying. In the former, one identifies the essence as explaining the properties, where explanation amounts to knowing that the properties belong to the identity of things with that essence; in the latter, there is no explanation sought, but rather a recognition of the identity of that which is otherwise cognised. Specifically, it is the recognition of the essence that is cognised through sense-perception. It is through sense-perception that we come into contact with individual substances and their particular accidental attributes. Our goal is to know that which we encounter in this way.

---

[6] One can also have non-demonstrative knowledge of axioms, definitions and hypotheses. Cf. *EN* 6.6.1141a7; 6.8.1142a25–6.

Clearly, demonstrative knowledge is not possible without non-demonstrative knowledge or intellection. Equally clearly, intellection is the end of the road; there is no possibility of acquiring demonstrative or non-demonstrative knowledge of why things with such and such a nature have the nature they do. It is not even possible, within an Aristotelian framework, to ask *why* things with such and such a nature exist, as if the substances in nature were in fact artefacts that are, by definition, constructed for a purpose. It is, though, entirely appropriate to ask how the structure or functioning of some substance existing by nature fulfils its nature. The latter question will reduce to another question about properties – in this case structural or functional properties of a species – and the essence with which they are to be identified.[7]

The above apparatus is necessary for understanding some of the remarkable things that Aristotle says about knowledge and belief in *Posterior Analytics*. He maintains, for instance, that there is no demonstrative knowledge of 'destructibles' (*phtharta*) (1.8.75b24). Further, knowledge does not arise from sense-perception (1.31.87b28). And finally:

Knowledge and the knowable differ from belief and the object of belief in this: knowledge is universal and proceeds through necessary [premises], and that which is necessary cannot be other than it is. But there are some things that are true or real but may be other than as they are. It is clear, however, that there is no knowledge of these things, for otherwise things that are capable of being other than they are would be incapable of being other than they are. Nor is there intellection of such things, for this is the true judgment of an immediate premise (1.33.88b30–7).[8]

Aristotle's rejection of the possibility of what eventually came to be termed 'empirical knowledge' is much clearer than any reasons given for this rejection.[9] It is one thing to say that cognition of necessary truths is

---

[7] At *Post. An.* 2.1.90a15, Aristotle says, 'it is clear that what a thing is and why it is are identical'. We must here understand 'identity' with sufficient capaciousness to enable us to talk about the identity of a thing apart from its properties, or with its properties, or even with its accidental attributes. The capaciousness of the identity of something is why explanation is necessary or even possible. If something were, as we might say, only strictly or formally identical with itself, there would be nothing to explain in an Aristotelian framework.

[8] Cf. *Met.* 7.15.1040a1–2. *EN* 6.3.1139b19–24: 'We all judge that what we know cannot be otherwise than as it is; as for the things which can be other than as they are, when they are outside of our observation, whether they are or are not is concealed from us. So, the object of knowledge exists necessarily and so is eternal, for all things which exist necessarily and without qualification are eternal, and what is eternal is ungenerable and indestructible.' Cf. *Post. An.* 1.8.75b24, 1.18.8165–7, 1.31.87b37–9.

[9] Cf. *EN* 6.5.1147b15–17 where Aristotle can be taken to imply that there is such a thing as perceptual knowledge. But the context of the passage, wherein Aristotle is discussing how Socrates in Plato's *Protagoras* is in a sense right when he says that one cannot act against 'knowledge in the primary sense' makes this unlikely. Acting according to or contrary to primary knowledge does not imply that there is primary knowledge of sensibles.

different from cognition of contingent truths and quite another to say that
the modes of cognition relative to each must be different. Why, for example,
should we not insist that we may have beliefs about contingent matters and
beliefs about necessary matters even if we agree to call the latter 'knowledge'? The fact that some of the things we believe might have been
otherwise seems beside the point. Our beliefs about them, so long as we
have those beliefs, seem to be no different as beliefs from our beliefs about
necessary states of affairs which, it may be granted, are never otherwise than
as they are. That is not, however, what Aristotle does. On the contrary, he
appears to endorse Plato's contention that knowledge is a mode of cognition
really distinct from belief. Why?

Aristotle seems to hold that the cognitive state of believing that something
is the case is different from the cognitive state of knowing why something is
the case, where knowing the 'why' includes both demonstrative knowledge
and intellection. A further clue to his meaning is his additional remark that,
'belief is unstable (*abebaion*), and nature is like this' (1.33.89a6).[10] The clue is
that the instability of nature is like the instability of belief. This does not
mean, as Aristotle argues elsewhere, that nature is constantly changing such
that it is beyond our cognition (*Met.* 1.6.987a33; 4.8.1012a30–b31). The
instability of nature and the instability of belief go together.

Belief is, for Aristotle, a state arising in us from sense-perception, when
there is already present in us *logos* such that what we experience we can
classify and express in a proposition. Generally, we could not have beliefs
if we were incapable of *logos*. When we have a belief, we identify something
as the subject of a predicative judgment. A predicative judgment is a type
of identity statement. Normally, it attributes an accident to a substance,
wherein the attribution is equivalent to a claim about what that substance
is, that is, what it is actually. And to 'actually' we always need to add 'now'.
As we have seen, the identity of the subject goes beyond what that subject
is actually now. There is no doubt here that beliefs can be true. The instability
of the belief does not consist in the believer's wavering over whether the
belief is true or false any more than does the instability of nature consist in
its making the truth value of the proposition indeterminate now.

The ineradicable instability of the belief consists rather in the fact that
it also and necessarily only attains to a simulacrum of real identity. No
accidental predication can be otherwise. To believe that Socrates is white-
haired is to make a claim about identity that is compromised from the start,
for Socrates' real identity is found in his essence, and his essence is not

---

[10] Cf. Plato, *Meno* 98A2–4 where true beliefs are said to 'wander' until tied down.

available to us through sense-perception. Socrates was, after all, Socrates before he had white hair and he would be Socrates even if he were to lose his hair altogether. In a strictly parallel manner, the instability of nature consists in the fact that nature is always what is here and now; its own identity is other than what is actually now before us; its identity is found in the essences of species and genera of individual substances and their parts. That is why Aristotle maintains that 'the cause always exists to a higher degree (*mallon huparchei*) than that of which it is a cause' (*Post. An.* 1.2.72a30).[11] What exists to a higher degree is that which does not have a compromised or qualified identity, that is, something whose reality and actuality are not diverse.

When we turn in the next section to *De Anima*, we shall explore further the differences between the cognitive states of the believer and the knower. For now, we may focus on the claim that cognition of accidental identity in belief is distinct from cognition of non-accidental identity in knowledge. There is no knowledge of that of which there is belief because that of which there is belief is or has an accidental identity. Of course, if there were no non-accidental identities, there would be no bar to designating as knowledge a belief that had met a particular standard of reliability or clarity, whatever that might be determined to be. If, though, there really were no non-accidental identities – and here I take it that Aristotle is following Plato exactly – then there no more could be belief than there could be knowledge. Heraclitus or Protagoras would have been right after all. So, protecting belief either by making knowledge a type of belief or by denying the non-accidental identities that knowledge seeks to attain is not on Aristotle's agenda.

The diversity of belief and knowledge is, according to Aristotle, balanced by their generic unity (*DA* 3.3.427b24–6). They are both types of judgment (*hupolēpsis*).[12] As Aristotle tells us at the beginning of *Metaphysics*, 'Craft (*technē*) occurs when there is judgment of the single universal arising from the many thoughts (*noēmata*) that come from the experience of things that are the same' (1.1.981a5–7).[13] The association of judgment with universality sets knowledge and belief over against sense-perception and imagination that are always of particulars. In belief, the universality is cognised as being manifested in an accidental identity; in knowledge the universality is

---

[11] Cf. *Met.* 2.1.993b23–31 where Aristotle claims that 'that is most true which is the cause of the truth of that which is posterior to it' in reference to eternal causes.

[12] Aristotle seems to be the first to use this as a technical term for the generic unity of certain types of cognition.

[13] Cf. Plato, *Phdr.* 249B8–C1 where recollection is described as a process of achieving 'unity' from many sense-perceptions by reasoning.

cognised as being manifested in a non-accidental identity. This raises the possibility that what is in fact a non-accidental identity should be judged to be an accidental one. So, Aristotle argues that one can believe that man is an animal, but not know it, because one also believes (falsely) that the identity is an accidental one (*Post. An.* 1.33.89a33–7).

It seems that if one can have a belief about the species man, one can have a true belief about that species. And if one can have a true belief, how does this differ from knowledge of that of which there is a true belief? This question is evidently generalisable for anything of which there can be knowledge: for any knowable identity, why cannot one have a true belief in regard to that identity, though fail to have knowledge owing to the additional false belief that the identity is an accidental one?

The answer to this question resides in the fact that there is no justificatory condition – as per the Standard Analysis – that would turn a true belief that man is an animal into the knowledge that man is an animal. What the former is missing, namely, the knowledge that man cannot not be an animal, is not the evidence or the reason for the claim to know that man is an animal. That is, the modality of the proposition 'man is an animal' is not evidence or a reason for the truth that man is an animal. What one knows when one knows this is a non-accidental identity; what one believes when one believes this is in regard to an accidental identity.

This suggests that the believer does not cognise the non-accidental identity and take it for accidental, but rather he cognises something else. He cognises the 'single universal' arising from his thinking about individual men and another 'single universal' arising from thinking about individual animals. He supposes, say, that what all animals have in common, as opposed to plants, is self-motion. He thinks that, though it is the case that all men are self-movers and so are animals, a man *could* be immobile or made so. In that case, he would no longer be an animal. The reason for his failure to achieve knowledge is that the identity he judges is an accidental one. He does this owing to his failure to cognise the identity of the species man and the genus animal. He does this evidently because he fails to cognise the essence of animal. What he is *not* doing is cognising man; for him to do that would be for him to cognise its identity, in this case the generic identity with animal.

The way Aristotle distinguishes the object of belief from the object of knowledge in this context is to say that belief is of the 'what it is' (*ti estin*) whereas knowledge is of the essence (*to ti ēn einai*).[14] The latter is prior to the

[14] 'What it is' can refer to any category of accidental being as well as to substance. Accidents do not have essences in the strict sense (cf. *Met.* 7.4.1030a28–31). Individual substances do have essence but they

former, meaning that a thing is what it is owing to its essence (2.4.91a25–6). The reason there can be no knowledge of the object of belief ('the things that can be other than they are') is that knowledge is cognition of non-accidental identity. By contrast, belief is always of accidental identities, accidental because only accidental identities come to us through sense-perception and beliefs arise in us through sense-perception. This, of course, presents Aristotle with the problem of how, after all, non-accidental identities are cognised, a problem that is addressed both later in *Posterior Analytics* and in *De Anima*. To this we shall turn in a moment. First, though, we need to consider the question arising from Aristotle's insistence that knowledge and belief have a generic unity. What is this unity?

It might seem that all the types of judgment are best construed as propositional attitudes. If this were so, there would be no reason to deny that the identical proposition can be known and believed. We have seen that Aristotle rejects this view. So, the generic unity of knowledge and belief cannot reside in this. It is more likely to be understood by Aristotle along the lines of the generic unity of types of sense-perception.[15] The basic idea is that there is a single faculty of sense-perception that operates in distinct ways according to the proper objects of each of the five senses. It is owing to this single faculty that we can with distinct senses sense something white and sweet as the identical thing. I shall return to the role of sense-perception in the next section. Here, I make the suggestion that the generic unity of knowledge and belief is analogous to the generic unity of the five senses.

What unites knowledge and belief is that both are acts of identification. In both cases, one affirms an identity underlying things that are thought to be the same. The identities subject to judgment in knowledge are non-accidental; the identities judged in belief are accidental. The formulation of a belief results from sense-perception. The belief transcends the sense-perception in the specific sense that one who has the belief judges an identity of that which appears to the senses. My belief in regard to an identity – as in 'a man is sitting here' – is, roughly, my belief that there is an identical substance that appears to me thus and so here and now. In the sentence 'that which seems to me to be a man also seems to me to be sitting', I identify the one thing as seeming to be a man and seeming to sit. Stated thus, beliefs are always inferences from appearances to reality.

---

cannot be unqualifiedly identical with these; otherwise, it could not be the case that more than one individual could have the identical essence (cf. *Met.* 8.3.1043b3). Therefore, since knowledge is of essence, there is no knowledge of individual substances. Cf. *Met* 7.15.1039b27–8.

[15] See *DA* 3.1; *De Sen.* 7.449a5–19; *De Som.* 2.455a12–20. Cf. *EN* 9.9.1170a29–30.

In demonstrative knowledge, I judge the identity of the natural kind that is actualised as this individual substance and that is the cause of the property that is actualised as this accidental attribute present in this individual substance. In intellection or non-demonstrative knowledge, I judge the identity of the genus that is actualised as this species and that is actualised as this differentia (2.13.97a19–20). There is no demonstration of this because there is no cause of the identity. So, in demonstrative knowledge I judge that the cause of a triangle having angles equal to two right angles is the definition of a triangle. In intellection, I judge that this definition identifies the triangle; it states its identity. Intellection or non-demonstrative knowledge (*nous*) is more accurate (*akribesteron*) and truer (*alēthesteron*) than demonstrative knowledge (2.19.100b5–10). Its objects are more cognisable (*gnōrimōterai*) than the objects of demonstration. The reason for this is that the identity that it cognises is unqualified. That is, in demonstrative knowledge an identity manifested diversely is cognised; in intellection, the identical essence itself is cognised. It is true in a sense that, for example, some x is identical with x-at-t_1, but that identity is less true, that is, less real, than is the identity of x with itself. We need only add here that 'x' represents an essence or form, not a logical subject. Its unqualified identity does not preclude its complexity.

In the last chapter of *Posterior Analytics*, Aristotle gives a famous sketch of how it is possible to arrive at intellection of the principles of demonstrative knowledge beginning with sense-perception of particular or accidental identities. From many acts of sense-perception arise memories; from memories experience, and from experience or from the universals acquired in experience, arises intellection of the principles of craft or of that which is demonstrable, depending on whether the principle is of becoming (*genesis*) or of being (*to on*) (2.19.100a3–9).[16] The repeated use of the word 'from' (*ek*) in an explanation usually indicates a material cause or condition for Aristotle. These stages of the so-called induction (*epagōgē*) are represented by Aristotle in the metaphor of an army in retreat where one man, another and then another turns to make a stand, until a battle formation arises.[17] This battle formation is the 'principle' of the battle analogous to the principle attained in intellection. That is the essence or form cognised.

---

[16] The principle of a craft is a principle of becoming probably because it is equivalent to a skill in a craft, like understanding how to cure someone. This is always directed to the particular contingent state of affairs. By contrast, a principle of being is of that which cannot be otherwise than as it is.

[17] Cf. *EN* 6.3.1139b28–31 where induction is contrasted with a syllogism, that is, with demonstrative knowledge.

Aristotle adds cryptically that the soul is capable of being affected in this way. We have to wait for *De Anima* to have this explained.

The essence is the principle of every sense-perception in that it is the ultimate source of its intelligibility. But it is accessed through repetition and variation in sense-perception and memory and experience. It is like a shape becoming evident through the accumulated arraying of points, each of which contains information of its position in the whole. Just as one sense-perception is the matter for the actualisation of a sensible form in the soul, so a multitude of sense-perceptions and memories and experience are together the matter for the actualisation of intelligible form in the soul. The term 'intelligible form' can be misleading. It seems to suggest that there is another type of form, perhaps sensible form. This is, however, not so. Form is form and it is exactly co-extensive with that which is intelligible. A form is called sensible because the form comes to us through sense-perception. That same form is intelligible for one possessing an intellect. It is capable of being thought, whereas for an animal not possessing an intellect, the form is available or accessible only as an image.

One might suppose that intellection is the justificatory basis for demonstrative knowledge and hence that Aristotle does in fact provide at least a framework for the Standard Analysis. On this view, intellection would be analogous to something like primary or incorrigible mental or perceptual states that are supposed to provide the justification foundation for our knowledge claims. The principal bar to this is that the Standard Analysis is, paradigmatically, of empirical knowledge. We have already seen that Aristotle denies that there is such a thing.

Neither is it true that induction itself, leading to intellection, is the justificatory basis for knowledge. Aristotle recognises no inductive process such that if one believes truly some set of propositions arising from this process, necessarily one has intellection of the principle of the demonstration. First, there could be no such set since the intellection of first principles is not a generalisation from beliefs about contingent facts. Second, even if one did have a set of true beliefs about contingent facts, there is no necessary inferential connection between these and the first principle, which is to say nothing more than that induction is not deduction. And if this is so, what is the meaning of justification here? To take the externalist line that justification consists in the following of a reliable technique is to make an empty claim. For while there may be a reliable technique for arriving at what is termed empirical knowledge, there is in fact no reliable technique for arriving at knowledge of what cannot be otherwise. The modal leap from the contingent to the necessary inevitably undercuts the putative inference.

3 *DE ANIMA*

At the beginning of chapter three of Book Three of *De Anima*, Aristotle
remarks that his predecessors have tended to define the soul by two differ-
entiae: (1) the ability to locomote and (2) thinking, practical reasoning (*to
phronein*) and sense-perception (3.3.427a17–19). Chapters three to eight,
with which we are primarily concerned, focus on (2); chapters nine to
thirteen on (1). Aristotle has in this work already directed considerable
attention to sense-perception as a mode of psychic functioning.[18] Now, he
wants to distinguish thinking and sense-perception. He supposes that this is
necessary because some of his predecessors have fallen into the erroneous
belief that sense-perception and thinking are in fact the same kind of
thing.[19] They seem to argue like this. Thinking, like sense-perception, is a
kind of discrimination (*krisis*) and a kind of cognition. So, thinking and
sense-perception are fundamentally identical in nature. That is, whether we
discriminate or cognise with our senses or with our minds, we are basically
doing one thing. They reason this way because they believe that the things
we cognise are corporeal and cognition must be an activity of that which is
the same as that which is cognised, so thinking must be corporeal (*sōmatikon*)
(3.3.427a17–29). Cognition must be a corporeal activity because it is the result
of the corporeal acting on us.

Aristotle counters that sense-perception is not the same thing as thinking
because sense-perception (of its proper sensibles) is always true, whereas
thinking frequently involves error. So, if thinking truly is an activity which
is the same as what is thought, that is, corporeal, thinking falsely must be an
activity which is different from what is thought. But recognising contraries
and being deceived with respect to contraries is a function of the identical
faculty (3.3.427b2–6). So, generally, if error shows that thinking falsely is an
activity which is different from what is thought, thinking truly is an activity
which is different from what is thought, for thinking falsely and thinking
truly belong to the identical faculty.[20] Thus, thinking truly could not be a

---

[18] Book 2, chapters 5–12 (416b32–424b18) and Book 3, chapters 1–2 (424b22–427a16) are devoted to the
general nature of sense-perception and to particular remarks about the five senses.

[19] Cf. *Met.* 4.5.1009b12–17. In this passage, Empedocles and Democritus are specifically mentioned as
embracing this error.

[20] Strictly speaking, a proof that the faculty of knowledge is not the same as that which it knows is not
sufficient to prove that thinking in general is not the same as that which is thought. I suppose,
however, that it is the generic nature of knowledge that Aristotle has in mind here, namely, judgment
(*hupolēpsis*). All judgments can be true or false (cf. 3.3.428a24–6). The contrary of knowledge is
ignorance as a disposition. If one believes falsely that nine is a prime number, one is ignorant with
respect to the truth that it is not.

corporeal event if thinking falsely is not, though we do not as yet have a clear idea why this should be so. In addition, all animals have sense-perception, though only animals with a capacity for reasoning can engage in thinking (3.3.427b11–14).

If error is possible, even if sense-perception of proper sensibles is always true, it is false that all appearances are true, counter to Protagoras' claim (*Met.* 4.5.1010b1–3). For though it is true that the honey is sweet to me, nothing follows from this in regard to the honey itself. The gap between appearance and reality is maintained even if there is no falsity in sense-perception. This is different from the claim that *because* there is no falsity in sense-perception, there is no gap between appearance and reality. It is thinking alone, generically speaking, that is able to attain to reality.

Aristotle's argument here should bring to mind Plato's argument in *Theaetetus* against the identification of knowledge with sense-perception. Yet unlike the dialectical procedure in Plato's dialogue, Aristotle will not now take up the claim of true belief to be knowledge. That claim has been dealt with elsewhere. His argument stays within the general ambit of thinking, focusing gradually on what is truly distinctive about it. This is in line with the basic orientation of *De Anima* which is to show how a soul defines a species of living thing, and in particular how a soul is characterised by its highest functioning. For a human soul, this is thinking, which includes both knowledge and belief as well as practical wisdom.

There is, though, perhaps another consideration. Although thinking is a species of cognition distinct from sense-perception, thinking does not occur in human beings without sense-perception. Even though, as Aristotle says in *Posterior Analytics*, knowledge does not arise by means of sense-perception, thinking in general does not occur without imagination and imagination does not occur without sense-perception.[21] So, Aristotle's central task in these chapters is to show the correct way to conceive of thinking and to avoid the errors of his predecessors who maintained that because thinking is so closely connected with sense-perception, it is really the same sort of thing.

As we saw briefly in the previous section, the direct objects of sense-perception are the particular accidental attributes of individual substances, parts of substances, and artefacts. Every sensible object is composed hylomorphically, which means that it is analysable into a formal aspect and a material one. Its formal aspect consists in that which makes it the kind of thing it is, to have a certain structure or arrangement of parts, to produce one sort of

---

[21] For the claim that there is no thought without imagination see 3.7.431a17; 3.8.432a8. On imagination as being the result of sense-perception see 3.3.429a1–2.

effect rather than another, and so on. Its material aspect is that in virtue of which that sensible has the ability to be altered in any respect. Its formal aspect constitutes what the object is actually; its material aspect constitutes what the object is potentially. Together, formal and material aspects – principles of actuality and potentiality – constitute the reality of the sensible object.

These objects have the capacity to undergo change and also to produce specific changes in perceivers. Something that is red can turn blue or be perceived to be red; something that has an odour can lose it or be perceived to have that odour; something that is in one position can be in another or seen to be in a position or to be moving. We need not consider the details concerning the question of whether the matter of an accidental attribute is distinct from the matter of the substance that possesses it or not. The central epistemological point is that the sensible object (directly the accident, indirectly the substance that possesses it) is capable of acting on something with the capacity for sense-perception.[22] Again, the details of sensing a red colour or a particular smell need not concern us. The result of sense-perception, however, is that the sensible form is present to the perceiver without the matter being present.

The idea of sensible form raises for Aristotle much the same problems as the idea of the intelligibility of the sensible world does for Plato. If thinking and sense-perception are, as Aristotle wants to insist, fundamentally distinct, we seem pulled in the opposite direction by allowing that sensibles are intelligible. The *tertium quid* that connects the two is actuality. Aristotle claims, 'the actuality of the sensible object and the actuality of the sense-perception of it are identical or one, whereas the being [*einai*, that is, what it means to be in each case] is not identical' (3.2.425b26–7). He here rejects the supposition that the being of the sense-perception of red is identical to the being of red when not sensed. This is not equivalent to a capitulation to the Democritean 'sweet to me, bitter to you, neither sweet nor bitter in itself'. It is a recognition that actuality is form and sensible form is never identical to 'what the sense-perception of x feels like'. Rather, the intelligibility of red or of the form of this colour is present in one way in the rose and another way in the perceiver. The connection between the former and the latter is the identity of their actualities.

Since sense-perception is always of a particular sensible object in a particular place and time, the inability to associate acts of sense-perception

---

[22] It is important to realise that we do sense indirect sensibles, namely, the substances possessing the accidental attributes that we directly sense; we do not infer their existence from the direct sensible. Cf. *De Insom.* 1.458b14–15.

and sensibles in some meaningful way would render sense-perception practically useless. This meaningfulness is owing entirely to the formal aspect of the sensible that is present to the one who senses it. Imagination is the power to associate sensibles via their forms. For animals incapable of thinking, imagination functions solely as a tool for action.[23] To associate what is sensed now with what was sensed previously via the imagining of the latter is to enable an animal to act in a way that is most likely to satisfy its desires. Because *this* smells like something that in the past was in fact eaten, the present sensible is pursued as edible.

For Aristotle, it would be a mistake to characterise the employment of imagination by animals in this way as involving conceptualisation. To match the sensible form present owing to a previous experience to the sensible form now present does not require cognition of a universal, the *sine qua non* of all thinking. This is so because cognising a universal is, minimally, thinking that there is an identity present in multiple 'samenesses'. The inability to distinguish among sensible forms, even if they are in fact the same, is not equivalent to this. Thus, following a practical associative rule regarding sensible form is not, according to Aristotle, an instance of thinking.

A further difference between conceptualisation and the non-human use of imagination bears emphasising as it will concern us in a bit. This is that thoughts (*noēmata*) are employed not just in thinking of an identity present in multiple samenesses, but also as representing the cause of these instances that are the same. *Intelligible* form is, somehow, to serve in the explanation of the presence of sensible form as per the basic structure of reality sketched in the previous section. Here we touch again on the problem of how knowledge is attainable given that the knowable is not directly available to us in the sensible.

Images, which are just sensible form without the presence of the sensible object, are thus used differently by animals and humans. They are indispensable for both; for animals in action and for humans in thinking, whether this thinking is relevant to action or not. In order, finally, to address the question of the distinctiveness of thinking, Aristotle turns in chapter four to an account of intellect (*nous*). By 'intellect' here, Aristotle means that by which the soul engages in thinking (*dianoia*) and judges (*hupolambanei*) (3.4.429a23). It appears that this thinking is the activity leading up to judgments, whether these are beliefs or knowledge or manifestations of practical wisdom. It remains to discuss intellect and to show that thinking and judgment are not to be assimilated to sense-perception.

---

[23] See *DA* 3.3.428a1–429a9 for Aristotle's extended discussion of imagination.

To do this, Aristotle recurs to the point made in chapter three, namely, that sense-perception is corporeal.

Chapter four begins by conceding the fact that thinking is analogous to sense-perception. Just as the form of sensibles must be somehow in the perceptual faculty, so intelligible forms must be in that which thinks, the intellect (3.4.429a17–18). Since the intellect can potentially think anything, it must be unmixed (*amigē*) with any corporeal element.

Therefore, it is not even reasonable that it [intellect] should be mixed with body, for it might then acquire some quality, for example, coldness or heat, or there might even be an organ for it, just as there is for the faculty of sense-perception. But as it is this is not the case. And those who say that the soul is the 'place of forms' speak well, except that it is not the whole [soul that is the place of forms] but only the thinking part, and this part is not actually the forms, but is them in potency (3.4.429a24–9).

The notion of being 'mixed' with a body seems to indicate having the attributes of a body or perhaps being capable of being affected by these attributes, such as being cooled by the body with which the intellect is putatively mixed. The reason why the intellect must be unmixed with that which it thinks is clear enough. The reason why it must be unmixed with body is not so clear. Since the intellect cognises intelligible forms without their matter, why is it 'not even reasonable' to suppose that it is itself mixed with some corporeal elements? As Aristotle emphasises, he is speaking here not about a form or property of a body, that is in a way unmixed with matter by definition, but of an entity, the intellect, that is not a property and obviously, since it is pure potency, not a form either. The fact that it is to be receptive of all possible intelligible forms hardly seems to disqualify it from being corporeal. Evidently, there is something about the 'information' of the intellect by intelligible forms that makes it impossible for it to be like a body similarly informed.

Aristotle immediately gives us the explanation:

And whenever it [the intellect] becomes each [intelligible] in the way that someone who knows is said to actually know (this happens when he is able to actualise his knowledge by himself), even then it [the intellect] is somehow still in potency, but not in the way it is in potency before it learned or discovered. And it is then that it is able to think itself (3.4.429b5–9).[24]

---

[24] I alert the reader to the fact that some scholars emend Aristotle's text here. The word in the mss. 'itself' (*de hauton*) in the phrase 'think itself' has been thought by some to be unintelligible and the words 'through itself' (*dia hautou*) substituted. The substitution is in my view unjustified. The words 'think itself' are in fact readily intelligible in the context of Aristotle's account of the intellect.

The basic distinction here is between (1) the intellect becoming or acquiring an intelligible form and (2) a further actualisation of the intellect. It is this actualisation that enables the intellect to 'think itself'. It is this latter actualisation that constitutes thinking in the primary, definitional sense.[25] The distinction between (1) and (2) is, we may recall, exactly the distinction Plato makes in *Theaetetus* between 'possessing' and 'having' knowledge. Aristotle has already anticipated the distinction earlier when he distinguishes two sorts of actualisation of cognition: (1) 'acquiring' the intelligible form and (2) 'bringing it to mind at will' (*DA* 2.5.417a27–8; b24). I have characterised this as the awareness of the presence of the form in the intellect in contrast to its simple presence. If this is correct, the question we face is why fully fledged, actual thinking consists in intellect thinking itself and why this requires that the intellect is unmixed with body.

The answer to this question appears in the striking claim repeatedly made by Aristotle that in thinking, one 'thinks oneself' or, stated otherwise, that one is identical with that which one thinks.[26] This is a claim that perhaps causes more consternation among critics of Aristotle than it should. In fully fledged thinking, one is aware of the presence of intelligible form in oneself. The identity of thinker and object of thinking consists in the fact that if thinker and object of thinking were *not* identical, the object of thinking would be like the object of thinking *prior* to its being cognised, that is, prior to 'possessing' it. Once we realise that we have to distinguish between first actualisation and second actualisation or between 'possessing' and 'having' intelligible form, we see that in order to avoid an obvious infinite regress, we have to recognise the identity of thinker and object of thinking. In addition, since a thing's identity comes, as we have seen, from its form, and since the intellect is, prior to thinking, without forms in it, the presence of form is its acquisition of an identity. The intellect becomes what it thinks formally, not materially; therefore it is not *really* what it thinks, except in those cases, Aristotle says, where what is thought has no matter in reality (*DA* 3.4.430a3–4).

The need for there to be an identification of thinker and object of thinking explains why thinking cannot be corporeal. Suppose that the presence of intelligible form were the presence of form in a body. After all, apart from cognition, that is how form is typically present. If that were so, the 'having' of form or the awareness of form's presence would have to be

---

[25] Cf. *Met.* 9.8.1049b12–17, on the priority of actuality to potency in 'definition'.
[26] Cf. *DA* 3.4.430a4–5; 3.5.430a19–20; 3.6.430b25–6; 3.7.431a1; 3.7.431b17; 3.8.431a22–3. Cf. also *Met.* 12.9.1074b38–1075a5.

by that which is not identical with that form, something that, say, 'monitored' the form's presence. But this monitoring would just be a prelude to what would in fact be the real first actualisation of form in cognition, namely, the presence of form in *it*. So, the need for the distinction between first and second actualisation or between possessing and having intelligible form requires the identity of thinker and object of thinking that in turn requires that thinking is not corporeal. The necessary physical separation of the putative corporeal subjects of the states of (a) the presence of form and (b) the awareness of the presence in fact precludes thought.

One might object to this line of reasoning as follows. If thinking is not corporeal because the second actualisation of incorporeal form requires the identification with it, cannot the same be said for sense-perception? That is, should we not be led to hold that perceivers are also incorporeal? Yet Aristotle maintains that animals are perceivers, though they are not capable of thinking because they do not have *logos*, and they do not have *logos* because they are not in any sense incorporeal subjects of cognition.

I believe that Aristotle's reply to this objection requires him to insist upon a distinction between the presence of sensible form and the effects produced in a perceiver by that 'information', on the one hand, and the cognition of form on the other. Animals are capable of sense-perception in the first sense, but not in the second.[27] In sense-perception broadly construed, the presence of sensible form can produce an array of physiological effects or responses without the cognition of that form; in sense-perception narrowly construed, cognition of sensible form is continuous with cognition of the form as intelligible, particularly in the classification or conceptualisation of that which was sensed. Cognition of sensible form is a sort of 'seeing as' as opposed to mere seeing. This 'seeing as' is equivalent to cognising the form universally as opposed to particularly, which is the way it is present in the sense-faculty. Aristotle thinks that this universal cognition could not occur in a corporeal subject because its putative occurrence could then only be the presence of a particularised (i.e., enmattered) form transformed into or represented by another particularised form. Cognising universally does not occur without sense-perception and imagination, but these are only the conditions for the 'seeing as'.

---

[27] Cf. *DA* 3.10.433b29–30 where Aristotle distinguishes imagination (*phantasia*) that is either 'with *logos*' (*logistikē*) or merely 'sentient' (*aisthētikē*). Animals are only capable of the latter whereas humans are capable of both. But imagination is 'a motion produced by the activity of sense-perception' (3.3.429a1–2). I take it that 'imagination with *logos*' is continuous with rational or fully fledged sense-perception and 'sentient imagination' with non-rational sense-perception.

That thinking is not corporeal does not, of course, mean that there could not be necessary corporeal conditions for thinking. The forms of all things that exist by nature have a corporeal basis, that is, these things are composed of form and matter. The corporeal basis means that the particular instance of the form cannot exist separately from the composite. So, when Aristotle defines the soul as 'the first actuality of a natural body with the potential for having life' (2.1.412a27–8), he is convinced that he has given the reason why the soul cannot exist separately from the composite. And yet, Aristotle also says that 'intellect is a kind of thing different from soul' (2.2.413b25–6), which is precisely why it is *not* so obvious that it cannot exist separately from bodies. In fact, when in chapter four of Book Three Aristotle focuses on intellect, he assumes that the requirement that it be unmixed with corporeal elements means that it is in fact separable from body (3.4.429b5; cf. 3.5.430a17).

I have already spoken of Aristotle's account of thinking as identification, specifically, as the cognition of a unity behind things that are the same. In knowledge, this unity is an essence. This cognition is substantially one with the 'self-identification' that is the second actualisation of thinking or the 'having' of the intelligible object. Thinking, however, includes modes of cognition other than knowledge. And yet the *logos* of belief is, as we have also seen, different from the *logos* of knowledge. Belief is cognition of an accidental identity; knowledge of a non-accidental one.

Thought, says Aristotle, thinks intelligible forms in images (*DA* 3.7.431b2; cf. *De Mem.* 1.449b30–450a7). An image is particular, arising from a particular sensible; yet, it has a measure of intelligible content. The reason sensibles are available, indeed, necessary for thinking is that they do possess intelligible content, even though the sensibles in all their particularity include more than what is strictly intelligible, i.e., matter. A thought (*noēma*) is the intelligible content considered now not merely as the remnant of sense-perception, but in relation to the intelligible form of which it is a manifestation. So, for example, in thinking about the properties of an insect, we may imagine a particular one. At the same time, we are thinking about that insect while leaving out the particularities of its composition. To do this is to think about it, or to think discursively about it. The result of this thinking is perhaps a true judgment. The judgment may be the true belief that this insect is winged. It may be the knowledge of why such insects have the properties they do, that is, the knowledge of the 'middle term' as the explanation. Or it may be the intellection (*nous*) of the essence. In the case of knowledge, the intellect identifies itself with the intelligible form. In the case of the true belief, an accidental identity is affirmed. Thoughts are combined in an affirmation or a denial. That is, one has a thought about a subject, a thought about an accidental attribute that is supposedly identified with the subject, and one makes an affirmation or denial of their accidental identity.

The capacity for making judgments – including beliefs – belongs to one faculty, that of thinking. So, one who is capable of having beliefs must, at least ordinarily, be capable of making the judgments that require self-identification because it is in virtue of one faculty that she is capable of both. The principal characteristic of belief indicating that it belongs only to that which is capable of knowledge is that belief is always attended by conviction (*pistis*) (3.3.428a19–21). To be convinced that, say, this moving object is a man is, for Aristotle, different from an animal's using its imagination to identify one thing with another for the purposes of action. The image is sufficient for this. In belief, however, it is the intelligible aspect of the image that becomes crucial. Conviction requires that one affirm or deny a combination of thoughts as representing reality. It requires, we might say, a propositional attitude. This attitude is precisely a judgment that there is an accidental identity in reality that is as the identity affirmed in thinking. In other words, one must judge that the state in which one is in represents reality. This judgment about one's self could not occur in something corporeal for the same reason that knowledge could not occur in something corporeal. An affirmation or denial is not possible without thoughts and thoughts require the sort of self-participation that is not required for the use of images.

The connection between the possibility of error or false belief and the incorporeality of thinking that we saw above to be left unexplained seems in part to be this. False belief is impossible for a corporeal entity because false belief, like true belief, requires self-reflexivity. But self-reflexivity, wherein the subject of a state is identical with the subject that is aware of being in that state, is not possible in a corporeal subject. If false belief did not exist, one might have supposed that belief is neither true nor false but like sense-perception in the sense of sensation, occurrent or non-occurrent, and explicable solely in corporeal terms. The falsity of a belief – as opposed to the falsity of the proposition expressing that belief – is not so explicable.[28] A false belief is not equivalent to the absence of a belief either, something which in corporeal terms would be like a switch failing to be

---

[28] The requisite contextualisation of the belief and its falsity or truth suggests another reason why Aristotle thinks that there is no belief about things that cannot be otherwise.

turned on. The falsity requires the self-reflexive awareness of the subject of one's belief as well as the self-reflexive awareness of what one is attributing to that subject.

One might suppose that the underlying argument rests on the idea that sense-perception is an event in which we are passive, but that having a belief, whether true or false, is something we do with or on the basis of our perceptual states. So, this line of reasoning goes, having a belief is not just one further corporeal state; it is something that we are actively engaged in realising. But apart from the obvious objection that a belief could be a corporeal state initiated by us in the way that the production of antibodies is a corporeal state initiated by us, Aristotle himself does not seem to be thinking in this way. For he maintains that our acts or states of believing are not 'up to us' (3.3.427b20). Minimally, this puzzling claim seems to mean that we acquire the beliefs we do because we believe that these beliefs are true, that is, we accept as epistemic the appearances that entail their truth. Of course, the reason we accept certain appearances as epistemic and certain others as not may well depend upon beliefs we already have. Nevertheless, it is well to emphasise that Aristotle maintains the general passivity of humans in acquiring beliefs at the same time as he maintains that beliefs are not something that strictly corporeal subjects can acquire.

The propositions to which one may assent may be true or false whereas in the thinking that is intellection, there is no falsity (*Met.* 5.29.1024b17-21). Specifically, in the intellection of essence what one cognises cannot be other than as it is. It is tempting to suppose that this means simply that if S knows p, then p, whereas if S believes p, either p or not-p. That this is not Aristotle's point is clear from the example of the previous section of one who has a true belief that man is an animal, but does not know it because he believes that this could have been otherwise. In this case, S believes p and p could not be otherwise. It does not follow, though, that S knows p. In other words, the two possibilities, p and (p or not-p) do not differentiate knowledge from belief.

Aristotle in this passage compares knowledge with sense-perception of proper sensibles, which he declares to be, like knowledge, always true. Another temptation is to take this to mean that the beliefs that affirm propositions about sense-experience are always true. But it is not so, for belief is of that which could be otherwise. Just as sense-perception is here taken to be apart from the realm of propositional attitudes, so is knowledge. The parallel is that the presence of sensible form and the awareness of this presence is like the presence of intelligible form and the awareness of this presence. The truth in knowledge, analogous to the truth in sense-perception, is not propositional truth. Aristotle says:

Concerning being as truth and non-being as falsity, being is true if it is united being but false if it is not united. But in the case of that which is one, if it is just a being, it exists in just this way, and if not in this way, it does not exist. And the truth about such being is the thinking of it, and there is neither falsity nor mistake about it but only ignorance, yet not the kind of ignorance that is like blindness, for blindness exists as if one were able to think of it as having no power at all (*Met.* 9.10.1051b34–1052a4).

The truth of 'united being' and the falsity of 'non-being' is the 'ontological truth' we already found in Plato.[29] For example, (a) the equality of base angles in an isosceles triangle is truth in this sense because being an isosceles triangle and having equal base angles are (in this case, always) united; (b) the diagonal of a square being commensurate with a side of that square is falsity in the sense that it has non-being (cf. *Met.* 5.29.1024b17–21). Propositions asserting (a) and (b) are true and false because one does and one does not 'correspond to' ontological truth. But in regard to what is self-identical or incomposite, that is, in regard to essence, the truth about these is the thinking of it and falsity is ignorance, not assent to a false proposition. In this thinking, no mistake is possible (*Met.* 9.10.1051b27–31; cf. *EN* 6.6.1141a3–5).

If the thinking of essence is infallible, is the same equally true for demonstrative knowledge? After all, such knowledge is paradigmatically expressed in the propositions that comprise the syllogism. In addition, if there is no thinking without images, how are we to suppose that the immediate 'touching' of essence suggested here by Aristotle is even possible? Just as we represent our sense-perception, as soon as we are aware of its occurring in propositional terms about which we spontaneously formulate a propositional attitude, so it would seem that our touching of essence, that is, our awareness of the presence of intelligible form in us must be immediately represented to ourselves via thoughts and hence, propositionally.

The answer to this question requires at least some attention to the part of *De Anima* that has always been rightly regarded as the most difficult and even mysterious, namely, the cryptic chapter five. The general purpose of this chapter seems to be to further explain the nature of intellect, that which owing to its thinking itself is intelligible. At the beginning of the chapter, Aristotle situates his remarks about intellect into his fundamental hylomorphic analysis of things that exist in nature. In every kind of thing there is

---

[29] See above, 49.

that which is the matter or, in other words, that which is the thing potentially, and there is that which is the productive cause of the thing (3.5.430a10–12). This productive cause acts like art in relation to its material. We expect the correlate of the material cause to be a formal cause, yet here Aristotle identifies the correlate as 'productive', presumably an efficient cause. There is, however, no discordance. In his *Metaphysics*, Aristotle explains that 'the medical art and the building art are the form of health and of the house' (7.7.1032b13–14; cf. 12.4.1070b30–5; 12.10.1075b10). They are the forms precisely by being productive.

This general principle about nature is now going to be applied to intellect in the soul. Intellect is in one way matter, because, as we have seen, it is capable of becoming all things, that is, all things intelligible. In another way, it is capable of making all things, like light that makes potential colours actual (3.5.430a14–17). This intellect, says, Aristotle, 'is separable, incapable of being affected, unmixed, and its essence is actuality' (3.5.430a17–18).[30] The central interpretive problem with the whole chapter is evident here: is this separable intellect *different* from the intellect that has hitherto been discussed, something that deserves to be called by a different name, for example, an active intellect or agent intellect? Or, is the intellect being analysed here just the intellect that has concerned Aristotle since chapter three?

In favour of the former interpretation is the consideration that if we suppose that the intellect that has hitherto been under discussion is a part of the soul and we know that the soul is inseparable from the body, the intellect that is here said to be separable must be different. Those who take this approach are typically inclined to go on to identify the active or agent intellect with the divine intellect, the Prime Unmoved Mover. This seems to me to be highly implausible because chapter five sits in the middle of a detailed discussion of human intellect and because the introduction of the divine intellect here adds nothing to the analytic function of this chapter.

Even more important, there are good reasons for denying that Aristotle is here introducing out of the blue an intellect that is different from the one already discussed as opposed to analysing further the one human intellect. Aristotle has already emphasised that intellect is a kind of thing different from soul, and so the fact that it is separable does not contradict the claim that soul is not. Further, the characteristics of being 'unmixed' and 'separable' have already been attributed to the 'other' intellect, the one supposedly different from the agent intellect. Finally, Aristotle has already stated

---

[30] Or, as some manuscripts have it 'in essence it is in actuality'.

clearly that within intellect we need to distinguish a part that acquires an intelligible form (first actualisation) and a part that is aware of the acquisition (second actualisation). Accordingly, if a second intellect is being introduced here, it looks very much like the 'first' intellect. That putative second intellect is, it would seem, indistinguishable from intellect hitherto discussed. If that is so, what does this compact chapter add to the previous discussion?

In the remainder of the chapter, we do get further information:

> Actual knowledge is identical with its object. In the individual, potential knowledge is prior to actual knowledge, but absolutely it is not prior, even in time. It does not sometimes think and sometimes not think. When separated, it is just what it is, and this alone is immortal and eternal. But we do not remember because while this is impassive, intellect that is passive is destructible. And without it, [the individual] thinks nothing (3.5.430a19–25).

We do have here an explicit distinction between passive and impassive intellect, but this is not presented as a distinction between two intellects; rather, it appears to be a distinction between intellect as it is 'in us' available for use in thinking, and intellect as it is apart from us, when it is 'just what it is'. Since this intellect, when separate, is just what it is, it is present in the individual in some *other* way. More important, there is a clear distinction here between intellect and the individual accessing or using intellect.

I shall begin with the last point, because it is only indirectly relevant to our central concerns. In several places in his *Nicomachean Ethics*, Aristotle discusses the relation between a human being and his intellect.[31] He claims that the intellect is 'us especially' or 'that which we are in the primary sense'. Intellect identifies us. It is what is most distinctive about us. Although human beings, composed of body and soul, are not immortal, our passage adds that our intellects are. We may leave aside the deeply obscure matter of how the immortality of 'us especially' is related to the human being here and now. In any case, the main point for our purposes is that this passage indicates that when we are talking about embodied human cognition, we are talking about our accessing of our intellects which, when separated from us, are fully or actually what they are.[32]

---

[31] See *EN* 9.4.1166a23; 9.9.1168b35; 9.9.1169a2; 10.7.1177b2.

[32] Note that Aristotle here is faced with the same problem we noticed in the previous chapter on Plato, namely, how the individual intellect is related to intellect in general. Those scholars who want to identify the intellect in *DA* 3.5 with the Unmoved Mover are following the same line of thinking as those who want to identify the disembodied intellect for Plato with the Demiurge. These very difficult matters cannot be pursued here.

When intellect is separate, it is identical with that which is intelligible. There are here no images or thoughts, insofar as the latter depend on images and ultimately on sense-perception. If, though, it is only when separated that the identity of intellect and intelligibles is unmediated by thoughts or images, what are we to say about the identity between intellect and intelligibles in those passages in *De Anima* already discussed? Drawing again from material found in *Metaphysics*, Aristotle says that in the knowledge sought in the theoretical sciences, the intellect is unequivocally identical with its objects. Even in the productive sciences, the intellect is unequivocally identical with its objects (*Met.* 12.9.1074b36–1075a5; cf. 12.7.1072b21). Qualified identity occurs only insofar as the objects known are composites, that is, only insofar as they are individuals or things that are not completely intelligible owing to their possession of matter. So, intellect is always just what it is, identical with the intelligible. In us, however, our accessing it is always through images and thoughts. We are not identical with intellect; neither are the things we encounter in sense-perception identical with that which is perfectly intelligible. Our thinking is the result of our perceptual encounters and includes our accessing of intellect. Without intellect, we could not have beliefs.

If intellect is identical with that which is intelligible, what I have termed the 'accessing of intellect' is equivalently the accessing of the intelligible. A bit of the oddness in saying this should be mitigated by the fact that Aristotle explicitly identified 'primary essence' or 'primary substance' with thinking in the first principle of all, the Prime Unmoved Mover.[33] Aristotle's notorious conclusion in *Metaphysics* that the Unmoved Mover is 'thinking thinking about thinking' (12.9.1074b33–5) is really a special application of the general principle that in thinking, the thinker is identical with the object of thinking. In the case of the Unmoved Mover, since there is no distinction between thinker and the activity of thinking, the Unmoved Mover is not a thinker who is identical with its objects of thinking, but *thinking* that is so identified. The point, of course, is that this identification is with all that is intelligible, that is, with *content*. So, it would seem that our accessing of the activity of thinking is simultaneously the accessing of that which is intelligible.

Intellect in us is not as it is when separated. Our access to it is through images and thoughts. Since we acquire these images and thoughts in sense-perception, we are passive with respect to them. The universals that become evident to us in these thoughts are the way we cognise intelligible objects;

---

[33] See *Met.* 12.7.1072a31; 12.8.1073a20.

they are not the intelligibles themselves. This follows from the fact that it is the identical intelligible form that is present in the intellect when we think and in the particular sensible objects of thinking. For example, the intelligible form that is the triangle is present both in the particular triangle and in the intellect when it makes universal judgments in regard to the triangle. If the intelligible form were identical to the universal, it could not be present in the particular. It could not be individualised. As Aristotle emphasises in his *Metaphysics*, universality and particularity are mutually exclusive (3.6.1003a5–12; cf. 7.13.1038b8–15). So, when we think universally, we mediately access intellect and intelligibles. We do not do what the Unmoved Mover does eternally or what our immortal intellects do when separated.

The apparatus of embodied thinking is thus distinguished from the paradigms of intellection. Aristotle, though, has insisted that in knowledge there is infallibility. This would seem to be exactly what we should *deny* if our embodied cognition does not possess the immediacy of the Unmoved Mover's cognition of intelligibles. Alternatively, we should deny that knowledge or intellection are available to us 'here below'. Aristotle certainly does not want to do this.

In the chapter immediately following the brief discussion of separate intellect, Aristotle turns to what at first appears to be a different subject:

> The thinking of indivisibles, is among those things in which there is no falsity. But in things in which there is truth and falsity, there is some combination of thoughts (*noēmata*) already there, just like the unity of things ... As for that which produces a unity in each case, it is the intellect (3.6.430a26–430b6; cf. 6.4.1027b25–8).

As in the *Metaphysics* passage quoted above, there is no falsity in the thinking of indivisibles (cf. *Met.* 5.6.1016b1–3). The 'unity' that is produced in each case of thinking by intellect when it combines thoughts is distinct from the 'indivisible' cognised in thinking. That indivisible is immaterial (*DA* 3.6.430b30). The combining intellect produces a unity of thoughts; the intellect that cognises indivisibles has the unity of its objects. In the former, one arrives at knowledge of the identity that explains some diversity or plurality, as in the self-identical middle term in a demonstrative syllogism or in the self-identical universal predicate manifested in its instances. In the latter, the intellect is itself identified with the intelligible form that is subsequently represented in thinking as 'one' concept or thought.

There is no doubt that the expressions of both demonstrative knowledge and intellection involve the combination of thoughts. The propositional expression of knowledge of an axiom, for example, or of the explanation for the possession by a species of animal of a certain property, is inseparable from the act of judgment that is an affirmation of its truth. What Aristotle here seems to be getting at, however, is that a necessary condition for such expressions (even to oneself) is the 'contact' with the intelligible object or form or middle term that makes the knowledge true. This contact is the state of the soul in which there is an identity between intellect and intelligible. Our access to these intelligibles requires images and thoughts. It turns out that the access is to intelligibles through the expression of the combination of thoughts. And it turns out that the word 'knowledge' (*epistēmē*) refers both to the 'intellection' (*noēsis*) that is the necessary condition for the representation of that state and to the representation itself.

Aristotle's account of thought in general drives his conclusion that knowledge is distinct from belief, and even from true belief. For Aristotle's account of thought as distinct from sense-perception means that the dependence of belief on sense-perception will guarantee that knowledge is not a type of belief. Still, belief is only possible for one capable of knowledge, that is, for one capable of thought. If it turned out that knowledge of necessary and universal truths were not possible for us owing to other incapacities or owing to the simple fact that there are no such truths, the capacity for belief would still depend on one possessing the capacity for thought, that is, the capacity for not merely 'possessing' form but 'having' it as well. This capacity depends on the intellect being 'unmixed' with body. If one is otherwise convinced that there can be no thing so unmixed, one will have to construe knowledge and belief and thought in general in a different way. We may, for example, revisit the claim of Aristotle's predecessors that thought is not substantially different from sense-perception. And the way is also open to stipulate that knowledge is nothing but true belief that happens to be arrived at in a certain canonical manner. In the next chapter, we meet the first generation of post-Aristotelian philosophers whose materialistic metaphysics inspires their approach to epistemology.

CHAPTER FIVE

Epicureanism and Stoicism

I INTRODUCTION

In this chapter, I turn to the responses made to Plato and Aristotle and, indeed, to the entire epistemological tradition by those in the first and second generations after Aristotle. Specifically, I will focus on Epicurus and the members of the so-called Old Stoa, Zeno, Cleanthes and Chrysippus. My justification for treating together two schools of philosophy that are deeply divergent in many ways is that they share a type of naturalism in epistemology that is self-consciously materialist. Owing to the fragmentary nature of our evidence and to considerations of space, I am going to try to express what I take to be the common ground among Epicureans on the one hand, and Stoics on the other, relating to epistemology. To this end, I shall make use of relatively late testimony by friends and foes alike of these two great schools of ancient philosophy. I hope that suppressing any of the philosophical differences that might have existed between, say, Chrysippus and Zeno will not compromise my basic account.

We saw in the last chapter that Aristotle criticised his predecessors for failing to distinguish thinking and sense-perception. They did so, says Aristotle, because they believed that (1) sense-perception is corporeal; (2) reality is corporeal and (3) cognition must be by that which is the same sort of thing as that which is cognised. So, (4) thinking, like sense-perception, must be corporeal. Aristotle does not dispute (1). His reaction to (2) and (3) is nuanced. Even if no non-corporeal entities exist, the bodies that do exist in nature have a hylomorphic composition. All that is cognisable in bodies is owing to form. Cognition of form occurs both in sense-perception and in thinking. So, if it is the case that the sense-perception of form is a corporeal process, there is at least one reason for inferring that thinking, too, is a corporeal process. Why, we may ask, is the reception of form in the intellect not the same thing as the reception of form in the sense-perception faculty? Aristotle maintains that the answer is indicated by the fact that in thought, as opposed to sense-perception strictly speaking, error is possible. The possibility of error or false belief depends on the incorporeality of thinking.

Both Epicureans and Stoics want to show that, though error is possible, this fact does not count against the corporeality of thinking. Attention to the possibility of error is of considerable importance to these philosophers for another reason as well. They both insisted that substantive error – particularly about the nature of reality – was at the root of human unhappiness. Human misconceptions and illusions were the principal impediments to living satisfying lives. What we might term the therapeutic aspect of Epicureanism and Stoicism is focused on the elimination of error in the most significant areas. Accordingly, they paid close attention to the development of rules and practices for identifying and removing falsity from the mind. Given this practical orientation to their epistemological reflections, one might have expected that their declared goal would be the replacement of false belief with true belief. In fact, Epicureans and Stoics also paid a good deal of attention to the difference between true belief and knowledge, unquestionably privileging the latter over the former. Why?

One additional introductory note is in order. Much of the philosophical excitement in Hellenistic epistemology generally is owing to the dialectical give and take among Epicureans, Stoics and their sceptical Academic rivals.[1] No doubt, some of the expressions of Stoic epistemology especially by Chrysippus are best understood in the light of Academic attacks on Stoicism and 'dogmatism' generally. For the sake of simplifying what is a rather complicated story, I shall in this chapter refrain from inserting the Academic objections to some of the dogmatic Epicurean and Stoic claims. As we shall see in the next chapter, some of these claims may themselves actually have been made in response to sceptical arguments.

2 EPICUREAN EPISTEMOLOGY

Epicurus' deep concern with epistemological matters flows from the explicitly practical orientation of his philosophy. In his *Letter to Menoeceus* (D.L. 10.121–35; cf. Sextus, *M* 11.169), he urges his disciple to take up philosophy for the sake of happiness. He identifies philosophy, first, with the acquisition of true beliefs about the universe and human beings. But there is

---

[1] Cf. Plutarch, *On Common Conceptions* 1059B–C (= *SVF* 2.33) who tells us that the Stoic Chrysippus philosophised after the Academic sceptic Arcesilaus and before the Academic sceptic Carneades. We are given to understand that Chrysippus sharpened or even changed Zeno's expression of Stoic doctrine in the light of Academic criticism and that Carneades attacked these responses.

more: Menoeceus is urged to 'accustom' himself to Epicurean precepts or
doctrines (124) and to 'practise' them 'day and night' (135). It is not enough,
it seems, to have acquired a true belief; one must be completely convinced of
it in order for the belief itself to make the requisite change that is actually
constitutive of happiness, or tranquility of soul (*ataraxia*). The factor that
transforms a mere true belief into one that is psychologically effective is the
firmness (*bebaiotēs*) and clarity (*enargeia*) with which it is held. When our
conviction (*pistis*) is as firm as possible, that is, when the truth of what we
believe is self-evident, we shall have knowledge.[2]

The emphasis on knowledge as opposed to mere true belief is not difficult
to appreciate. Epicurus will offer criteria for the acquisition of true beliefs,
especially sense-perception. Yet the fact that a belief is true because it was
acquired in the 'canonical' manner does not guarantee that the one holding
the belief knows that it is true. Consider the case of someone who holds
the belief (true, according to Epicurus) that the gods live a blissful life and
so have no care for us. Such a person may hold this belief with tepid
conviction, perhaps owing to his possessing another false belief that tends
to undercut this one such as that evil-doing will be punished some day.
What is needed in order to make the true belief effective is the firmest
possible conviction that this belief is true.[3]

Plato, we will recall, has differentiated true belief from knowledge by
claiming that a knower has 'bound' his belief with a 'figuring out of the
explanation' (*Meno* 98A). The belief is unstable and tends to 'run away'
until it is tethered. The instability of true belief is not removed by the
accompanying reasonable claim that true belief is as serviceable as knowledge for practical purposes. Epicurus' insistence on the superiority of
knowledge to mere true belief is probably not because the actions of a
knower will differ from those of a true believer, but rather because a knower
will be psychologically transformed in the right way by his knowledge
whereas a true believer will not be so transformed by his true belief.

---

[2] In our woefully incomplete primary sources for Epicurus' teachings, he does not appear to use the
word *epistēmē*, opting instead for the word *gnōsis*, a vaguer or more general term neutrally translatable
as 'cognition'. But cf. Lucretius, *On the Nature of Things* 4.469–521 who is defending and explicating
the Epicurean philosophy and uses the word *scire* (from which is derived the word *scientia*, the Latin
translation of *epistēmē*) in his argument that sceptics are wrong in denying the possibility of knowledge. Cf. Epicurus, *Letter to Herodotus* D.L. 10.78, where the accurate representations (i.e., the
'knowledge') of the causes of celestial phenomena are a crucial means for our 'blessedness'.

[3] Cf. Epicurus, *Letter to Pythocles* D.L. 10.85: 'Furthermore, do not believe that there is any other goal to
be achieved by the knowledge of meteorological phenomena … than freedom from disturbance and a
secure conviction, just as with the rest of physics.'

We also recall that Aristotle claimed that every belief is attended by conviction (*DA* 3.3.428a22). Presumably, the conviction attendant upon the infallible mental state that is knowledge or intellection would be greater owing at least in part to its greater accuracy. Yet, infallibility, as we have seen in the previous chapter, is purchased by separating the objects of knowledge from the objects of belief. By contrast, Epicurus seems to assume that knowledge, along with its maximum conviction, will be of that of which one can also have mere true belief.

One may suppose that the measure of conviction attendant upon knowledge is just whether the true belief has or has not produced the desired result in the philosophical aspirant. So, Epicurus' definition of knowledge might be: a true belief of which one has sufficient conviction for that belief to put one's soul in a state of tranquility. Such a definition, however, is clearly too broad. For one who is, say, about to be tortured may have maximum conviction in his belief that this is about to happen without thereby achieving the desired psychological tranquility. We might emend the proposed definition to refer only to those true beliefs that pertain to ultimate matters or first principles. These would be something like the province of wisdom or *sophia*. The limitation in this way is certainly apt, for the ancient Greek philosophers generally concurred in holding that *sophia* was indeed knowledge about matters the possession of which was intrinsically life-enhancing as opposed to being necessarily practically applicable. If this is what Epicurus wants to maintain, a different sort of problem arises. For as we shall see presently, the criteria of truth according to Epicurus all serve to justify empirical knowledge claims. How the contents of wisdom are supposed to be reduced to these is not readily apparent.

The essential metaphysical context within which Epicurus' epistemology must be understood is his view that nothing exists except bodies and the void (*Letter to Herodotus* D.L. 10.39–40).[4] Bodies are either atoms or compounds of atoms (41). Bodies and bodies alone have causal efficacy; the role of the incorporeal void is to make possible the motion of bodies. Hence, cognition is a corporeal event occurring in the bodies of the cognisers and caused by the bodies cognised. For this reason, if the soul is supposed to be involved in cognition, it cannot be incorporeal (67). Atoms possess size, weight and shape, and the attributes that necessarily go along with shape (54). Bodies, which are compounds of atoms, have permanent

---

[4] Epicurus is said by Diogenes Laertius (*Lives of Eminent Philosophers* 10.2) to have been inspired by the treatises of Democritus. Elsewhere (9.69), he is said to have been taught by Nausiphanes of Teos, though Epicurus himself is reported (10.8) to have spoken of Nausiphanes only in disparaging terms.

and impermanent attributes, the latter of which are termed, in the traditional way, 'accidents' (*sumbebēkota*) (68–72). The former belong alone to
the nature of bodies, that is, these cannot be separated from the body
without causing its destruction (Lucretius, 1.451–54). The body is thus
constituted by its permanent attributes in the sense that the 'aggregate
conception' (*athroa ennoia*) of it will always include these.

  This aggregate conception is itself derived from a 'basic grasp' (*prolēpsis*) or
a 'primary conception' (*prōton ennoēma*) arising from our sense-perceptions
(*Letter to Herodotus* D.L. 10.38). The basic grasp is, like sense-perception
itself, one of the criteria of truth. It arises from repeated sense-perceptions
retained in memory and it is equivalent to a true belief. If a primary
conception is a criterion of truth, no primary conception should be equivalent to a false belief (*Letter to Menoeceus* D.L. 10.124).[5] False beliefs will have
to be explained otherwise. With the possibility of false belief at issue, we need
to focus on sense-perception and basic grasps as criteria of truth.[6]

  Epicurus notoriously maintained that all sense-perceptions are true.
For, as Epicurus says:

every sense-perception is non-rational (*alogos*) unreasoning and incapable of
remembering. For neither is it moved by itself nor can it add or subtract anything
when moved by something else. Nor is there anything that can refute sense-
perception. For a perception from one sense cannot refute another of the same type,
because they are of equal strength; nor can a perception from one sense refute one
from a different sense, because they do not judge the same objects. Nor indeed can
reasoning (*logos*) [refute them]; for all reasoning depends on the sense-perceptions.
Nor can one sense-perception refute another [from the same sense], since we attend
to them all. And the fact of our awareness of sense-perceptions confirms the truth
of the sense-perceptions. And it is just as much a fact that we see and hear as that
we feel pain; hence, it is from the apparent that we must infer the non-evident.
Moreover, all conceptions are formed from sense-perceptions by direct experience
or by analogy or by sameness or by compounding, with reasoning also making a
contribution. And the appearances that madmen have and those in dreams are true,
for they cause motion [in us], and what does not exist does not move anything (*Letter
to Menoeceus* D.L. 10.31–2; cf. Lucretius, 4.469–521; Sextus, *M* 7.206–10; 8.63).

---

[5] Cf. *Letter to Menoeceus* D.L. 10.34 where true and false belief are given as types of judgment
(*hupolēpsis*). If this is accurate, *prolēpsis* is one type of *hupolēpsis*.
[6] The third criterion of truth is *pathē* (feelings) (*Letter to Herodotus* D.L. 10.37–8, 82; D.L. 10.31).
Diogenes lists a fourth criterion, the 'presentational applications of the intellect' (*phantastikas epibolas
tēs dianoias*), which is perhaps a universal thought derived from the consideration of primary thoughts
or basic grasps. That would make it much like the 'one universal' that Aristotle says arises from many
thoughts, that is, from thought about the intelligible content of images. Although I shall have a bit
more to say about these two criteria, I shall largely focus on sense-perceptions and basic grasps.

The motive for maintaining this apparently extreme position is evidently recorded by Cicero (*Acad.* 2.32.101; cf. 2.25.79): if any sense-perception is false, nothing can be grasped (*percipi*). This seems highly counter-intuitive, to say the least. Common sense has it that the perception of the stick in water as bent is false on the grounds that we have other perceptions of the stick as straight and we have good reasons to privilege the latter over the former. Indeed, a propos the last line in the above quotation, we designate some as mad precisely because their perceptions are false. One must suppose that all this was as plain to Epicurus as it is to us. So, what is his point and why does he make it a cornerstone of his epistemology?

Epicurus appears to reason as follows. If there are any false sense-perceptions, the intelligibility of such a notion depends on our understanding how to distinguish false ones from true ones. Epicurus then considers the ways that one might suppose we have for making such a distinction: (a) the perception of one sense cannot be refuted by another of the same type because they each have equal probative force; (b) the perception of one sense cannot be refuted by that of another sense because their objects are different; (c) one perception (of the same thing) cannot refute another because, again, of their being equally probative; and (d) reason cannot refute perception because reason relies on sense-perception. The reasoning is perhaps not unlike that of Aristotle who also insisted that the sense-perception of proper sensibles is without falsity.[7] And like Aristotle, Epicurus claims that falsity arises in our reasoning about our sense-perceptions.

If this is the case, why then go on to insist that sense-perceptions are *true* rather than simply to claim that they consist of a real event in the perceiver?[8] We today would find no difficulty in maintaining that the neurological events in the brain of a madman are no less real than those in the brains of the sane. What does Epicurus add by saying that all sense-perceptions are true, particularly in light of the fact that he also maintains that they are non-rational atomic events?

It seems that the general answer to this question is that Epicurus wants to ensure that knowledge is possible, where knowledge is evidently a *true* belief accompanied by maximum conviction. Yet the fact that Epicurus needs criteria for truth indicates that he takes cognition in general to be something more than an atomic event. As we saw in chapter 2, epistemology arises just

[7] Aristotle adds 'or has the least possible falsity' (*DA* 3.3.428b20), perhaps willing to concede that illness could yield falsity even with the perception of proper sensibles.

[8] The word used, *alēthēs*, can connote 'genuine' or 'real' as well as 'true'. But Epicurus seems to want to insist on more than that here.

at the point that the appearances of nature are put into question. To insist on the truth of sense-perceptions as opposed to just their reality is to insinuate the criteriological into the natural. As we have seen, Aristotle would not disagree. The disagreement starts at precisely the point where Aristotle wants to make the natural extend beyond the corporeal by including thought. And his initial reason for doing this is that error or false belief are possible. By contrast, Epicurus identifies the natural with the corporeal. He has no grounds for maintaining that all sense-perceptions are true unless he can show that error is, nevertheless, possible on his atomic assumptions. He certainly wants to do this, since it is, in his view, human error about the most important matters that is the cause of unhappiness.

Epicurus' claim that all sense-perceptions are true cannot, accordingly, be just the Protagorean relativist claim that man is the measure of all things. Epicurus is not subject to Plato's refutation of Protagoras which works by showing that knowledge, unlike sense-perception, is of objective reality (*ta koina*). Nor does he fall unwittingly into the Democritean trap of relativising sense-perceptions and therefore being unable to show how these provide evidence for that which is non-evident (*Letter to Herodotus* D.L. 10.38–9).[9]

Epicurus' response to the problem of how sense-perceptions can all be true and yet still be evidence for that which is objective is perhaps in line with Aristotle's own. As we recall, Aristotle does not just say that the sense-perception of proper sensibles is true; he adds that falsity is possible in regard to the sense-perception of things of which the proper sensibles are actualisations (*DA* 3.3.428b20–2). These are objects accidentally or indirectly perceived. It is crucial here that the objects about which falsity is possible are *perceived*, that is, they are not, in the language of Epicurus and Hellenistic epistemology generally, non-evident. Epicurus himself seems to use the term 'appearances' (*ta phainomena*) for such objects. Thus, Epicurus describes the atoms that actually impinge on our senses as 'images' (*eidōla*) and the objects themselves as appearances from which these images arise (*Letter to Herodotus* D.L. 10.46, 47, 54; cf. Lucretius, 4.255–8). Although the Aristotelian way of describing proper sensibles as actualisations of that which is accidentally or incidentally perceived is unacceptable to Epicurus owing to the implication that potentiality is a principle of reality, still, these atomic images are something like a manifestation of the bodies that appear.

---

[9] It may be that the testimony that Epicurus maintained that all 'presentations' (*phantasiai*) as well as all sense-perceptions are true (Sextus, *M* 7.203–04; Plutarch, *adv. Col.* 1109B) is an inference from the claim that sense-perceptions are indeed evidence of objective reality. A presentation, in Stoic usage, is that which is caused by an external object and indicates both itself and its cause. In Epicurean usage, presentations are external things – named 'appearances' (*phainomena*) – as these appear to us.

In this way, appearances, which had been typically contrasted with reality, turn up as reality itself, or at least the causally effective part of reality.

Sense-perception itself, as we have seen, is non-rational whereas the presentations of appearances or external things are rational in the sense that they are propositional. Epicurus adds:

> Falsehood or error always resides in the added belief. For the sameness of appearances (which are like what is grasped in a representational picture and occur in dreams or in some other application of the intellect or the other criteria) to what are called real or true things would never occur if some such thing were not added [to the basic experience]. And error would not occur if we did not have some other motion, too, in ourselves, which is linked to but distinct from [the sense-perception of the appearance]. Falsehood occurs because of this, if it is not testified for or is testified against; but if it is testified for or is not testified against, truth occurs (*Letter to Herodotus* D.L. 10.50–1; cf. Sextus, *M* 7.210).

Epicurus seems to reason in this way. A belief is a natural result of an atomic event constituted by atomic images acting on the atoms of our bodies. A true belief arises when the atomic images originate in the appearances; a false belief originates in *another* atomic event occurring as a result of one being affected by atomic images from elsewhere. Clearly, what should be the explanation of the error is the 'link' that the motion has with the genuine sense-perception and the fact that it is nevertheless 'distinct'.[10]

Sextus records the Epicurean example of Orestes who believed that the images he was encountering were those of the Furies, mythical women with snakes for hair (*M* 8.53). This was owing to his false belief that the Furies were bodily creatures. Presumably, what he did actually encounter were images of women or snakes and based on his false belief, he had another false belief that what were before him were Furies. This does not account for the original false belief in the existence of bodily Furies. How was that acquired? On the basis of the last line of the above quotation, we may suppose that Epicurus treats the true sense-perception as prima facie evidence of the appearances. An original false belief – one that can be implicated in subsequent false beliefs – is in fact a belief arising from a true sense-perception that is prima facie evidence for appearances, but can be defeated either by lack of supporting evidence or by counter-evidence.

This explanation, however, seems to confuse that which makes a false belief false with the cause of the false belief. The belief that the distant tower is small is false because the tower is not. If one moves close to the tower, the

---

[10] Cf. Plato, *Tht.* 193B–194B on the genuine cases of false belief that involve the 'misfitting' among two memories and two sense-perceptions.

true sense-perception of it will, of course, be different and so supposedly count as counter-evidence of the tower being small. As sceptics will point out, however, the sense-perception from afar is also counter-evidence for the sense-perception up close. If the privileging of one or more sense-perception over others is not to amount to the trivial claim that only real appearances produce true beliefs, some way of distinguishing among the sense-perceptions themselves has to be offered. It is not open to Epicurus to argue on pragmatic grounds that true beliefs are merely those beliefs that have at this moment not been subject to counter-evidence. For the whole point of trying to acquire true beliefs is that true beliefs will lead to happiness, whereas beliefs we regard as true because we have no evidence against them do not if they are in fact false. Epicurus cannot say that a true belief is one that has been arrived at by having a true sense-perception of a real object. All sense-perceptions are like this.

A false belief is apparently one that arises from the malfunctioning of our atomic systems. False beliefs are like the physiological malfunctionings that cause pathological responses in animals. Epicurus could point out that when Aristotle is forced to come up with an explanation for the possibility of practical error, that is, someone acting counter to his own best interests as he conceives of them, he himself appeals to the 'physiologists' for enlightenment.[11] Aristotle will reply that incontinence is not possible for corporal entities, since these do not have the capacity for making the universal judgments that comprise practical syllogisms. So, the appeal to physiology to account for error is only available if one has the capacity for theoretical error, and that capacity is not explicable if we assume any form of corporealism. Indeed, Aristotle will want to insist that atomic composites cannot have false beliefs because they cannot have beliefs at all.

It is clear enough that Epicurus' response to this argument must be couched generally in naturalistic terms. So, he has to reject the view that would make a belief a state of an incorporeal subject. A natural substitute for such a view is based upon a dispositional analysis of belief. Thus, to claim that S believes p is to claim nothing more than that S is disposed to act in various ways under given circumstances. Thus defined, cognitional dispositions may be held to arise from atomic corporeal states exactly as do the behavioural dispositions of non-rational creatures. The disposition that is a false belief is then analogous to atomic malfunctionings in behaviour generally, like Alexander the Great's slave who, Sextus reports, was marvelled at because he sweated in the cold and shivered in the sunshine.

---

[11] Cf. Aristotle, *EN* 7.5.1147b5–10.

The only real evidence we have that Epicurus looked upon belief in this way is his indexing belief to conviction. If a belief is a mental state rather than a disposition of a corporeal state, it would make little sense to speak of degrees of conviction.[12] Yet we manifestly seem to maintain our beliefs with varying strengths. For Epicurus, one who knows has maximal conviction, which amounts to a disposition not to become agitated or troubled. On this interpretation, the purpose of the acquisition of many true beliefs is to bolster or stabilise the maximal conviction in regard to the most important truths.

If a dispositional analysis of belief does indeed underlie Epicurus' epistemology, the distinction between true and false beliefs begins to seem not as sharp as his predecessors made it out to be.[13] So long as one maintains the basic criteria of truth, a false belief honestly reasoned to on their basis is likely to be as practically useful as a true one. One must add, of course, that according to Epicurus, no true belief that did not have these two principles could ever be arrived at otherwise. As we shall see in the next chapter, the Sceptics will find in the disassociation of justification and truth a wedge for attacking those forms of dogmatism that open this possibility.

Epicurus' elaborate though, unfortunately, sketchily attested theory of scientific methodology is evidently constructed to differentiate the true sense-perceptions that form the basis of true belief from the true sense-perception that leads to falsity.

Therefore, according to Epicurus, some beliefs are true and some are false; those which are (1) testified for (*epimarturoumenai*) and those which are (2) not testified against (*ouk antimarturoumenai*) by clear facts (*enargeiai*) are true, while those which are (3) testified against (*antimarturoumenai*) and those which are (4) not testified for (*ouk epimarturoumenai*) by clear facts are false (Sextus, *M* 7.211–12).

As Sextus goes on to explain, (1) and (4) are criteria for the truth of beliefs about bodies; (2) and (3) are criteria for the truth regarding things non-evident, such as the void and the atoms themselves. The clear facts are,

---

[12] Aristotle, for example, seems to distinguish a *hexis* from a *dunamis* in cognition. Cf. *EN* 6.13.1144a29–30. The former is a state in virtue of which the latter, a power, is possessed. As we recall, underlying the reason for distinguishing these is the argument that higher cognition requires an incorporeal subject and this in turn follows from the argument about the possibility of error and ignorance. Only one capable of knowledge can be ignorant or have false beliefs. Only an incorporeal subject is capable of knowledge. If one can explain the possibility of error or false belief or ignorance otherwise, the motive for distinguishing the state and the power (disposition) disappears.

[13] Lucretius, 4.500–6, gives powerful expression to the idea that a false belief about the causes of things based on the conviction that all sense-perceptions are true is better, that is, more useful to us, than a true belief that is not so based.

presumably, sense-perceptions and basic grasps. They are the basis for inference to true beliefs according to the relevant inferential criteria.

None of our accounts of Epicurus' theory indicate any modalisation of these criteria, that is, any inclination to say that a true belief is one for which there could not be testimony like (3) and (4). Accordingly, a true belief is always 'so far as we know at the present time'. And this seems admirably scientifically minded in its modesty. Yet as we have seen, Epicurus wants beliefs – especially about things not evident – embraced with maximum conviction. It is not easy to see how degrees of conviction could be rationally correlated to the status of beliefs whose supposed truth cannot be but recognised as *pro tem*.

At the end of his *Letter to Herodotus* (D.L. 10.80), Epicurus acknowledges a somewhat mitigated standard. Regarding the various possible explanations for meteorological phenomena, he says that 'we must not believe that our study of these matters has failed to achieve a degree of accuracy which contributes to our undisturbed and blessed state'. I take this to mean that for practical purposes, it is enough that our explanations are based on the basic Epicurean principles even if they turn out to be supplanted by superior explanations similarly based. It turns out then that maximum conviction is a desideratum only for the basic principles. One may suppose that this conviction is achieved by the compilation of successful explanations for particular phenomena using the basic principles. The contemplation of any mysterious phenomena could weaken our conviction of these. Remove the mystery and conviction is fortified.

Epicurus' embrace of the traditional Greek philosophical idea that knowledge is supposed somehow to be life-enhancing along with his principle that the only sort of knowledge possible is empirical knowledge sets ancient epistemology on a new path. Epicurus was joined on that path by the Stoics.[14]

3 STOIC EPISTEMOLOGY

The practical orientation of Epicurus' philosophy is matched by that of the founder of Stoicism, Zeno of Citium (334–261 BCE). Zeno pronounced the goal in life to be 'living in agreement with nature' (Stobaeus, *Eclogues*

---

[14] There is no space here to consider the connection between the Epicurean and Stoic rejection of the possibility of incontinence and their emphasis on the motivational effect of knowledge (as opposed to mere belief). If it is not possible to act counter to one's own knowledge, the practical and even transformative power of knowledge is plain. This is already a point made by Plato in his *Protagoras* (cf. 352D). For Epicurus and the Stoics, however, knowledge is exclusively empirical.

2.75.11–76.8). This amounts to 'living in accord with a single consonant rational principle' (*kath' hen logon kai sumphonon*). At least part of what is meant by the last phrase is living without false beliefs, including those that are constituted by the passions. The coherently rational life is the happy life; it is the life belonging exclusively to the Stoic sage. He alone possesses knowledge. And yet this knowledge has as its objects exactly the same objects as those of true belief. In order to understand the Stoic's distinctive and subtle view, we need to sketch briefly the metaphysical context within which it is developed.

The Stoics rejected atomism but shared the materialism of Epicureanism. They hypothesised two principles of the universe, an active and a passive principle (D.L. 7.134 = *SVF* 2.300; Sextus, *M* 9.75–6 = *SVF* 2.311).[15] The latter they called 'matter'; the former they called *logos* or 'god'. Everything is either corporeal or incorporeal (Sextus, *M* 10.218 = *SVF* 2.231). Only the corporeal is capable of acting or of being acted upon (Sextus, *M* 8.263 = *SVF* 2.363). Incorporeals include space, time, void and 'sayables' (*lekta*), roughly, propositions ('complete sayables') and their meaningful parts ('incomplete sayables'), that is, parts that can be understood to have reference. I shall have more to say about sayables in a bit. Corporeals are divided into four kinds: (1) substrate (*hupokeimenon*); (2) the qualified (*poion*); (3) condition (*pōs echon*); and (4) relative condition (*pros ti pōs echon*). The distinction between (1) and (2) is, it seems, a distinction between that which underlies a body's identity through time and the constituents of its identity (Stobaeus, 1.177.21–179.17). The distinction between (2) and (3) is not apparent, though the few examples given suggest that (3) includes a qualification subsequent to or supervenient upon fundamental qualities, perhaps indicating a principle of action. (4) is more clearly a straightforwardly relative property, one which can be altered by an alteration in one of the relata.

The distinction between (1) and (2) is a successor to Aristotle's hylomorphism with the crucial qualification that the qualified includes only that which is corporeal. These are divided into (a) the 'commonly qualified' (*koinos poion*) and (b) the 'uniquely qualified' (*idiōs poion*). The identity of an individual is found in (2) (a) and (b), that is, in that to which general terms refer when they are used of it and in that to which a proper name refers when used of it. It is natural to conjecture that (2) (b) is in fact the locus of an individual's identity. This only works perspicuously if (a) is related to (b) as potentiality to actuality, a distinction that has no basis for justification in Stoic materialism. Probably, (a) is best understood to refer to

[15] *SVF* = *Stoicorum Veterum Fragmenta*, ed. H. von Arnim, repr. (Stuttgart: Teubner, 1979).

portions of a corporeal whole, like pieces of gold, whereas (b) refers to those bodies that are uniquely identifying, presumably within a spatio/temporal matrix. Under (a), for example, falls that bodily nature that is conceptualisable as 'man' or 'dog'; under (b) falls the bodily nature that is conceptualisable as the referent of a singular proper name in a proposition. Our concepts in general are representations of the individualised portions of nature, typically expressed in sayables.[16]

The Stoic criterion of truth is the 'graspable presentation' (*katalēptikē phantasia*) (D.L. 7.54 = *SVF* 2.105). A presentation is a state (*pathos*) in the soul revealing (*endeiknumenon*) both itself and its cause (Aëtius, 4.12.1 = *SVF* 2.54).[17] Presentations can be acquired either through sense-perception or thought (D.L. 7.49 = *SVF* 2.52). The latter are of incorporeals and non-evident corporals, like god.[18] In a rational animal, presentations are all rational, that is, they are events that include as an essential part our thinking; in a non-rational animal, they are all non-rational.

Presentations may be either true or false. A false presentation is one about which it is possible to make a false assertion, e.g., that the oar in water is bent (Sextus, *M* 7.244 = *SVF* 2.65).[19] As Sextus reports:

Of true presentations, some are graspable and some are not. Non-graspable ones are those experienced by people in an abnormal state. For countless people who are deranged or melancholic receive a presentation that, though true, is non-graspable; rather, it occurs externally or by chance, such that they often do not respond to it or do not assent to it. A graspable presentation is one which (1) comes from that which exists and (2) is stamped and impressed according to the identity of that which

---

[16] Sextus, *M* 8.13, implies that Epicurus rejected sayables, claiming that he recognised only signifiers and things signified (cf. Plutarch, *adv. Col.* 1119f.). If the concept of a *lekton* was, as is perhaps likely, introduced by Chrysippus, it is not clear that Epicurus could have not admitted it as opposed to not ever having thought of it. But in *Letter to Herodotus* (D.L. 10.38), Epicurus does in fact seem to place between signifier and things signified the 'primary concept'.

[17] Sextus, *M* 7.227–36, adds that Zeno called this state an 'impression' (*tupōsis*) and understood literally, like an impression made in wax. But Chrysippus rejected this on the grounds that if impressions were like this, the presence of one would preclude the simultaneous presence of others, something which is manifestly false. This is a point related to Aristotle's argument that the soul must itself be without form if it is to receive all forms. Instead, Chrysippus took the impression to be an 'alteration' (*heteroiōsis*). Thus, a soul could be variously affected by different impressions simultaneously. Other Stoics noted that there could be impressions in the soul that were not presentations, e.g., a blow to the finger or a scratch on the hand. So, the definition of presentation was amended to refer to an impression on the soul 'insofar as it is a soul'. This seems to mean an impression in the 'leading part of the soul', the so-called *hegemonikon*, the subject of cognition.

[18] Sextus, *M* 8.409 = *SVF* 2.85, says that presentations of incorporeals are received not directly by them, but in relation to (*ep' autois*) to them. This seems to mean that some bodies affect us such that we think that they could not do this were an incorporeal such as space or time not involved.

[19] The Stoics hereby reject the Epicurean claim that all presentations are true. Cf. Cicero, *Acad.* 2.83–5.

exists and (3) of such a kind as could not come from that which does not exist (Sextus, *M* 7.247–9 = *SVF* 2.65).

Sextus goes on to note that (3) was added in response to the Academic sceptics who argued that it was possible to have a false impression indistinguishable from a true one. Later Stoics, we are told, added (4) 'provided that it [the presentation] has no obstacle' (*M* 7.253), meaning that sometimes though there is a graspable presentation, one may give it no credence owing to an antecedent false belief that conflicts with the present presentation.[20]

Let us begin by noting that the graspable presentation is a criterion of truth; it is not a criterion of knowledge. The Stoics insisted that knowledge is available only to the wise, whereas the having of graspable presentations was possible for any rational creature. It is clear enough why a criterion of truth is alone not sufficient. If we look carefully at the elements of the criterion, (1)–(3), it is entirely possible for one to have a graspable presentation and be unaware that it is such. If one is unaware that the presentation one is currently having is graspable, the practical value of such a presentation is at once diminished. Adding (4) does not help matters at all. For no one has beliefs that he thinks are false. Yet if it is a false belief that obstructs the assent to a current graspable presentation, one would need to be confident that one is not bringing to the current situation any false beliefs that would obstruct assent. How could this be done, given that we are not aware of any of our beliefs as false? So, one would seem to be in need of an internal criterion to distinguish a true presentation from which assent is improperly withheld owing to the presence of false beliefs and a true presentation to which one ought to assent since there is no false belief obstructing it.

The problem here encountered is similar to the one looming over proponents of the Standard Analysis, as we saw in chapter 1. A true belief is one for which there is, presumably, an evidentiary or justificatory story to be told. It does not follow that the one who has the true belief has the story or even has access to it. Moreover, even if one does have the story, one must face the dilemma of whether the 'having' is equivalent to believing or knowing. One can opt for the former and dispense with knowledge as

---

[20] The examples that Sextus gives are odd, but revealing. One is the case of Admetus who has a true presentation of his wife Alcestis, brought back from the grave by Heracles. But Admetus did not believe that people return from the grave, and so he took the presentation of Alcestis as a certain *daimōn*. The other example is of Menelaus who, receiving a true presentation of Helen on the island of Pharos, did not believe it to be so because he thought he had left Helen under guard on his ship. In fact, what was on his ship was only a wraith of Helen.

nothing more than the name for beliefs that have been acquired and are believed by the believer to have been acquired through some suitably recognised practice. Here, though, where justification is implicitly severed from truth, there is no guarantee that beliefs acquired in the canonical way are true. Alternatively, one can opt for the latter, but in that case it is useless to insist that knowledge is true belief with the added condition that one know why the belief is true.

It is noteworthy that the Stoics refused to reject the distinctiveness of knowledge from belief and even from grasping, especially given their claim that knowledge was extremely rare. For the Academic sceptics' attack on the graspable presentation is, as we shall see more fully in the next chapter, simultaneously an attack on the possibility of knowledge. It might have seemed to the Stoics that the ubiquity of graspable presentations and the rarity of knowledge would make the latter dispensable, particularly if dispensing with its possibility meant that the former could be more effectively defended. What is at stake here is in fact whether rational belief is possible if knowledge is not. This might seem a question as easy to answer in the affirmative as one regarding the possibility of a long and healthy life even if immortality is not possible. This is not, however, what later sceptics will argue.

Again, we may appeal to Sextus' admirably clear statement of the Stoic position:

For they [the Stoics] hold that three things are linked to (*suzugounta*) each other: knowledge, belief and placed between these, grasping. Of these, knowledge is sure and stable grasping unalterable by reasoning; belief is weak and false assent; and grasping is what is between these, assent to a graspable presentation. According to the Stoics, a graspable presentation is true and such that there could not be a false one just like it. They say that knowledge is present only in the wise, belief is present only in base men, but that grasping is common to both groups, and that this is the criterion of truth (*M* 7.151–2; Stobaeus, 2.73.19 = *SVF* 1.68–9; Cicero, *Acad.* 1.41 = *SVF* 1.60).

Minimally, the 'linkage' that exists between belief, grasping and knowing is that they all require assent and that they all may be of identical truths. On the basis of the description of the criterion of truth above, it seems that what we may call a 'mere' belief generates weak and false assent because it is unjustified. Yet as we have seen, the justification cannot simply consist in the fact that there is a justification to be had independent of whether the one who assents has that. Let us grant the Stoic claim that a graspable presentation is such that there could not be a false one just like it. This hypothesis would seem to offer no comfort to one who cannot tell the difference between a true and a false presentation. So, the Stoic might have replied that graspable presentations are such that their force is *irresistible* – like being dragged by the hair, they would say (Sextus, *M* 7.257) – and their distinction from false presentations manifest. If, though, this is the case, why continue to maintain that there is a difference between grasping and knowledge?[21] For if knowledge is essentially unalterable by reasoning, and knowledge is different from grasping, it would seem to follow that mere grasping *is* alterable by reasoning. And if this is so, the irresistibility of a graspable presentation is, to say the least, suspicious. If a grasp is alterable by reason, it is hard to see exactly what the difference is between the 'weak' assent of mere belief and the stronger assent of a grasp. We must envision the possibility that one who is 'dragged by the hair' into assenting is still in a position to be reasoned out of the assent she has given.

In the continuation of the above passage, Sextus records that the Academic sceptic Arcesilaus saw the problem with the utmost clarity:

These being the Stoics' views, Arcesilaus countered them by showing that grasping is in no respect a criterion midway between knowledge and belief. For that which they call grasping and assent to a graspable presentation occurs either in a wise man or in a base man. But if it occurs in a wise man, it is knowledge, and if in a base man, it is belief, and there is nothing else left besides these two but a name (*M* 7.153).

According to the dilemma posed, a grasp is either a mere belief or knowledge. There is no middle ground. The Stoics made the graspable presentation the criterion of truth. If there is no graspable presentation, there is no grasping. Worse, if there is no criterion of truth, the assent of the base man is no different from the assent of the wise man. And so, it would seem, the wise man is either base or is one who will refuse to assent to anything. That is, he will, like the sceptic, suspend judgment.

Perhaps we can now see more clearly why the Stoic's insistence on the possibility of knowledge and the identification of this as the preserve of the wise man is so odd. If we say farewell to knowledge, the putative dilemma can be reconfigured into an easily made choice: either irrational assent or rational assent. Grasping would become the *ne plus ultra* of cognition and the true preserve of the wise. The Stoics had grounds, though, for not making this concession. The graspable presentation is only rational if it is knowledge, that is, if it does not just happen to be true belief. So long as it is possible for one to be disposed such that one's assent is unalterable by

---

[21] Aristotle, *Topics* 5.2.130b16; 5.4.133b29ff.; 4.133b29ff.; 5.5.134b17; 6.8.146b2, seems to acknowledge a common definition of knowledge as '*hupolēpsis* incontrovertible by *logos*'.

reasoning, an analysis of the way one acquires that disposition is intelligible. The problem is that as soon as one sets knowledge apart from grasping, the alterability of assent in the latter makes it indistinguishable from mere ungrounded belief.

The Stoics, like the Epicureans, identified knowledge as a condition, in the third category of corporeals.[22] Thus, the wise man will be disposed differently from one who grasps true presentations owing to his condition. As the Stoics insist, the one who is not wise is a fool; the one who does not have knowledge is ignorant. The dilemma Arcesilaus wishes to foist on them is actually encouraged by this stark division. In the *hegemonikon* (leading part of the soul) of one not wise, there might well be a disposition to utter a true proposition (Sextus, *PH* 2.83). How can it do him any good, though, if he does not know that it is true? The Stoics are not willing to recognise a realm of rational, measured beliefs populated by holders of these beliefs who are not wise but who are not fools either. The assent that one gives to a graspable presentation is no doubt stronger than the 'weak and false assent' accompanying mere belief. This stronger and truer assent is only available to the wise, to someone whose assent is impervious to alteration by reasoning.

The true proposition to which the fool gives assent is not equivalent to knowledge of the truth (Sextus, *M* 7.42; *PH* 2.83). The point of distinguishing true and truth is not the relatively uninteresting point of a coherentist account of truth according to which no single proposition contains the *whole* truth but that without possessing the whole truth, one's grasp of a single truth is qualified in some way. If that were the case, grasping would be doomed anyway. The point is rather that the wise man does not assent to anything that is false as a result of which there is nothing to obstruct or diminish his assent to a graspable presentation (Cicero, *Acad.* 2.59, 66, 77). His assent differs not in degree but in kind. For his assent is to what is evident to him, that which he could not even conceive of as being false.

To reason thus is to approach a position that is in fact but a hair's breadth from scepticism. The last step would consist in acknowledging that any proposition – any complete 'sayable' – is true or false, that is, it does not present itself to us as inconceivably only one way (D.L. 7.65 = *SVF* 2.193; cf. Sextus, *M* 8.74 = *SVF* 2.187; Cicero, *De Fato* 38). As Arcesilaus noted, assent is to a proposition, not to a presentation (Sextus, *M* 7.154). The position of the putative reasonable man who is not a fool in relation to the putative wise

---

[22] Cf. Sextus, *M* 7.39; *PH* 2.81, 'knowledge is a disposition of the *hegemonikon* just as the fist is a certain disposition of the hand and the *hegemonikon* is a body, for according to them [the Stoics] it is breath'.

man is not the position of one who possesses an admittedly inferior though respectable degree of evidence, but rather of one to whom the truth of the proposition is not evident at all. As far as he is concerned, he assents to a proposition the truth of which is adventitiously connected to the reasoning behind his assent.

The Stoic may reply that the presentation to which one gives assent when one has a grasp is revelatory both of itself and of its cause. The cause in this case is presumably equivalent to the indirect or accidental object of sense-perception in Aristotle and *ta phainomena* of Epicurus. So, it might be supposed that even if assent includes belief in the truth of a proposition, it also includes something else, namely, direct cognition of what makes the proposition true. That is, indeed, why the presentation is graspable as opposed to being ungraspable.

If this is the authentic Stoic defence of their position, the obvious reply is that this direct cognition of the cause should be no more alterable by reasoning than is the knowledge of the wise man or the sense-perceptions of Epicurus and of Aristotle. The Stoics, though, resolutely deny that every grasp is an instance of knowledge. Presumably, what makes some grasps *alterable* is that reasoning has gone into the grasp in the first place, that is, the one with the grasp has essayed an inference from the presentation qua proposition to the presentation qua cause. If this is the case, the presentation is no longer the criterion of truth. Stated otherwise, assent to the truth of a proposition is not a criterion for the cognition of truth, that is, for grasping. One will need another criterion to justify inferences from the propositions to which one assents to the conclusion that they are in fact true, that is from the belief that p is true, to the truth of p.

The Stoics want to maintain that the appropriate inferences fall within the nature of the presentation because only one particular individual could cause this particular presentation. This is a fair Aristotelian point if indeed the sense-perception is both of a proper and of an indirect sensible. The inadequacy of this response is evident as soon as one is asked about the grounds for assent to anything other than a particular proposition. The problem is not that the general propositions may not be true; the problem is that the Stoics have to maintain that one can grasp their truth without knowing them. This will require that one be able to justify one's claim to grasp the truth, even to or especially to oneself. The justification, however, is in principle always open to being overturned by reasoning. This is precisely what Arcesilaus' argument from illusion is designed to do.

The Stoics will not relent on the high or even unattainable standard of knowledge. One might have thought that in, say, rejecting Plato's Forms, and therefore in rejecting the claim that knowledge is of Forms, they might have decided that there is actually no such thing as knowledge as traditionally conceived. In addition, one might have thought that faced with Academic attacks, they could have made a strategic elision of knowledge with grasping. The Stoics, however, maintain the possibility of knowledge as distinct from grasping precisely because they need graspable presentations. Graspable presentations are in fact not, practically speaking, available to anyone who is not so disposed that it is inconceivable to him that these presentations are other than as they are. This inconceivability or unalterability by reasoning is, it appears, the Stoic version of the impossibility of error as characterised by Aristotle.[23] The crucial difference is that Aristotle holds that the impossibility of error is in regard to the knowledge of essence or of that which cannot be otherwise; all error resides in belief about what can be otherwise. By contrast, the Stoics maintain that knowledge is of the same things of which grasping and mere belief are possible. The reason for this is, of course, not that the Stoics want to deny that there are necessary truths to be known. The reason is rather that in the Stoic universe, necessary truths all pertain to a single subject – the cosmos – and these are available to us only through our presentations.

The designation of knowledge as a condition of the *hegemonikon* is exactly right if knowledge is the result of the (corporal) action of the cosmos upon our (corporeal) souls. The state of the *hegemonikon* in virtue of which one is disposed to behave in a certain way is a corporeal state. For Aristotle, the state that is knowledge consists in the presence of a non-corporeal form and the awareness of this presence by the subject that is identical to the subject that is 'informed'. So, for the Stoics, knowledge has to have as its objects corporeal presentations and their corporeal causes, exactly what the putative grasping and belief have as their objects.

That the Stoics reject the Platonic/Aristotelian theory of forms as objects of knowledge is clear from their treatment of universal propositions as conditional statements pertaining to individuals (Sextus, *M* 11.8–11). A universal proposition like 'man is a rational mortal animal' differs only verbally from a definition of man. It is a generalisation whose subjects are individual men and falsifiable by a single counter-example. Knowledge of the essence or form of man reduces to a grasping of a true universal proposition. Even if it is true that there are in fact no individuals called

---

[23] As the Stoics themselves seem to admit. See Stobaeus, 2.88.4 = *SVF* 3.171: 'Propositions are the objects of acts of assent.' The proposition to which one assents is also describable as an intentional object of belief or knowledge. See, e.g., Seneca, *Letters* 117.13.

'man' who are not rational mortal animals, it is difficult to see how one could know this in the Stoic sense of 'know'. According to that sense, knowing is the sort of thing about which one could not conceivably be in error.

Taking knowledge to be fallible, as in 'I know but I could be mistaken', or, it having been determined that I was not mistaken, 'I could have been mistaken', is an eminently reasonable approach given the Stoics' nominalist metaphysics.[24] One suspects that the immediate reply to this suggestion by the Stoics is that one should not 'take' knowledge in any way other than the way knowledge is in reality. Why, then, did they suppose that knowledge must be infallible? One clue is the above distinction between 'truth' and 'true', the former of which is identified with the knowledge possessed by the wise man. It is identical with the corporeal condition of his *hegemonikon*.[25] The second clue is found in a passage in Cicero's *Academica* (1.41 = *SVF* 1.60) where we learn that the opposite of knowledge is ignorance. Yet just as for Aristotle, ignorance is not nescience but a relation to reality owing to false belief, so for the Stoics, one who is ignorant is also one who has weak and changeable assent (Stobaeus, 2.111.18–112.8 = *SVF* 3.548). This weak and changeable assent is belief.[26] Such a belief may well be true, yet one who possesses it is nevertheless ignorant (Sextus, *M* 7.42). He is ignorant of that of which he has a true belief! How can this be?

The belief of one who is ignorant is assent to a proposition which supposedly represents the corporeal truth that is the cause of the proposition's being true. But he does not know that it is true. To know it, he would have to know that the proposition to which he assents is true. By contrast, the wise man is the truth he knows. The identification of knower and known that Aristotle argued was available only to an incorporeal entity is here ascribed to the body that is the *hegemonikon*. And the division Plato made between the highest type of cognition, namely, knowledge, that consists in identification with the known and all other types of cognition that are representational is here retained, albeit in altered form. Weak and changeable assent is all that is available to one who is assenting to the truth of a proposition. And this is so for a good reason. Incorporeal representations

---

[24] See chapter 4, above 168ff. The Stoics treated universal concepts as 'no-things', that is, as quasi-real entities because they do not represent anything other than individuals. See Stobaeus, 1.136.21–137.6 = *SVF* 1.65; Simplicius, *In Cat.* 105.8–16 = *SVF* 2.278.

[25] Cf. Sextus, *M* 8.409 = *SVF* 2.85, who reports on the Stoic description of the reception of presentations by the *hegemonikon* as a sort of 'touching' or 'contact'. Cf. Aristotle, *Met.* 9.10.1051b25; 12.7.1072b20–1.

[26] Sextus, *M* 7.151, says that belief is 'weak and *false* assent' where 'false' must mean 'unjustified'.

of corporeal reality *are* changeable and subject to the vagaries of language. The wise man has no beliefs; he knows because he assents to the truth, not to supposedly true propositions. This is not to say, of course, that he does not also assent to true propositions. His assent, though, is not belief; it follows from his knowledge. It is not a substitute for knowledge as is the assent of one who believes.

The state of one who has *katalēpsis* (grasping) in comparison to the one who has *epistēmē* is compared by Zeno to the one who 'grasps' the object with his fist to the one who grasps that fist with the other one (Cicero, *Acad.* 2.145 = *SVF* 1.66). This could be interpreted to mean that the one who knows has an even firmer grasp than the one who 'merely' grasps. But this alone does not explain why the grasp is firmer. Given the above, I suspect that Zeno's point is that the one who knows knows that he knows. What he knows is self-evident to him. That is, the truth is self-evident to him because it is actually present to his *hegemonikon* and he is aware that it is. If this is so, *only* one who knows that he knows indeed knows for even the ignorant man may have his *hegemonikon* affected in the same way that the *hegemonikon* of the wise man is affected. There is, in other words, no suggestion that the sense-perceptions of the ignorant are inferior as sense-perceptions to those of the wise.

On the above interpretation, for a Stoic to deny the possibility of knowledge would amount to conceding that all cognition is representational. It might occur to us that this concession is entirely salutary. The Stoics would no doubt find it entirely unacceptable. And incredible, too. If all cognition is representational, there is no way to discern the difference between good and bad representations. The graspable presentation is a criterion of truth when had by a wise man because he really does possess the truth, not a representation of it. The criterion of the truth of the propositions to which he does assent is the truth in him. He will assent to nothing but that.

The wise man is the corporeal analogue of Plato's disembodied knower and Aristotle's intellect which only comes into its own when separated. The parallel is actually even closer than this. The wise man is not just a notional ideal that we all could theoretically attain to, but he is what we all are in the absence of our (perhaps irremovable) defects. The Stoics refuse to forgo the possibility of infallible knowledge because to do so would be to render the distinction between true and false belief problematic. In this they agree with their Academic critic Arcesilaus and with their later Pyrrhonian critics as well. What makes it possible to discern the difference between true and false belief is that the truth really is in us. All but the wise fail to access the truth, instead supposing that they have an independent means of access to a criterion of true propositions.

Stoic epistemology rests upon a general principle of cognition as a natural process or event. This naturalism precludes representation from being exclusively the medium of cognition. A true proposition is an expression of the truth when the truth is known, not the truth itself. The relationship that a wise man has to the truth is not a propositional attitude. In this regard, the Stoics are deeply imbued with the naturalistic approach to knowledge and belief developed by Plato and Aristotle. Where they set themselves apart is in their materialism. The combination of naturalism and materialism on behalf of a defence of the possibility of knowledge provides scepticism's main target.

CHAPTER SIX

Scepticism

I PYRRHO AND THE BEGINNING OF SCEPTICISM

Pyrrho of Elis (*ca* 360–270 BCE), painter, student of atomism, of Indian philosophy, and certifiable eccentric was taken by the ancients to be the founder of scepticism. As usual, things are not quite so straightforward. The first sceptic of the philosophical schools was the Academic Arcesilaus (316/ 15–241/240 BCE), perhaps some two generations younger. It is not implausible that Arcesilaus was inspired by Pyrrhonian philosophising but there is no direct evidence that he was. The Academic Aenesidemus' 'Pyrrhonian revival' in the first century BCE certainly stakes itself to a Pyrrhonian inspiration, as indicated by two of the titles of his works – *Pyrrhonian Discourses* and *Outline Introduction to Pyrrhonian Matters*. It is, though, given the paucity of evidence, difficult to judge to what extent Pyrrho was more than a vivid personage whose name and notable character were his sole contributions to later scepticism.

In any case, the first century BCE or CE Peripatetic philosopher Aristocles of Messene wrote an extensive and, as far as we can judge from the remaining fragments, acute history of philosophy in which he tries to summarise Pyrrho's philosophical position. The account is preserved for us by Eusebius, the fourth century bishop of Caesarea in his *Praeparatio Evangelica*. It contains most of what we know of Pyrrho apart from his colourful life and will serve as a useful starting-point for my account. Aristocles tells us that:

It is necessary above all to consider the issue of our cognition (*gnōseōs*). For if by nature we cognise nothing, there is no need to consider other things. There were some ancients who made this pronouncement, and Aristotle argued against them. Pyrrho of Elis gave a powerful exposition of this view, but left no written treatment of it himself. His student Timon says that he who is going to be happy must look to these three things: (1) what things are like; (2) what our disposition ought to be with respect to them; and (3) what will be the result for those who are so disposed. [Timon] says that [Pyrrho] declares that things are equally indifferent (*adiaphora*) and unmeasurable (*astathmēta*) and undecidable (*anepikrita*), and that for this reason neither our sense-perceptions nor our beliefs tell the truth or lie, and so we ought not to put our trust (*pisteuein*) in them but ought instead to be without beliefs (*adoxastous*) and uncommitted and unswayed, saying of each and every thing that it no more is this than is not (*ou mallon*), or both is and is not, or neither is nor is not. Timon says that the result for those who are in this disposition will be speechlessness and then freedom from disturbance (*ataraxia*). Aenesidemus [says they will attain pleasure]. These then are the main points of what they say (Aristocles, *apud* Eusebius, *Praeparatio Evangelica* 14.18.758c–d).

In this highly suggestive report, our main focus will be on the first two questions that Timon says must be answered: what is the nature of things and what should our response be to this. The realisation that things are 'indifferent', 'unmeasurable' and 'undecidable' should lead us to be 'without beliefs', 'uncommitted' and 'unswayed'. To each thing or matter proposed for our judgment, we should say 'no more one way than the other'.

This concise testimony suggests no reason for arriving at the above realisation. If we suppose that Pyrrho's actual reasoning was of a Democritean sort ('sweet to me, bitter to you, neither sweet nor bitter in itself'), we might take him to have felt obliged to offer an explanation why our sense-perceptions are incapable of cognising things as they are in themselves. We recall, though, that Democritus had a definite – and therefore from the Pyrrhonian perspective, dogmatic – view on the non-evident nature of things.[1] If Pyrrho was a Democritean, it would, therefore, be surprising for him to go on and maintain that we should be, as Democritus certainly was not, without beliefs. If, on the other hand, we suppose that Pyrrho's reasoning was influenced by the philosophical pronouncements he evidently heard on his travels to India, we might take him to be claiming that things themselves really are indeterminate as opposed to being merely indeterminable, in which case the urge to renounce beliefs would be more intelligible. If, however, this is so, we seem to be left in the dark as to why he held such a view.

We might, however, suppose that an indication of the latter interpretation is that Pyrrho is reported as claiming that 'neither our sense-perceptions nor our beliefs tell the truth or lie', which must mean minimally that from the fact that one has a sense-perception or a belief, nothing follows regarding reality. The assumption of the indeterminacy of things would certainly block such inferences. Strictly speaking, though, all that we are entitled to conclude from the claim that sense-perceptions and beliefs are neither true nor false is

---

[1] See chapter 2, above, 21–6.

that whatever it is that would make these so is indeterminate. We are not entitled to conclude that there is not some other means of cognition that can produce statements that are true or false because what these statements represent is other than what is sensible and an object of belief. Parmenides naturally comes to mind as one who would maintain this view, arguing that intellect alone is able to attain to (determinate) being. A belief, say, neither tells the truth nor lies in the sense that there is no entailment from 'S believes p' to 'p is true' or to 'p is false'; similarly for a perceptual judgment.

I think we cannot say for sure whether Pyrrho believed that all things were indeterminate or indeterminable.[2] It is clear, though, that all later sceptics who claimed Pyrrhonian inspiration took the latter alternative as the basis for their arguments. There are at least four good reasons for this. First, if things are indeterminable, that should be enough to defeat the dogmatists all of whom propose to deliver to us the good news about how things are determined. Second, if one claims that things are indeterminable rather than indeterminate, it is easier to defend oneself against the rebuttal that one is thereby being inconsistent. To claim that things are indeterminate seems like a dogmatic utterance; to claim that they are indeterminable is to make the more modest and hence more defensible point that neither I nor anyone else has hitherto determined how things are. Third, if things are indeterminable, the claim that beliefs and sense-perceptions neither tell the truth nor lie does not need to rest upon the previous dogmatic assumption. It need only mean that beliefs and sense-perceptions do not reveal themselves as either telling the truth or lying. Thus, my belief that p is not true just because I believe it. As we shall see in a moment, the possibility that one could change one's belief for a reason means that a belief is held for a reason. That fact constitutes a crucial vulnerability in the dogmatist. Fourth, we need to keep in view the goal of the sceptical strategy, which is to arrive at a tranquil state through the forswearing of cognitive commitments. If one can defeat any claim that things are *determinable*, this should be enough to enable us to attain this goal. The longer and harder road, which consists in showing that things are indeterminate, is superfluous.

The second question posed by Pyrrho is answered by saying that we ought not to put our trust in our sense-perceptions and in our beliefs but ought instead to be 'without beliefs and uncommitted and unswayed, saying of each and every thing that it no more is this than is not, or both is and is

---

[2] The words he uses can be taken in either way.

not, or neither is nor is not'. This is what Pyrrhonists characterise as 'suspension of judgment' (*epochē*) (D.L. 9.61–2). Later in the passage (76), Diogenes quotes Timon, the disciple of Pyrrho, as using the term 'decline to assent to' (*aprosthetein*). Sextus (*M* 7.157), says that 'suspension of judgment' is the same thing as 'refusing to assent' (*asugkatathein*).

The suspension of judgment or, equivalently, the withholding of assent is, according to Timon, not incompatible with admitting that things appear (*phainetai*) one way rather than another (D.L. 9.105). How, we may well ask, is it possible for one to hold both that 'I do not believe p' and 'It appears to me that p'? Superficially, at least, these seem to be contradictory utterances. And yet making sense of the suspension of judgment is clearly essential to understanding why it should be thought to be a necessary prelude to tranquility.

In the last chapter, I quoted a passage from Sextus in which Arcesilaus challenges the Stoic distinction of grasping from belief on one side and knowledge on the other. In that passage (*M* 7.154–8), Arcesilaus is reported as arguing further that (1) the Stoic wise man is supposed to give assent only to a graspable presentation, but (2) if there is no such thing, the wise man will not assent to anything. We have already considered the sceptical argument against (2). Here we must focus on the reasoning behind (1). Arcesilaus says that assent arises in relation to reason (*logos*), not in relation to presentation (*phantasia*). That is, the mere fact that one has a presentation – that one is 'appeared to' – is not a sufficient ground for giving assent. After all, one gives assent to a reason because one supposes that given that reason, what one believes is true. The Pyrrhonian position is arrived at by adding the claim that, since no belief 'tells the truth or lies', there is no reason for that belief, and hence no basis for assent. Since this is also the case for any sense-perception, it, too, can neither find any reason to warrant assent to it and cannot serve itself as the reason for belief.

One might object that, after all, there are various sorts of reasons. To have reason sufficient to warrant the assent that belongs to belief is not necessarily to have reason to warrant the assent that pertains to a claim to knowledge. To see the Pyrrhonian answer to this objection it will be useful to recall the problem facing the Standard Analysis. That problem is how to formulate the evidential condition such that when it is met (along with the belief and truth conditions), one will then possess knowledge. The dilemma is that evidence that entails what it is evidence for is hard to come by and the meaning of evidence that does *not* entail what it is evidence for is deeply obscure. One response to this dilemma is to reject the claim that knowledge is anything more than true belief that meets the best criteria of evidence that one could set down. What might appear to be only a minor concession to the sceptic, namely, that there is no such thing as knowledge if that is taken to be a mental state distinct from belief, will hardly do the trick. For by thus collapsing knowledge and belief, one must still appeal to reason to justify assent. And now the dilemma appears again: does the evidence, that is, the reason, for the belief entail that the belief is true or not? If entailing evidence continues to elude us, what makes the reason for the assent anything other than arbitrary, which is to say, no reason at all?

We can make the point in a slightly different way. If I concede to you that things appear to you in a certain way, what reason will you adduce for going beyond that to an assent (that is, to a belief) that they are that way? Any reason you care to bring forward is inevitably going to rest upon some large claims about the world, claims that are surely not more, but rather less, compelling than the experiences that led you to say that things appear to you thus and so. One might counter by saying that if one agrees that things appear to one in a certain way, one really does believe that they are so. I reply that this so-called belief is without assent, which makes it quite different from ordinary belief. Why? Because ordinary belief, accompanied by assent, is either amenable to questioning or it is not. If it is, that is, if I can be reasoned out of the belief, my holding it was constituted by my assenting to a reason. If it is not, that is, if there is no reasoning that will dislodge the belief in me, your assent is indistinguishable from your mere acknowledgement that you are being appeared to thus and so.

According to the Pyrrhonian strategy, if the dogmatist admits that belief requires assent to a *logos*, it will be possible to show him that there is no *logos* that can entail the truth of any belief. By contrast, to admit that one's belief is held for no reason is equivalent to believing that one has no reason to believe that one's belief is true. But we *only* hold beliefs that we believe are true. If one admits that one has no more reason to believe p than not-p, one is not faced with a cognitive black hole. On the contrary, one can embrace the sceptic way, insisting that it appears to one that p (or not-p).

The technical apparatus of this general sceptical strategy is found abundantly on display in the writings of Sextus Empiricus. We shall examine these in section three. I turn first back to Arcesilaus and his Academic cohorts.

2 ACADEMIC SCEPTICISM

Sextus tells us that Arcesilaus was the head of the 'Middle Academy' (*PH* 1.232; cf. D.L. 4.28). This classification was apparently made with a view to contrasting his philosophy with that of Carneades (214–129/8 BCE), the supposed head of the 'New Academy'.[3] Arcesilaus, as we have seen, focused on the Stoic criterion of truth and argued against the existence of the graspable presentation. The conclusion that is supposed to follow from this argument is that all judgment should be suspended (Sextus, *M* 7.155; Plutarch, *adv. Col.* 1120C).[4] The two reasons given for the non-existence of the graspable presentation are (1) assent is always to a proposition, not to a presentation and (2) no true presentation is found to be of such a kind as to be incapable of proving false (Sextus, *M* 7.154; cf. 7.247–52; Cicero, *Acad.* 2.77–8). We have briefly discussed the argument for (1) in the previous chapter. Here we need to address the bolder second point, namely, the grounds for holding that no presentation can make it rational to assent to what is in fact a true proposition regarding it.

Our sources tell us that the Academics argued that a true presentation was 'indiscernible' (*aparallaktos*) from a false one.[5] Cicero presents the argument in this way:

Among presentations, some are true and some are false. A false presentation is not graspable (*percipi non potest*). But every true presentation is such that a false one of the same sort can occur. And where presentations are such that there is no difference between them, it cannot occur that some of them are graspable and some are not. Therefore, no presentation is graspable (Cicero, *Acad.* 2.40; cf. Sextus, *M* 7.402–10).

The central point of this argument – sometimes characterised as 'the argument from illusion' – is that we have no criterion for discerning the true from the false presentation. This claim is a direct challenge to the Stoic

[3] Carneades had a famous pupil, Clitomachus (187/6–110/09 BCE), who was the teacher of Philo of Larissa (158–84 BCE). Philo taught that the 'Old' and 'New' Academies were really one, in part relying on Carneades' revision of Arcesilaus' argument against anything being graspable. His pupil, Antiochus of Ascalon (*ca* 130–*ca* 68 BCE), rejected the sceptical interpretation of Plato implied by Philo, and upheld a return to the 'Old' Academy. Antiochus understood this Old Academy of Plato's to be harmonious with Stoic and Peripatetic philosophies. Cicero (*De Fin.* 5; *Acad.* 1.132, 137), in fact, identifies Antiochus' views as Peripatetic and Stoic. Among other things, this meant a positive reappraisal of the Stoic criterion of truth, the 'graspable presentation'. It was perhaps against Philo's alleged creeping dogmatism that Aenesidemus (first century BCE) reacted, paving the way for the foundation of a 'new' Pyrrhonistic scepticism.

[4] The question naturally arises as to whether Arcesilaus' admiration for Plato (cf. D.L. 4.32–3) extended to an interpretation of Platonism that made it compatible with scepticism. The usual answer to this question is that Arcesilaus tended to emphasise the aporetic nature of the so-called Socratic dialogues, perhaps generalising this for all knowledge. This is not a particularly satisfying answer, though it is perhaps the case that Arcesilaus supposed that Plato had such an exalted notion of what knowledge is that one could safely assume that he held it unattainable by embodied humans.

[5] Sextus, *M* 7.164, attributes this argument specifically to Carneades. Cicero, however (*Acad.* 2.77–8), attributes it to Arcesilaus. One may assume that the latter's penchant for arguing on both sides of a question (cf. D.L. 4.28) led him to maintain the indiscernibility argument.

criterion of truth. We are told that in response to Academic criticism, they added that the presentation 'is of such a kind as could not come from that which does not exist'. It is reasonable to suppose that the Stoics are responding to Arcesilaus' argument as represented here. What more can we say beyond the fact that there are here evidently irreconcilable views about the veracity of sense-perception?

The Stoics will maintain that in their corporealist and hence nominalist universe, every individual that is perceived has made its own unique presentation to us. This is something that the Academic sceptic need not deny. What he maintains is that the false presentation is in itself indiscernible from the true so that, for example, the straight stick in water really does look bent. Here the argument goes: if the presentation is not graspable, the true presentation is indiscernible from the false. The presentation is not graspable because if it were, there would be no possibility of error. That is, there would be knowledge of the proposition that expresses the true presentation. As we have seen, there is no way of demonstrating the impossibility of error or of providing entailing evidence for that which is supposedly known. One might, of course, assent to what is actually a true proposition, but unless one knows that one is assenting to a true proposition, there is no difference between assenting to a true one and to a false one. If we could discern the propositions that are true from the ones that are false, we could, presumably, discern a true presentation from a false one. But, alas, we cannot.

Arcesilaus' argument clearly depends on using knowledge as the standard by which we could theoretically discern true and false presentations. It is not enough to say that there *are* true presentations, and that these bear the unique marks of their sources, unless we can discern the true ones we are receiving from false ones. To do this, one would, presumably, need a criterion of discernment. Unless such a criterion is forthcoming, a *judgment* that one presentation is true and another false is without reason. Therefore, suspension of judgment is appropriate. There is, literally, no more reason to believe p than there is to believe not-p, where 'p' stands for a proposition that is true if and only if the presentation it represents is as it is represented. It is not even clear that it is *possible* to judge one way or the other when the truth or falsity of the presentation are equipollent. What, after all, would we say about someone who purported to judge that a fairly tossed coin is going to come down on one side or the other? Though he may hope that it goes one way rather than the other, he has no basis for judging this to be so. If assent is the act following upon a judgment, the impossibility of judgment would indicate at least the appropriateness of withholding assent.

In reply to Arcesilaus, it was and always will be said that human life speaks against his position every day. For people do make judgments on the basis of their presentations. The rationality of the judgments is always set before the court of experience. Even an Arcesilaus will make judgments about what is presented to his senses. He will, as Arcesilaus acknowledges, walk through a door and not into a wall when he wants to go to the market (Plutarch, *adv. Col.* 1122F). Does not the sceptic's own inevitable way of living belie his supposed suspension of judgment?

Arcesilaus' answer to this commonsensical complaint is subtle and reveals the pivot upon which turns the difference between the Standard Analysis and the ancient conception of knowledge. Sextus reports that the Academics, after arguing for the suspension of judgment, still had to reply to questions about the criterion for the conduct of life. Arcesilaus explains:

that he who suspends judgment about everything regulates choices and avoidances and, generally, actions by reasonableness (*to eulogon*), and, proceeding according to this criterion, will act correctly [i.e., morally perfectly] (*katorthōsei*). For happiness arises because of prudence, and prudence resides in correct [i.e., morally perfect] actions, and a correct [i.e., morally perfect] action is that which, having been done, has a reasonable defence (*apologian*). Therefore, he who adheres to reasonableness will act correctly and will be happy (*M* 7.158).

Our immediate response to this explanation might be that Arcesilaus has irrevocably undermined his own position by appealing to a criterion of 'reasonableness' for action. Is it not reasonable to go through the door instead of into the wall precisely because we have reasons for so acting? And these reasons are at least in part going to include our judgments about our presentations.

The implied charge of inconsistency is unjust or at least precipitous. First, the criterion of reasonableness is the Stoics' own as is the notion of 'correct action'. An 'appropriate action' (*kathēkon*) is 'one that is consistent with life, which when done admits of a reasonable (*eulogon*) defence' (Stobaeus, 2.85.13–86.4 = *SVF* 3.494). Among appropriate actions, some are 'morally perfect' (*katorthōmata*) and complete. Others are imperfect and they are called 'intermediate actions'. The former are those done by the wise man; the latter include actions done by those who are not wise. These may be the same actions, externally viewed. The appropriate action, like the graspable presentation, can thus cover the same action performed by different sorts of persons for different reasons. Its character is determined by the manner in which it is done, that is, whether it is done owing to the disposition of the wise man or the fool. What makes an incomplete appropriate action *complete* is the addition of this disposition.

The reasonable defence of the appropriate action, for the Stoics, is the *prima facie* case that can be made for it, the scenario in which this action belongs to a virtuous life. The reasonableness of the action would not be removed by its lack of success in achieving its goal. The charitable or just deed that inadvertently went awry is no less reasonable for that. So, just as the putative graspable presentation does not grasp the truth after all, neither does the reasonable action guarantee success. In fact, its reasonableness has nothing to do with the truth, just as a justified belief has nothing to do with the truth if the justification does not guarantee that the belief is true. So, the Academic criterion of action is not a criterion of truth. It presupposes no commitment to any belief that what is being done is the result of a judgment or an assent to any proposition.

It is essential to realise that the commitment to reasonableness here is being made by a thoroughgoing sceptic, one who challenges *any* claim to knowledge. The challenge to knowledge is also perforce a challenge to rational belief. Reasonableness is not here being viewed as a benign substitute for rational belief. By contrast, according to the Standard Analysis, reasonable behaviour is thought to be such because it has *something* to do with true beliefs. That is, the justification for behaviour is going to spring from and depend on justified beliefs, and a justified belief is one whose justification is supposed to at least make it more likely or probable that the belief is true.

This account depends heavily on a little conceptual illusion. It depends on there being in principle beliefs that are completely justified, where 'completely' indicates that the justification guarantees the truth of the belief. At the same time, a proponent of the Standard Analysis will typically want to deny that there is such justification, attributing the word 'knowledge' to some true beliefs that meet some stipulated standard of justification. In that case, though, the notion of the belief's rationality being indexed to justification becomes obscure. If we cannot tell what constitutes a justification that yields a probability of one for the truth of the belief, what content can be given to the notion of a justification making one belief more probable than another?[6] The illusion comes from thinking that there can be justified beliefs even if there is no knowledge, where 'knowledge' refers to an infallible mental state. Or rather, it amounts to thinking that a justified belief provides the justification for reasonable action. In fact, from the sceptic's perspective, there is no justified belief to provide such justification because there is no knowledge to

---

[6] One may compare the claim that one line is straighter than another which can only make sense if we antecedently understand what absolute straightness is.

provide the standard for justification. This, however, does not preclude an action from being reasonable or, indeed, preclude one from embracing 'the reasonable' as a criterion of action.

Arcesilaus' argument is in line with the founder of the Academy in that it takes as given Plato's account of what knowledge is. It supposes that knowledge is an infallible mental state the objects of which could not be the objects of belief. Accordingly, the only rational justification is found in that which is self-evident. An attempt to make knowledge a type of belief by giving to belief the justificatory structure of knowledge is bound to fail. That is, we may speculate, the entire point of scepticism from the Academic perspective. The Stoics retain the Platonic account of knowledge, but on their corporealist principles, naturally make the justificatory structure of knowledge continuous with that of belief. Zeno's example of the hand with closed fingers making a fist, grasped with the other hand illustrates this continuity perfectly. Arcesilaus saw that there is no such continuous justificatory structure where justification is supposed to have something to do with truth. He also saw that a mental state that is alterable by *logos* is not on the way to being a mental state that is unalterable by *logos*, at least where the latter has as its object that which is identical with the former.

Another obvious objection to Arcesilaus' approach is that in fact we all make judgments about relative degrees of justification, as in the case of the bent stick in water. The stick appears bent, but we do not believe that we are justified in acting as if it were. We are *more* justified in acting as if it were not. Carneades, Arcesilaus' illustrious successor in the Academy, took up the challenge to give a rationale for graded justification without a commitment to truth, and hence, without any claims to knowledge or to rational belief, where both of these are supposed to have some functional relation to the truth.

Sextus reports Carneades' position in an adversarial manner.

These were the counter-arguments that Carneades set forth against the other philosophers to the effect that the criterion [of truth] does not exist. But he himself when asked for some criterion for the conduct of life and for the attainment of happiness, is virtually compelled to take a position on this topic himself, introducing the persuasive (*pithanēn*) presentation, and the presentation that is at the same time persuasive, uncontroverted (*aperispaston*) and thoroughly tested (*diexōdeumenēn*) (*M* 7.166).

As Sextus goes on to maintain, these criteria together are the criteria of truth for Carneades and his school (7.173).[7] Sextus is clear that this position differs

---

[7] Sextus actually says that for them a presentation that is 'apparently true' and 'adequately representative' (*hikanōs emphainomenē*) is the criterion of truth.

both from that of Arcesilaus and from his own (*PH* 1.220–32). That is why he wanted to distinguish the 'Middle' Academy of Arcesilaus from the 'New' Academy of Carneades and his followers. The issue that needs to be faced is whether 'persuasiveness' (*pithanotēs*) is taken by Carneades to be a criterion of truth or of apparent truth.

Sextus explains that for Carneades a persuasive presentation is one that is apparently true and adequately representative, meaning that its appearance is not occluded by circumstances, such as a dim light or distance or the smallness of the object (*M* 7.171). Sextus adds that in this account, 'persuasiveness' is being used in three ways: (a) true and apparently true; (b) false but apparently true; (c) either true or false but apparently true (7.174). The cases left out as obviously unpersuasive are (d) true but apparently false and (e) false and apparently false. It is clear that (c) encompasses (a) and (b) and for this reason is the supposed criterion (174).

Readers will recall that we have here returned to the issue of epistemic versus non-epistemic appearances first broached among the Presocratics. The central issue now is whether the appearances that are to serve as a criterion are epistemic or non-epistemic, that is, whether an appearance is the 'face' of reality or a mask. Arcesilaus declined to take the bait and aver that it is either. Sextus interprets Carneades as being seduced by a perhaps Stoic-inspired inclination to take the former alternative. For he represents Carneades as holding that one should not be deterred by the fact that some apparently true presentations are false; rather, owing to the rarity of such cases, we should use as a criterion those apparently true presentations that are 'true for the most part' (175).

Talk about what is true for the most part only makes sense if we have some criterion of truth, not just the apparently true. The fact that in addition to persuasiveness, Carneades adds 'uncontroverted' and 'thoroughly tested' as further aspects of the criterion strongly suggests that it is truth, not apparent truth, that is the focus here. An uncontroverted presentation is one that is not in conflict with other apparently true presentations. It is one in which 'we trust more' (*mallon pisteuomen*) (177). And a thoroughly tested presentation is one where the collection of uncontroverted presentations along with the originally apparently true presentation are examined in all their potentially occluding circumstances (182–3).

The problem with this, however, is that when this criterion has been met we do not therefore have knowledge. Being persuaded is not equivalent to being certain. Nor does Carneades suppose otherwise. For as Sextus tells us, the three levels of persuasion – apparently true in 'normal' circumstances, uncontroverted and thoroughly tested – are held by Carneades to be a guide to action. Thus, for trivial matters, the first stage is sufficient; for more serious matters, the second stage is needed; and for the most serious matters, those upon which our happiness depends, the third stage is required (184). The apparently true presentation is the guide to action because, when uncontroverted and thoroughly tested, it usually turns out to be true.[8] If that is the case, however, Carneades would seem to be implicitly admitting an independent criterion of truth. He is not saying that the uncontroverted and thoroughly tested apparently true presentation is true since there are occasions on which such presentations only 'mimic' the truth. Furthermore, the apparently true presentation, even when it is uncontroverted, thoroughly tested and in fact true, is *still* only apparently true.

Carneades seems aware of this difficulty. Cicero tells us that Clitomachus praised Carneades for '[driving] assent – that is, belief (*opinationem*) and rashness (*temereitatem*) – out of our souls' (*Acad.* 2.108). Still, there is a sense in which the wise man can respond intellectually to the apparently true.

There are two senses in which the wise man is said to suspend judgment. In one sense, he gives assent to nothing at all; in the other sense, he suspends judgment by not responding to a query as to whether he approves of something or disapproves of it, so that he is not forced to deny or affirm anything. Since this is so, the one sense is accepted, so that he never assents to anything, and he holds to the other sense, so that, following persuasiveness wherever this should be present or absent, he is able to respond [to a question about acceptance] 'yes' or 'no' accordingly. Indeed, since we believe that he who withholds assent from everything is nevertheless moved and does something, there remain presentations of the sort that excite us to action and also those about which, when questioned, we would be able to respond either way, following only the claim that the presentation was like that, but still without assent. However, we do not give assent to every presentation of this sort, but only to those which nothing impedes (*Acad.* 2.104).

By distinguishing two types of assent, Carneades drives a wedge between the theoretical and the practical. He counters the obvious anti-sceptical objection that every time the sceptic acts, he admits his assent to the propositions relevant to action.

Carneades has here made a decisive break with the past in two respects. First, the apparently true presentation is really just the guide to action even if it is the criterion of truth. Second, by making the apparently true the criterion of truth, he removes that which is not apparent from the realm of truth or at least from the realm of that to which we need give any type of

---

[8] Sextus (*M* 7.175) says that for Carneades our 'judgments' (*kriseis*) as well as our actions are regulated by such presentations. I take it that these are practical judgments.

assent. With a view to the Standard Analysis, Carneades declines to call an uncontroverted and thoroughly tested apparently true presentation 'knowledge' because such a presentation may yet be false.[9] Even if it turns out to be true, it is only the apparently true that is able to serve as a guide. Accordingly, the 'strong' assent that is a property of knowledge is never given to any presentation.

Is the 'weak' assent that may be given to apparently true presentations of the relevant sort equivalent to rational belief? If it is, the sceptical denial of knowledge can be made to coexist happily with a robust embrace of knowledge conceived as equivalent to rational belief that is in fact true. It would seem captious to evince scepticism about those matters to which we have given assent – albeit weak assent – on the basis of the apparently true, uncontroverted and thoroughly tested presentation. As we saw above, Sextus rejected Carneades' sceptical credentials. He did so precisely because the distinction between weak and strong assent purports to create conceptual space for rational belief. For Sextus, the sceptical rejection of the possibility of knowledge makes rational belief impossible as well. In the last section of this chapter, we shall need to explore this radical view.

3 THE PYRRHONIST REVIVAL

Aenesidemus of Aigai in Macedonia, evidently unhappy with the dogmatist direction that Carneades and his disciples had taken the Academy, sought to reinvigorate the sceptical way of doing philosophy. The fact that he called one of his works *Pyrrhonist Discourses* probably indicates the inspiration he found in a distant enigmatic figure and not an intention to recount specific arguments that had been preserved over some two hundred years. Sextus, as I noted, found a harmony of views in Pyrrho and in the Academic Arcesilaus.

Luckily for us, the ninth century Byzantine bishop and scholar Photius undertook to set down in a book titled *Biblioteca* notes and extracts from his voluminous reading of the works of both pagan and Christian authors. One of these was Aenesidemus' *Pyrrhonist Discourses* (# 212 in his list,

---

[9] By contrast, the later Academic sceptic Philo of Larissa seems to have developed an account of knowledge such that something like ordinary empirical knowledge was possible, though philosophical knowledge was not. The Stoic criterion of the graspable presentation was held to be applicable to perceptual experiences, but not an infallible determinator of knowledge. Thus, against the Stoic concept of the all-knowing infallible sage, a true (sceptical) sage would manifest his wisdom in practical affairs based on fallible knowledge. The idea that knowledge can be fallible ('I know but I might be mistaken') is perhaps the crucial link between Academic scepticism and the beginning of the Standard Analysis as an articulation of the criteria of empirical scientific knowledge.

169b–170b). The 'whole purpose of this work', says Photius, 'was to establish securely that nothing could be securely grasped, either by means of our senses or even by means of our thought' (*noēsis*).[10] Those who are ignorant of this fact and who believe that they know things cause themselves needless trouble. Photius tells us that in the first book of his work, Aenesidemus stressed the difference between Pyrrhonists and Academics. Aenesidemus complained that the Academic introduced an obvious self-contradiction in maintaining at once that things were ungraspable and that, nevertheless, they could 'recognise' (*ginōskonta*) some things as true and some as false. If things could be recognised as such, they ought to be held to be graspable; if they are not graspable, they ought not to claim such recognition.

Aenesidemus' point seems to be that the appeal to the apparently true as a criterion implies some recognition of how this criterion operates. One who agrees that an apparently true presentation may come either from that which is true or from that which is false could be making a purely logical point, in which case he need not commit himself to the existence of any criterion or even to weak assent. The Academic, in offering the apparently true presentation that is uncontroverted and thoroughly tested, is doing much more. He is suggesting that with this presentation he is able to recognise some things as true and some as false. He becomes, as Aenesidemus notes, just another Stoic arguing with Stoics. His quarrels with the prevailing dogmatism of the time share the dogmatists' presupposition. He has abandoned scepticism altogether.

Sextus gives us by far the fullest account of the so-called 'modes' (*tropoi*) or argumentative strategies by which a sceptic may attack the supports for the dogmatists' claims. The goal of the modes is to produce a suspension of judgment. Sextus himself offers a list of ten modes. He says that Aenesidemus introduced eight modes against dogmatic causal explanation (*aitialogian*) (*PH* 1.180). He recounts five modes offered by 'later sceptics', possibly a reference to Agrippa (? first century BCE) (D.L. 9.88). Finally, he gives what is evidently a reduction of the various modes to two (*PH* 1.178–9). Clearly, the exact number of the modes is insignificant. The basic underlying strategy, as Sextus tells us, is

the setting of things in opposition. We oppose either appearances to appearances or concepts (*nooumena*) to concepts or appearances to concepts. We oppose appearances

---

[10] We may note a hint of sarcasm in Photius' remark that Aenesidemus is suggesting that he could *securely* establish that nothing could be securely grasped. Still, there is no reason to doubt the substance of his account of the position confirmed by Sextus.

to appearances when we say, 'The same tower seems round from a distance but square from nearby.' We oppose concepts to concepts when someone constructs providence from the orderliness of the things in the heavens and we oppose to this the fact that the good frequently fare badly and the wicked prosper, thereby inferring the non-existence of providence. We oppose concepts to appearances in the way in which Anaxagoras opposed to snow's being white the consideration that snow is frozen water, and water is black, therefore snow is black, too (*PH* 1.31–3).

Notice that this is a strategy that works nicely even against the crypto-dogmatism of Carneades. If one does not have a conclusive reason for a claim, the status of any reason for the claim is thrown into question. The 'oppositions' are aimed against reasons that are supposed to be conclusive but in fact are not. In the case of Carneades, since an appearance is supposed to be the criterion of truth, one need only oppose it with a conflicting appearance. The reply that there are no conflicting appearances if the original apparently true presentation is uncontroverted and thoroughly tested is met by pointing out that first, the resultant criterion is still only of the apparently true and second, that as such it is supposed to be explained by what is true. Accordingly, the opposition shifts from appearance against appearance to concept against appearance, that is, concept of the non-evident cause of the apparent. And here we are back to the problem faced by Democritus who wanted to argue that what is real is non-evident and fundamentally different from appearances, though capable of providing an explanation for these.[11]

If the above five modes plus Aenesidemus' eight serve to undercut the dogmatic pretensions of the Academics, the traditional ten modes serve to cast a wider net. They are aimed at any dogmatist who claims that one appearance or another is epistemic, that is, indicative of the truth. These modes are as follows:

[1] The first mode employs the variations among animals; [2] the second employs the differences among men; [3] the third employs the different conditions of the sense organs; [4] the fourth employs circumstances; [5] the fifth employs positions and distances and places; [6] the sixth employs mixtures;[12] [7] the seventh employs the quantities and structures of external objects;[13] [8] the eighth employs relativity; [9] the ninth employs the fact of constant or rare occurrences; [10] the tenth

---

[11] Sextus, *PH* 1.181, says that Aenesidemus' second mode was aimed at showing that no single dogmatic causal hypothesis exhausts the possibilities of explanation.

[12] Sextus means that external objects are composed of mixtures of elements and these may variously affect us owing to their combination (cf. *PH* 1.124).

[13] Sextus means that smaller or larger quantities of the bodies we claim to observe appear differently (cf. *PH* 1.129).

employs the practices [of ordinary life], laws, belief in myths, and dogmatic suppositions (*PH* 1.36–8).[14]

All of these modes are set in opposition to those who suppose that things are such as they appear to be (*PH* 1.22). By contrast, the Pyrrhonist sceptic 'adheres to appearances' as a guide for the conduct of life, and to our natural passions, laws and customs, and the arts, but he does so 'undogmatically' (*PH* 1.23–4).

Sextus proceeds to explain that these ten modes fall under three general categories:

based on him who judges, on the object judged and on both. The first four [1–4 above] are subordinate to the mode based on him who judges (for that which judges is either an animal or a man or a sense or is in some circumstance); the seventh and the tenth [7, 10 above] are referred to the one based on the object judged; and the fifth, sixth, eighth and ninth [5, 6, 8 and 9 above] are based [on the mode involving both]. Again, these three are referred to the relativity mode. So, the relativity mode is most general, and the three are specific, and the ten are subordinate (*PH* 1.38–9).

The generic primacy of the relativity mode and its appearance as well as a 'specific' mode [no. 8] is noted by Sextus (*PH* 1.37–40) and is justified by distinguishing the intrinsic relativity of an appearance as such and the two ways in which it is relative, that is, to other appearances and to the one who judges.

The Pyrrhonist's (non-dogmatic) strategy is to display the futility of the dogmatist's basic assumption: some appearances are intrinsically epistemic. For each particular dogmatic claim, an appropriate type of 'medicinal' trope in an appropriate 'dosage' is indicated (*PH* 3.280–1). Admit that appearance is *not* identical with reality, and a trope is ready to hand to show that the appearance is non-epistemic. That is, the sceptic will show that the particular claim about the reality that is supposed to explain the appearance is unjustified.

As Sextus carefully explains, this sceptical position is to be distinguished from Protagorean relativism precisely because Protagoras effaces the distinction between epistemic and non-epistemic appearances (*PH* 1.216–20). First, Protagoras holds that 'man is the measure of all things', meaning, Sextus says, that man is the criterion of the truth of things. The Pyrrhonist's

---

[14] Sextus means that if laws, customs and myths are taken to have epistemic force in regard to what is really good or bad, right or wrong, one can oppose to these others that suggest the opposite. The dogmatic suppositions are cases of analogical reasoning where it is uncritically supposed that if A explains B, something analogous to A (say, C) must explain D (cf. *PH* 1.146–7).

rejection of all criteria of truth covers the Protagorean one, too. Second, Protagoras proceeds to explain why to be is to be for a perceiver. Since all matter is in flux, existence or being only arise in the encounter between perceiver and perceived.[15] Things really are, for Protagoras, just as they appear. Accordingly, Protagorean relativism is a type of dogmatism, and must be distinguished from the relativism of the Pyrrhonist.

Because the sceptic insists on the theoretical distinction between epistemic and non-epistemic appearances, he is able to maintain with undeniable plausibility that he does not abolish appearances altogether, but only those appearances that are claimed as epistemic (*PH* 1.19–21). Indeed, his insistence that (non-epistemic) appearances are the natural guide to life is not, in this light, hypocritical. In addition, the endorsement by Sextus of Aenesidemus' disdain for the Academic's pseudo-scepticism rests reasonably enough on his insight that Carneades has – in a manner different from Protagoras, to be sure – tried to efface the distinction between epistemic and non-epistemic appearances.

The seemingly plausible strategy of starting with appearances, describable in purely phenomenological terms, and then proceeding to scrutinise them until we are able to say whether they are epistemic or not is, from the Pyrrhonist point of view, actually a gigantic bluff. As we saw in the case of Carneades, the uncontroverted and thoroughly tested appearance is still, after all, an appearance. It is one thing to say that you will be guided by this; it is quite another to say that it is (therefore?) epistemic. The latter claim is where the bluff enters. Sextus maintains that such a claim is the mark of the inveterate dogmatist. Either one is justified in saying that things are really this way because they appear this way or one is not. Unless the relation between appearance and reality is an entailment relation (as it is only for dogmatic Protagoreanism), there is no such justification. The idea that we can sneak up on reality and 'capture' it by being scrupulous about how we deal with appearances is just a naive dogmatic fantasy.

Sextus' argument suggests the following diagnosis of the dogmatists' problem. The dogmatist assumes that knowledge is possible, and that knowledge has the property of infallibility. With the use of careful testing or analysis or reasoning one can rationally conclude that a belief turns into knowledge, that is, our assent to things appearing a certain way turns into our knowledge that they are a certain way. The threshold between appearance and reality *could* actually be crossed and so, even if we do not do it in any particular case,

---

[15] It is difficult to know if Sextus is here relying on Plato's *Theaetetus* or whether he has independent access to Protagoras' work *Truth*.

we can give meaning to the idea that we are closer to it than before we began or that we are as close to it as anyone could come. To successfully argue that knowledge so conceived is impossible is not merely to leave the dogmatist with an unattainable ideal. It is to make the notion of a threshold between belief and knowledge meaningless and so, most importantly, to make the notion of rational belief meaningless. For rational belief was supposed to be belief that is closer to the threshold than irrational belief.

As we saw in the chapters on Plato, Aristotle and Stoicism, knowledge was conceived of as an infallible mental state, one in which what is known is self-evident. As Aristotle put it, in knowing it is the intellect that becomes intelligible by being aware of its identification with the object of knowledge. It is this self-reflexivity that, for Plato and for Aristotle, but not evidently for the Stoics, entails that the objects of knowledge cannot be corporeal. It also entails that to be in a state of knowing is not to be in a representational state. Sextus' argument against the possibility of the knowledge of incorporeals is couched in the distinction between appearance and reality (*PH* 3.51–5). He argues that these incorporeals are not knowable on the basis of sensible appearances or on the basis of non-sensible appearances, employing the various tropes.[16] The deeper argument is that self-reflexivity is impossible for corporeal entities such as human beings. If knowledge requires self-reflexivity, and if self-reflexivity is impossible, knowledge is impossible. And if knowledge is impossible, rational belief is impossible since belief does not cross the appearance/reality threshold.

Sextus' argument is this:

If intellect (*nous*) grasps itself, either it is as a whole that it will grasp itself or not as a whole, but using some part of itself for this. It will not be able to grasp itself as a whole. For if it grasps itself as a whole, it will as a whole just be the grasping and, in grasping, since the grasping is the whole [that is, all there is of it], it will not be that which is grasped. But it is the height of absurdity that the grasping should exist but not that which is grasped. Nor can intellect use some part of itself for this. For how does the part itself grasp itself? If as a whole, the object sought will be nothing; if with a part, how will that part in turn cognise itself? And so on indefinitely. So, grasping is without a beginning (*anarchon*), since either there is no first subject to be found to do the grasping or else there will be no object to be grasped (*M* 7.310–13).

Sextus adds the additional argument that if the intellect does grasp itself, it must also grasp the place in which it is. If this is the case, the question of where grasping occurs should not have been a matter of dispute among

---

[16] The argument here is primarily directed against Stoic incorporeals, but it is highly likely that Sextus maintained that the same argument would apply to the putative knowledge of any incorporeals.

philosophers. Yet some say it is the brain, some the breast and some say other bodily parts. This second argument makes it evident that Sextus is not merely targeting the Stoics.

Sextus clearly thinks that the highest type of cognition must be a non-representational state. The grasping that is here denied is the grasping that is, when it occurs in the mind of the Stoic sage, knowledge. It is the mental state that is supposed to be unalterable by *logos*. The argument is essentially that there are no non-representational cognitional states. If the object cognised is other than the cognition of it, the cognitional state must have as its content some sort of representation. If the cognition is of one part of the cogniser by another, the same problem arises. The subject cognising must have as its content a representation of the content of the state of the other part.

The argument is perfectly general and relevant to any epistemological theory that claims that knowledge is non-representational or, simply, that there must be a non-representational type of cognition. To concede that *all* cognition is representational is to play right into the hands of the sceptical argument that epistemic and non-epistemic appearances are in principle different but that there is no way for us to tell the difference. If the best we can have, cognitionally speaking, is a representation, we are bound to be bluffing when we claim to have a criterion of truth, that is, a way to distinguish true representations or appearances from false ones.

It might occur to us that an argument for the impossibility of knowledge is itself the product of a genuine dogmatist. Dogmatic ignorance may be susceptible to ridicule, but it is no less dogmatism for that. Certainly, Sextus was aware of the imputation of inconsistency by those who thought that a sceptical argument for any position *ipso facto* constituted a commitment to dogmatism (*PH* 1.13–16). Yet, the above argument only aims to indicate the destructive dilemma faced by those who hold that knowing requires self-knowing. The argument for the impossibility of knowledge is, therefore, hypothetically arrived at. As such, it operates in the realm of appearances and quite independently of reality just as analyses of the formal structure of arguments yield results about validity and invalidity but nothing about truth (*M* 8.473).

Sextus' argument reveals the vacuity of the strategy that concedes the impossibility of infallible mental states as a prelude to designating as 'knowledge' whatever beliefs are acquired in some accepted manner. For the establishment of any accepted manner is going to have to begin with the criterion of truth. The idea of such a criterion belies the unbridgeable gap between appearance and reality, unbridgeable that is, by those to whom reality is supposed to appear. For those who are 'appeared to' are bound to represent the appearances, whether to themselves or to others. No sum of appearances or representations, however scrutinised, amounts to reality, any more than does an endless heap of points amount to a line.

The position embraced by Carneades attempts – according to Sextus' understanding – to transform our natural inclination to follow appearances into a justification or reason for so doing. Sextus responds in effect that the only justification for belief is knowledge, but that knowledge is impossible. Stated in the context of the Standard Analysis, the severance of justification from truth leaves the former only with what Sextus would call a naturalistic meaning and what contemporary epistemologists would call a pragmatic meaning. This severance is effected via the tropes. The Pyrrhonist's generic tropic relativism translates accurately enough into contemporary terms of the linguistic contextualization of knowledge and belief. Sharing with Sextus the premise that appearances are necessarily representational, it is hard to see how it could be otherwise given that our representations are basically linguistic.

When the Pyrrhonist says, 'I suspend judgment', she does not reject action; rather, she rejects belief, where belief is a psychological state in which a proposition is asserted as true (*PH* 1.196). The suspension of judgment is a suspension of belief because any proposition and its contradictory have 'equipollence' (*isostheneia*). That is, neither the one nor the other is more trustworthy precisely because there can be no evidence to disturb the equipollence (*PH* 1.10). There is only authentic evidence when the evidence entails what it is evidence for. When that occurs, there is knowledge. But since knowledge seems to be unavailable to us because there seem to be no infallible mental states, the claim to have evidence fails. It would be a gross distortion of the Pyrrhonist position to interpret this as meaning that, though we do not have evidence sufficient for the knowledge of p, surely we could have evidence sufficient to make the belief that p more rational than the belief that not-p.

According to this line of argument, the only grounds one could give to justify a belief is that it is rational. If these grounds are removed, it is not at all clear how having beliefs is supposed to be superior to merely following appearances.[17] Indeed, Sextus is delighted to point out that because animals

[17] 'Adhering' (*prosechontes*) to appearances (*PH* 1.23; cf. *M.* 11.165, where the sceptics 'choose' and 'avoid') does not, as some scholars maintain, amount to belief if having a belief requires that one thinks that one has *some* reason for the belief, whether this reason be in fact a good one or a bad one. It would be very odd for one to acknowledge that one's belief that p is equivalent to one's belief that p is true but for one simultaneously to claim that there is absolutely no reason why he holds this belief. If he holds it *because* he believes it is true, having a reason for this seems constitutive of the belief. Further, if, as Sextus agrees, he may be appeared to in a certain way, his acknowledgement of this does not amount to a belief that he is being appeared to in a certain way, even if the proposition 'Sextus is being appeared to in a certain way now' is true.

follow appearances as we do – sometimes more and sometimes less success-fully – the designation of them as 'non-rational', especially by the Stoics, is particularly hollow (*PH* 1.62–3; 76). Here is, incidentally, the Pyrrhonist response to the Platonic *reductio* argument in *Theaetetus* (161C) to the effect that Protagoras must allow that a pig or a baboon is a 'measure' of the truth equal to a human being. This implication of the Protagorean position becomes considerably more plausible when it is accepted that the human cogniser is not a measure of the truth of things either, but only of appearances.

Diogenes Laertius (9.107) records a dogmatic response to this line of reasoning. When the sceptic is faced with contrary presentations (e.g., the round and square tower), either he will have to be inactive or he will act according to which appearance he thinks is correct. In the latter case, he will at least be acting like someone who believes that things are one way rather than another and the 'equipollence' of appearances will be disturbed. The pithy and somewhat obscure sceptical answer recorded by Diogenes is to the effect that sceptics acknowledge the contrary appearances as being just appearances, that is, as strictly non-epistemic. For this reason, the practical preference for one over the other is not a recognition that one is more likely than the other to be a criterion of the truth.

If a Pyrrhonist 'follows appearances', is this not equivalent to believing that one is appeared to in a certain way? Not according to Sextus, who argues that if one cannot tell the difference between an epistemic and a non-epistemic appearance, as far as the perceiver is concerned, the appearance is non-epistemic. To observe that one is in a state of being appeared to in a certain way is not to commit oneself to what the appearance is an appear-ance of, that is, to whether or not the appearance is epistemic. The objection that a sceptic has beliefs after all seems to suppose that beliefs are to be identified dispositionally: if one acts in a certain way that is because one is acting on beliefs. Here once again the comparison by Sextus with animal behaviour is apt. Animal behaviour, including the behaviour that depends upon expectations of future events, is not necessarily indicative of beliefs, viewed non-dispositionally.

The Pyrrhonist position as preserved for us in the works of Sextus Empiricus is aimed at the epistemological aspirations and pretensions of every single ancient philosopher so far discussed in this book, with the exception of Arcesilaus and Pyrrho himself, but including the backsliding putatively Academic sceptics like Carneades, Clitomachus and Philo of Larissa.[18] If Sextus is right, the enterprise of philosophy as gradually

---

[18] Aenesidemus (D.L. 9.106) is said to have written a book titled *Against Wisdom*.

articulated among the Presocratics and then developed for some six hundred years was effectively doomed. Although the activity of dialectic and the pursuit of happiness need not fall to scepticism, groundless would be the assumption that in between the dialectic and the achievement of the happy life the attainment of knowledge of serious matters must intervene.

As we are well aware, Sextus' writings did not succeed in stemming the tide of dogmatism, though Pyrrhonism in various forms has been insinuated into philosophical debate right up to the present. In the next chapter, we need to look at one dogmatic respondent to Pyrrhonism, namely, Plotinus.

CHAPTER SEVEN

Plotinus and the Neoplatonic synthesis

I INTRODUCTION

The term 'Neoplatonism' is an eighteenth-century label coined by German scholars ('Neuplatonismus') used pejoratively to indicate unwholesome contaminations of the pure stream of ancient Hellenic thought. I use that term here simply to refer to the last phase of ancient Greek philosophy, beginning with Plotinus (204–270 CE) and ending effectively with the pervasive domination by Christianity of the Greek world in the sixth century. I focus primarily on Plotinus, the 'founder' of Neoplatonism, because of his explicit engagement with the entire history of philosophy as he knew it, from the Presocratics up to contemporary Peripatetics. As we shall see in a moment, Plotinus provides one dogmatic response to the sceptical onslaught. In particular, it is, not surprisingly, a response made from a Platonic perspective. Precisely because Plotinus was so conscious of the ongoing eight-hundred-year long dialogue among the Greek philosophical schools, his dogmatic response is really something quite original. In regard to epistemology, it is a response steeped above all in Aristotle's analysis of cognition. Plotinus was more than willing to invoke Aristotle's assistance on behalf of a defence of Platonism against sceptical attacks on the possibility of knowledge and rational belief. Although Plotinus is critical of Aristotle on numerous matters, there is no indication that this critical stance included epistemology. Plotinus' originality lay in an attempt to articulate the position with regard to knowledge and belief that I outlined in the first chapter. He did not suppose that the core position was Plato's discovery, though he undoubtedly thought that Plato's expression of this position was superior to anyone else's.

2 THE PLATONIST'S RESPONSE TO THE PYRRHONIST

It will be convenient to begin with Plotinus' response to Sextus' argument discussed in the last chapter. We recall that in that argument Sextus tried to show that there can be no non-representational cognition. If this is so, the claim to possess a criterion of truth is baseless. Although we do not know for sure if Plotinus actually read Sextus, it is not improbable that he did given his well-documented extensive engagement with the entire Greek philosophical tradition. In any case, Sextus is recounting an argument that is likely not to be his own invention, but is one that other sceptics had employed. So if Plotinus is not directly responding to the argument in the passage quoted in the last chapter, he probably has its general strategy in mind.

The passages I am about to discuss are found in Plotinus' treatise 'On the Cognitive Hypostases and That Which is Beyond', third in order in the fifth *Ennead*.[1] The title of the treatise (probably provided by Porphyry) requires some explanation. For Plotinus, a hypostasis is generally speaking an extramental or objective principle of some sort, a starting point for understanding some irreducible phenomenon or other. The three fundamental hypostases of Plotinus' version of Platonism (and of Neoplatonism generally) are the One, Intellect (*nous*) and Soul (*psychē*). The One, identified with Plato's Idea of the Good, is the absolutely first principle of all, the explanatory basis for the being of everything. It is virtually everything that is in the sense, roughly, in the way in which white light is virtually all the colours of the spectrum. Intellect is the principle of essence or 'whatness' or intelligibility or substantiality *and* the principle of the activity of intellection. Following Aristotle, Plotinus affirms the cognitive identity of intellect and intelligibles. This principle is equivalent to Aristotle's Prime Unmoved Mover, interpreted as eternally cognitively identical with all that is intelligible and with Plato's Demiurge, similarly cognitively identical with the paradigms of intelligibility. The principle of Intellect is subordinate to the One owing to its complexity, that is, the complexity implied by there being a distinction between an Intellect and intelligibles, and among intelligibles. By contrast, the One is absolutely simple.

---

[1] Plotinus' pupil the philosopher Porphyry collected Plotinus' treatises into six groups of nine. The title *Enneads* is from the Greek word for the number nine. Porphyry has to divide up some long treatises in order to make the numbers come out right. There is no indication that Plotinus intended his works to be read in this or any other order. Porphyry does, however, in his *Life of Plotinus*, provide us with a relative chronology of the treatises, a chronology that does not correspond at all to his division. The treatise on which I am going to focus primarily is sometimes referred to as 5.3. [49] where the number in brackets indicates the relative chronology of the treatise. A reference such as 5.3. [49] 1.1–15 would indicate the first fifteen lines of the first chapter of 5.3 as found in the critical edition of Plotinus' *Enneads* by Paul Henry and H.-R. Schwyzer (eds.), *Plotini Opera* (3 vols., Oxford: Clarendon Press, 1964, 1976, 1982), vol. I, *Enneads* I–III, vol. II, *Enneads* IV–V, vol. III, *Ennead* VI.

The third hypostasis, ontologically subordinate to both the One and Intellect is Soul, the principle of embodied desire of all types. Every living thing has desire in two senses: all desire the Good, but all desire it by desiring something that answers to their embodied needs. The first sort of desire might be termed 'vertical' and the second 'horizontal'. For living things without an intellect, the only way that these things achieve their good is through the attainment of what their embodied selves desire. For living things with intellects, there is a constant lived ambiguity between the search for the satisfaction of embodied psychic desires and the satisfaction of the desire of intellect, a desire that is satisfied only in the contemplation of what the One is virtually, that is, all that is intelligible. The recognition that one's good is purely intellectual is supposed to follow upon the recognition that one is truly identical with an intellect, not with an embodied soul. Plotinus here is quite clearly relying on Plato's distinction between the immortal and mortal parts of the soul which he takes to be equivalent to Aristotle's distinction between soul and intellect.[2]

The three fundamental hypostases are the starting points for addressing the wide array of perennial philosophical problems that comprise the history of philosophy for Plotinus. We begin to explain psychic phenomena with an understanding of Soul; the intelligible structure of things with Intellect; and the being of everything with the absolutely simple One.

Returning to the treatise 5.3, the 'two cognitive hypostases' are Intellect and Soul. That which is 'beyond' these is the One. The One is beyond cognition because of its unqualified simplicity. One of the central problems Plotinus inherits from Aristotle and Plato is how the paradigmatic or highest type of cognitive activity – intellection – is related to other lower types of cognition, including belief, sense-perception, knowledge, discursive reasoning and so on. The problem may be expressed in several ways. If our intellects are permanently identified with all that is intelligible, why is it that we are not now aware of this? When we are acting cognitively other than as intellect acts, how do we access the activity of our intellects? Why is the supposed activity of our intellects not just irrelevant to our cognitive engagement with the sensible or embodied world in which we operate? These questions are also expressible in sceptical terms, as we saw in the last chapter. Let 'intellection' be another name for knowledge, the *ne plus ultra* of cognition. Let knowledge be an infallible mental state. Then knowledge is not possible for embodied human beings. And if knowledge is not possible – and here is the Pyrrhonist surprise – then neither is rational

---

[2] See *Tim.* 41C–D; 61C; 65A; 69C–D; 72D–E; 89D–90D; cf. *Republic* 611B–612A; *DA* 2.2.413b26.

belief. If belief is intrinsically fallible, what one actually has when one claims to believe in or assent to propositions is something else; it is at best a simulacrum of rationality, and at worst a constant snare and delusion.

In 5.3, Plotinus aims to explore the nature of cognition generally and the grounds for rebutting the above sceptical arguments. The treatise begins with Plotinus posing a question in apparent direct response to Sextus' claim, 'If intellect grasps itself, either it is as a whole that it will grasp itself or not as a whole, but using some part of itself for this.' Plotinus writes:

Must that which thinks itself be complex in order that, with one part of itself contemplating the others, it could in this way be said to think itself, on the grounds that were it altogether simple, it would not be able to revert to itself, that is, there could not be the grasping of itself (5.3.1.1–4)?

Plotinus answers the question by conceding that if something were complex in the way that Sextus supposes it must be, self-thinking would not be possible.[3] The sort of complexity Sextus has in mind is precisely the bodily complexity insisted on by the Stoics. A body has extensive magnitudes or parts outside parts so that insofar as cognition involves the awareness of the intelligible object as present in the intellect, one part must be aware of the presence of the intelligible in another part. In that case, such cognition cannot be self-thinking. The sceptic focuses on the dogmatic claim that the highest type of cognition is infallible knowledge, which is only possible if knowledge is self-thinking, that is, the awareness by the cogniser of the cognitive state in which it is.

Plotinus is also prepared to concede for dialectical purposes that all types of cognition other than the highest type, knowledge, might involve cognition of 'externals' (*ta exō*) (5.3.1.15–28). For the things we perceive or have beliefs about or reason discursively about are outside the intellect. Intelligibles, however, cannot be outside the intellect. Why not? Plotinus' answer to this question takes us to the heart of the issue. If intelligibles were outside intellect, what would be *in* intellect would be an 'impression' or 'representation' (*tupos*) of that intelligible. In that case, intellect would not have attained truth (5.3.5.19–26; 5.3.8.36).[4] This answer seems to play right into the Pyrrhonist's hands. As Sextus argues, it is precisely because of the distinction between reality and the appearances of reality that we are unable to make a rational inference from the latter to the former. It is because we are exclusively representational machines that we

---

[3] Plotinus will go on to argue that intellect *is* complex in two senses: (1) there is the complexity of thinker and object thought and (2) there is the complexity of the objects thought.

[4] See chapter 5 above, 106–7, on the soul of the Stoic sage as the locus of truth.

cannot attain the truth or, if we do attain it, know that we have attained it. Plotinus' response seems to be not a proof that we do or even can attain truth but an argument based on the unwarranted assumption that we do.

What Plotinus requires is the sort of transcendental argument along the lines of the one we briefly discussed in chapter 3 on Plato. We recall that Plato wants to argue that we could not make the judgments we do make about the deficient equality of equal sticks and stones if we did not already somehow possess knowledge of the Form of Equality. Our belief is that the sticks and stones are indeed equal, but that the equality of the sticks and stones is only deficient in relation to Equality itself. Plotinus seems to allude to this argument when he says that when we reason discursively and understand things, we do so by the 'rules' (*kanones*) that we have from intellect (5.3.4.15–17). The rules are not themselves, of course, the intelligibles; they are representations of them (5.3.2.12). They are that which supposedly enables discursive reasoning and thinking generally.

The modes of embodied cognition are defective versions of the cognition of intellect, just as the equal sticks and stones are defective versions of Equality. Plotinus later in the treatise provides a highly compact account of thinking (*noein*):

in general, thinking seems to be a consciousness (*sunaisthēsis*) of the whole with many things coming together into that which is identical, whenever something thinks itself, which is thinking in the principal sense (5.3.13.13–15; cf. 5.6. [24] 1).

The term *sunaisthēsis* is from the word for sense-perception plus the prefix indicating a union or completion. Thinking is like sense-perception in that it involves a direct cognition of a distinct object (cf. Aristotle, *DA* 3.3.427a19–21; 3.4.429a15–18). What Plotinus seems to mean by 'many things coming together into that which is identical' is this. To think an object is to identify it as that which is manifested in each of its appearances. The object we think is distinct from its indefinitely many appearances, whether these be in time or space or not. This is equivalent to Aristotle's universal cognition.

In the Platonic universe, to understand that two things are correctly called 'large' is to understand that there must be an identical nature or essence, largeness, in which each instance of largeness participates. Thinking is never reducible to sense-perception because it is in principle impossible to perceive with one's senses this (self) identical nature; anything we could perceive would be, by definition, a particular sensible instance of that nature. Unless we can understand that there is such a nature, we cannot think the thought that two things are the same in any respect and vice versa.

Thinking, for Plotinus (who is, we must recall, trying to articulate and defend the Platonic position), involves the 'mental perception' of the identity of several distinct immediate objects. This is true when the thinking is embodied and when the objects are sensible. It is also true – indeed, it is paradigmatically true – when the thinking is disembodied and when the objects are a multiplicity of purely intelligible objects. The understanding of the identity does not efface the multiplicity. The identity is owing to the One, which is virtually all that is intelligible. Regarding the second part of the definition of thinking, why is such understanding self-thinking? Because, following Aristotle, understanding occurs when the object understood informs the intellect and the cogniser is aware of its self-information. One 'sees' that nature which is identical in all its manifestations and one thus 'sees' oneself.

Returning to the original argument for the claim that if intellect did not know the truth, we could not engage in discursive reasoning or understand anything, Plotinus assumes that such embodied thinking is deficient in the sense that the identity of intellect with its objects is not found here unqualifiedly because we could not be identical with the things we encounter when embodied; these are external to us. Our ability to have even deficient awareness of the identities behind appearances depends on our ability to access and employ identities that are altogether non-sensible. My understanding that the man standing before me now is identical with the man who stood before me yesterday despite differing circumstances is itself dependent on my ability to understand that that self-identical thing is a man despite his appearing in countless ways different from other men. The 'rules' that come from intellect are, I suspect, the propositional claims that such and such an intelligible nature is real and variously manifested as opposed to the case in which there is no real intelligible nature but only a name used to classify sensibles.

Still, it seems a gap remains, for when Plotinus speaks of the possession of truth he does not mean a belief that is adventitiously connected with the truth; he means that all intellects have the truth as a permanent possession. So, it is not enough for him to claim that we can know eternal truths or that there is eternal truth to be known. He must show that scepticism is wrong because we do eternally know the truth and that without this knowledge we could not have the understanding we do have.

Plotinus' response to this challenge, found in his treatise 'That the Intelligibles are not Outside the Intellect, and on the Good' (5.5. [32] 1–2), is this. There is no way to access the intelligible natures representationally. For there to be successful access, we would have to be able to differentiate a 'correct' representation from an 'incorrect' one. This could only occur if we had a criterion of correctness, and this in turn could only be our direct access – our mental 'seeing' – of intelligibles. Representations of them are, therefore, the result of, not a substitute for, knowing them. So, if we do have their 'rules' in us, we must already know them. If we did not know them, these supposed rules would be completely bogus. Then, counterfactually, we would not possess the ability to cognise identities among things that are the same and different. Following both Plato and Aristotle, Plotinus maintains that in the highest type of cognition the intellect possesses the intelligible and is aware of the possession; hence, it is identical with what it knows. Our difficulty in grasping the point comes, I think, from our assuming that even if there are eternal intelligibles, our knowledge of them would have to be a case of seeing something we had never seen before. We suppose that we discover intelligibles the way we discover, say, new species of insects. This Plotinus emphatically denies (5.5.1.46–9). *Aisthēsis* is of that which is outside; *sunaisthēsis* is of that which is inside, that is, identical with the knower.

For Plotinus, my understanding that before me is a man is not equivalent to my using the word 'man' correctly, though it is undoubtedly the case that owing to my knowing the intelligible nature man, I can use the word correctly. My ability to access this intelligible is identical with my ability to access my own knowledge. It is analogous to a skill that one has internalised, like playing a musical instrument. Accessing the skill is identical with accessing whatever was learned.

Plotinus' strategy in relation to Sextus is to maintain that unless we know eternal truth, we understand nothing. 'Exactly my point', Sextus will happily reply. But then Plotinus will want to insist on the disingenuousness of the Pyrrhonist position. Sextus himself quite obviously *understands* all sorts of things even if he claims to *believe* nothing. Declining to assent to an appearance does not preclude one's understanding that the appearance is of a man and not of a horse. Sextus might reply that it is only custom that has brought us to agree that what appears to us is called one thing rather than another. In one sense, this is obviously so, since language itself is the product of custom. Plotinus' point, though, cuts somewhat deeper. The ability to use language (as opposed to the ability to mimic the use of language) presupposes understanding; it is not equivalent to it. For understanding consists in the identification and re-identification of objects. And these are not reducible to mere physical responses to sense-perceptions because these objects are not sensible. In addition, the identification and re-identification of these objects are prior to their linguistic or conceptual representation.

Plotinus describes the process by which we arrive at understanding as fitting the representations that come from sense-perception to the representations that come from intellect (5.3.2.11–14). The latter are, apparently, intellect's rules. Plotinus does not deny Aristotle's point that there is no embodied thinking without images, that is, images obtained originally from sense-perception. Along with Aristotle, he does deny that thinking is unqualifiedly possible only with images. With Aristotle, he also claims that we have to be able to access intellect and the intelligibles with which it is eternally identical for us to be able to do anything beyond responding to sense-perceptions and to images with our behaviour.

Plotinus has the identical difficulties found in Aristotle with explaining how we access intellect without being unqualifiedly identical with it.[5] He says that though intellect is not a part of the embodied soul, it is both 'ours and not ours'. For this reason, 'we use it and do not use it' (5.3.3.25–9). Intellect is ours though not a part of the embodied soul because we are neither soul-body composites nor souls, but intellects. That is, we are intellects when we identify ourselves with our intellects. Plotinus is here drawing out the implication of Aristotle's claim that 'the human being is especially intellect' (*EN* 9.8.1168b35–9a2; 10.7.1178a2–7). We embodied persons use our own intellects and are identical with them whenever we think. Since intellect is identical with intelligibles, our accessing of what is intelligible is identical with our accessing or use of our own intellects. Since intelligibles are eternally separate from their sensible manifestations, so, too, are our intellects. Accordingly, Plotinus maintained the view, rejected by some later Neoplatonists, that our intellects are 'undescended', that is, permanently separate from embodied persons (4.7. [2] 13; 4.8. [6] 8).

Plotinus follows Plato and Aristotle in arguing that there is no knowledge of that which can be otherwise. But knowledge is not propositional. It is direct contact with – and, hence, identification with – that which is knowable. What are knowable are the paradigms of intelligibility, those entities which make it possible for us to understand that two things can be the same, though they are different. The sceptical challenge is addressed by denying that knowledge is belief that is justified by evidence that entails what it is evidence for. Plotinus' response does not consist in arguing that we can have knowledge about that of which the sceptic says we can only have unjustified beliefs. It consists in arguing that knowledge is the sort of thing that we must have if we are to have understanding of anything and hence belief.

[5] See chapter 4 above, 86–8.

3 KNOWLEDGE AND CONSCIOUSNESS

The anti-sceptical Plotinian argument might be termed the argument from self-consciousness. Indeed, Plotinus is the first philosopher to thematise consciousness in epistemology. Consciousness is primarily self-consciousness in 'primary thinking'.[6] 'In it [intellect] as primary thinking it would have the thinking that it is thinking as one being and so it is not double there even in thought' (2.9. [33] 1.50–1). The 'thinking that it is thinking' is not a propositional attitude.[7] It is the recognition or awareness of an occurrent cognitive state. This thinking is something other than introspection. It is not the awareness of a substantial 'self' that is other than the intelligibles cognised. The awareness of one's substantial or true self is, paradoxically, possible only for embodied individuals who are, as embodied, other than their own true selves.

Consciousness is paradigmatically of what is unqualifiedly intelligible; its derivative manifestations are of what is only qualifiedly intelligible. Consciousness is paradigmatically self-consciousness because what is unqualifiedly intelligible is identical with the intellect. In the latter aspect, it is 'self-reflexivity' (*epistrophē pros heauton*) (5.3.6.3–6). Without self-reflexivity, intelligibles could be present, though they could not be thought. Without self-reflexivity, there could be representations, too, of that which is intelligible, but there could be no thought. Of course, the presence of representations is no more equivalent to thinking than is the presence of intelligibles. One must think the representations as representations. Thinking is not equivalent to a behavioural response to a representation such as an image, even though a response may follow from thinking. Thus, self-reflexivity or self-consciousness is an essential property of all thinking, though when what is thought is external, thinking and self-reflexivity are manifested in a diminished manner.

The opposing view that all thinking is representational is the source of the fundamental divide between the ancient and the modern conceptions of knowledge and belief. This counter-claim is no doubt facilitated by the wholehearted adoption of the Aristotelian slogan 'no thinking without

---

[6] Plotinus uses the term *antilēpsis* for consciousness that apprehends external objects through the senses or for consciousness of the process of discursive reasoning about externals. Cf. 4.4. [28] 13.11–16; 5.1. [10] 12.5–14; 6.7. [38] 7.24–31. The phrase 'primary thinking' refers to the paradigmatic instance of thinking, from which all other types of thinking are derived. The criterion for 'grading' thinking hierarchically is the degree of unity or identity of thinker and object of thinking.

[7] See 1.3. [20] 5.17–19 where Plotinus contrasts cognition of the truth with cognition of propositions. The former is a condition for the latter.

images', where images obviously have a representational role. As indicated above, in antiquity neither Aristotle nor any of those influenced by his epistemology confused the instrumentality of images with thinking itself. This divide over thinking as representational or not actually rests upon an even deeper split. For suppose that thinking is direct contact with intelligibles analogous to the putative direct contact with sensibles. Should we nevertheless not still insist that thinking and sense-perception are the *result* of that contact, not the contact itself? In the case of sense-perception, the contact must be described in physical terms and if the sense-perception is to be other than that – if, say, we distinguish sensation from perception proper – then it must in some sense consist in a representation of that contact. Analogously, even if contact with intelligibles is not described in physical terms, that is, even if we concede that thinking consists in an immaterial entity contacting another immaterial entity, the supposed presence of the intelligible will have to be distinguished from the awareness of that presence. And it is the latter, not the former, which the ancients agree is the actual thinking. So, must not this thinking be some sort of representation of the intelligible that is present to the intellect?

It is precisely this problem, I suggest, that Plotinus is addressing when he claims that thinking in the principal sense is self-thinking. The relation between intellect and intelligible is thus analogous to the relation between an individual and the embodied states of which he is the subject. Consider in the latter circumstance someone who announces that he has a headache. The Neoplatonic analysis of this report is as follows. The one who is aware that he has a headache is a subject identical with the one who has the headache. There are no headaches of which one is not aware. Nevertheless, the awareness is distinguishable from the having of the headache. The last statement seems, however, to be entirely gratuitous. If headaches are not things separate from the having of them, how can the awareness of having a headache be distinct from the headache? To make such a distinction would seem to turn the headache into something like an intentional object. In doing that, one seems to undercut the claim that there are no unfelt headaches. Plotinus would, I think, agree that a headache is not an intentional object, but that 'my-being-in-a-headachy-state' is. The justification for this claim is that my awareness of the state I am in has a cognitive component that my being in that state does not. This component is constituted by my awareness that what I am feeling is a headache. My feeling the headache does not have this component.[8] The awareness is

---

[8] So, for Plotinus, animals can be in pain but not understand that they are in pain.

not a representation of the headache, for if it were, the representation would not be the headache. Since it is the identical subject that is aware of the headache and that is having the headache, there is no way to distinguish the subjects.

Self-reflexivity means that one's cognition of one's own states is not representational. This does not mean, of course, that one is thereby precluded from representing one's own states. Assenting to the proposition 'I have a headache now' is justified by my now being aware of having the headache; the belief is not identical with that which justifies it. Even if it were true that we could not be aware of having a headache without assenting to the proposition 'I have a headache now', that assent is explained by the awareness and is not identical with it. All propositions have the property of being either true or false. Awareness is true only in the ontological sense recognised by Plato and Aristotle; 'false' awareness, by contrast, is only the absence of awareness. One might object that between feeling the headache and assenting to the proposition 'I have a headache now' there is no conceptual space for the awareness. Plotinus' position, as I understand it, is that to eliminate the awareness or to conflate it with the assent to the proposition is to miss altogether what is distinctive about human cognition, namely, its self-reflexive character. If it were not *self*-evident to me that I have a headache now, it would not be absurd (as it surely is) to ask for the evidence that I am aware of my own state. By contrast, there is no absurdity in asking why I believe the proposition 'I have a headache now' is true. It is extremely easy to make the illicit conflation just because of the absurdity of the former question. The only question it makes any sense to ask is in regard to propositions to which one has assented. For example, we might ask someone if she is sure that she is feeling headachy and not anxious. Just because it is absurd to ask for one's evidence for one being in a certain state, it does not follow that the state of which one is aware is identical with the assent to a proposition. The absurdity derives from ignoring the self-reflexivity of the state ('I cannot have a headache without being aware that I have a headache'), not from the supposed fact that the awareness is identical with the assent to a proposition, much less with the proposition 'S has a headache now' when asserted by S.

Let us recall that the self-reflexivity present in one's awareness that one has a headache is only analogous to primary thinking. It is analogous in the way that an image is analogous to that of which it is an image. In primary thinking or intellection, the awareness is of the presence of an intelligible object, not of a bodily state. Just as in the case of the bodily state, there are no intelligibles existing 'free floating' outside an intellect. To think of Plato's Forms in this way is not only to overlook what he says in *Timaeus* about the Demiurge, but more importantly it is to misconceive them as something like separately existing bodily individuals (5.5.1.46–9). If they were actually like that, our access to these would be through sense-perception (5.5.1.62–6; cf. 5.3.5.19–29). What would be present to the intellect would be some sort of representation of that intelligible entity, not the intelligible itself. Of such representations, the relevant mode of cognition is belief. Understanding in general and intellection in particular are, however, not like this. For when one understands, one sees the reason for something being true, especially that two things that are the same are so owing to an identical nature. It is not a representation of this nature that explains; it must be the nature itself. As Plotinus puts it, 'if intellect contemplates [intelligibles] as outside of it, necessarily it cannot possess the truth of these and it must be deceived in everything that it contemplates' (5.5.1.52–3). If intellect or intellects do not possess the truth, understanding is not possible. If understanding is possible, intellects do actually possess the truth, where 'truth' of course refers not to propositions but to the intelligibles themselves.

For Plotinus, the identity of intellect and intelligibles does not negate the complexity of intellection, that is, the 'internal' real distinction within one entity between intellect and intelligibles (4.8. [6] 3.10; cf. 5.1. [10] 8.26; 5.3.15.11, etc.).[9] Self-reflexivity necessitates a complex identity. The identity of intellect and intelligibles means that, since the actuality of intellection is the activity (*energeia*) of intellection, the intelligibles themselves are identical with an activity (5.3.5.36–9; 5.9. [5] 8.15–16). All types of cognition other than the primary type are hierarchically ordered images of the primary just as every manifestation of an intelligible is within a hierarchically ordered series of images. Admittedly, the idea that, say, doubleness or beauty are activities takes some getting used to. Here Plotinus is in line with Aristotle in identifying form, that which is intelligible, with actuality, and perfect actuality with the activity of thinking. The further notion that thinking is not absolutely primary, but that 'above' it is to be found the absolutely first and simple principle of all, is the Platonic notion that, according to Plotinus, Aristotle failed to grasp (5.6. [24] 1.1–14; cf. 3.8. [30] 9.8–13; 5.3.11, etc.).

---

[9] A real 'minor' distinction, in the useful Scholastic terminology is within one entity; a real major distinction is between two entities. For example, a substance and its accidents are really distinct according to a real minor distinction whereas one substance is distinct from another according to a real major distinction. Both distinctions are real as opposed to conceptual distinctions which exist only in the mind of one who makes them, for example, between the substance considered as a human being and the identical substance considered as an animal.

The identity of intellect and intelligibles entails that primary thinking is both non-propositional and non-representational. As with the above example of a headache, intellection is primarily a self-reflexive activity, whereas the assumption of propositional attitudes is derived from this activity (5.5.1.38–42; cf. 5.8. [31] 6.6–9). It must be emphasised that Plotinus agrees that such propositional attitudes are constitutive of all types of cognition other than the highest. His position, however, is more extreme than one that maintains that there is *one* type of cognition among many that is non-propositional. His position is that primary cognition, that is, intellection, is the type of cognition without which none of the others would be possible. So, if we wish to use the word 'knowledge' for the highest type of cognition, we have to admit that knowledge is non-propositional. If we refuse to say that knowledge is non-propositional, that does not, from Plotinus' point of view, negate the fact that wherever on the hierarchical scale knowledge is to be located, it could not exist if non-propositional thinking were not ours. We have to be able to access our own intellect's activity in order to engage in any type of cognition.

If we were to agree with Aristotle in calling knowledge (*epistēmē*) a type of cognition inferior to the highest or paradigmatic type, and that it is propositional, we would expect that self-reflexivity would be manifested therein, but in a derived manner. This is similarly true for all other derivative modes of cognition. Even the most elementary type of belief will manifest self-reflexivity. Further, any belief requires an understanding of the qualified identity of a subject with its predicate. That understanding is not reducible to rule following. The understanding is prior to any disposition arising from it.

So, my belief that Theaetetus is sitting requires that I understand that what appears to my senses as that which I am accustomed to call 'Theaetetus' also appears to my senses as being seated. The identity is *not* between the sensible object Theaetetus and the sensible object of his position. It is strictly correct to insist that the only thing identical with Theaetetus is Theaetetus whether he is sitting or not. The self-identical object is that which appears to my senses as *this* man *and* to my senses as seated. The understanding operating here requires self-reflexivity because it requires both that I perceive a sitting Theaetetus and that I judge that what I see are two materially identical manifestations of one thing. To do the first without the second would reduce my belief to nothing more than a recording device or scanner. The subject making this judgment must be identical with the subject who perceives; otherwise, the judging subject would just be another device recording the original perception. That is why, ultimately, anything without an immaterial or incorporeal intellect cannot possess beliefs. Only an immaterial intellect can be aware of its own states (4.7. [2] 8.1–11).

We might concede that our capacity for understanding is indeed a remarkable one. Plotinus, however, will insist that the understanding we exercise in our belief states is in fact inseparable from the eternal intelligible objects of understanding. The exercise of our embodied understanding requires the use of what our undescended intellects eternally have intellection of. This is so because intellection and intelligibles are really two aspects of the identical reality. So, in some sense when we do exercise understanding, we are using the 'rules' derived from intellect.

4 IMAGINATION

Plotinus posits two image-making powers, one for the deliverances of our senses and one for the deliverances of our intellects (4.3. [27] 31). From the latter, we receive 'understandings' (*noēseis*) and from the former 'sense-perceptions' (*aisthēseis*) (4.3.30.16). These 'understandings' in the imagination are apparently the 'rules' derived from intellect. The fitting of the images or impressions derived from sense-perception to those derived from intellect is what, according to Plotinus, Plato meant by 'recollection' (5.3.2.11–14; cf. 3.5. [50] 1.35; 3.7. [45] 1.23).

In the so-called recollection argument in *Phaedo* (72E–78B), Socrates argues that unless his interlocutors Cebes and Simmias possessed knowledge of Equality, they could not make certain judgments about equal things they encounter with their senses. This argument is widely misunderstood to be maintaining that we could not *re*cognise things as being equal unless we had, apparently prior to our embodiment, cognised the Form of Equality. It is naturally objected that it is perfectly possible to explain how we learn to use the general term 'equal' and to apply it correctly to equal things without recourse to the extreme metaphysical position that is the conclusion of this argument, namely, the disembodied pre-existence of the soul. It is not Socrates' point that the disembodied knowledge of Forms is necessary to explain how we apply general words or universal concepts. In particular, what Cebes and Simmias agree that they are able to do is to recognise the deficiency of equal sticks and stones, that is, a deficiency with respect to the Form of Equality (74D4–7). And such recognition is not accounted for by our learning how to use words or how to internalise concepts for the simple reason that no sensible equal is deficient with respect to a general word or to a universal concept.

We have already seen that for Plato this knowledge is neither propositional nor representational in any way. That certainly does not preclude the representation of what is already known. Indeed, in our encounters with the sensible world what we are most in need of are representations to ourselves. Our ability to cognise the deficient equality of the equal sticks and stones manifests itself, for instance, in our statement to this effect and in our understanding of what it is we are saying. No one who has ever learned a mathematical formula and then failed to apply it correctly in an examination will deny that there is a difference between being able to express the formula correctly and understanding what it means. We can also add that the understanding is only available to us by means of the image that the formula is.

This is, for Plotinus, exactly parallel to the case of sense-perception where a perceptual image is necessary for our cognising what we sense (4.4. [28] 1.1–20; cf. 4.3.26.39–46). The relation between intellection and perception in cognition is further explained in this way:

> Therefore, even though the soul [i.e., the highest part of the soul, the intellect] is always moved to intellection, it is when it comes to be in the image-making power (*to phantastikon*) that we have an awareness (*antilēpsis*) of it. The intellection is one thing and the awareness of the intellection is another, and we are always intellecting, but we are not always aware that we are. This is so owing to the fact that that which receives does not only receive these [i.e., the 'intellections'], but also receives sense-perceptions from the other side (4.3.30.11–16).

As Plotinus explains elsewhere (5.1.12.11–12; cf. 1.1. [53] 11.1–8), cognitional awareness occurs when there is a communication (*metadosis*) between the intellect and the perceptual faculty. This communication involves more than the presence of an intelligible image alongside the presence of a sensible image. If mere co-presence were occurring, we could not understand what it is we perceive. The communication consists in the use of the thought (*noēma*) of that which is intelligible to cognise the identity of that which is perceived. It is the thought of equality, itself a representation of the intelligible, that enables one to understand that the sensible equals are also deficiently equal. Their deficiency is with respect to intelligibility, because that out of which the equality of equal sticks and stones is constituted is not constitutive of equality itself. The thought of equality must be other than a concept of equality if the latter is taken to be a representation only of that which all equal things have in common (5.8. [31] 11.19).

This thought is also to be distinguished from the intellection of the Form of Equality that the undescended intellect enjoys. In intellect, there is no representation; there is only complete cognitional identity. Therefore, 'we have it [intellect] either collectively or individually, or both collectively

and individually. We have it collectively because it is indivisible and every-
where one and identical; we have it individually, because each one of us has
the whole of it in the primary part of the soul. We have the Forms in two
ways, in the soul in a way unfolded and separated, but in intellect all
together' (1.1. [53] 8.3–8).

It seems that the 'unfolded' and 'separated' Form is the intellectual image
of what intellect contemplates. The distinction between a concept consisting of an image derived from sense-perception and the kind of image
intended here seems clear. A concept is obviously more than a visual
image. Its generality or universality resides in the intrinsically general or
universal rules that one internalises for the use of words. The rules may
remain when the connection between the internalisation of the rules and
the original image (Epicurus' 'basic grasps') is lost. I take it that Plotinus'
central point is that the images or representations derived from sense-
perception do not account for our ability to understand anything, even
though they are part of the aetiology of our ability to apply rules. If we are
able to apply rules with understanding, that is owing to the presence in the
cogniser of a different sort of image or representation as well.

Thus Plotinus wants to distinguish on the one side the physical event that
is sensation of the equal sticks and stones, the perceptual awareness of this
physical event, the perceptual images arising therefrom, the ability to
employ such images for classificatory or communicative purposes, and on
the other side, the understanding of material identities in the sensible world,
the latter mode of cognition being only possible with the presence of
intellectual images or thoughts.

This sharp separation of images and their role in understanding appears
to be controverted by the phenomenology of cognition. We do not seem to
be aware of anything other than the sorts of images that are derived from
sense-perception, including words. In our internal speech, when we wonder
or calculate or apprise a situation leading up to the application of a word, we
do not seem to be aware of a distinct intellectual image of the sort Plotinus is
confident is present. His response to this objection is as follows:

When one soul [i.e., the part of the soul capable of sense-perception] is in harmony
with the other [i.e., the part of the soul capable of higher cognition], and the image-
making faculty of each is not separate from the other, and that of the better soul is
authoritative, the images become one, in a way as if a shadow followed the other or
as if a little light moved under a greater one. But when there is war and disharmony
between them, the other image [i.e., the perceptual] becomes itself manifest, and
we do not notice [the image] that is in the other [part], and generally we do not
notice the duality of psychic parts (4.3.31.9–14).

The unity of phenomenal consciousness is the default state for embodied cognisers. The analysis of what makes it possible for us to see, that is, to understand, something's identity does not require that we be aware of the elements of understanding any more than does our ability to engage in physical activity require that we be aware of the elements making this possible (1.4.10.21–33).

Plotinus seems to be offering a sort of transcendental argument: understanding is possible only if certain conditions obtain. Among these are: the existence of paradigmatic intelligible reality with which intellect is actively cognitively identical, the existence of an ability in us to access this activity and hence its contents, and the existence of a complex immaterial subject, capable of self-reflexivity. This complex apparatus is developed to explain irreducible cognitive phenomena, including belief, understanding and knowledge. The irreducibility of these to sense-perception or to other physical processes seems to require the hierarchical inversion. That is, if knowledge is not reduced to belief and belief is not reduced to sense-perception and/or a purely physical response to the environment, all cognition is going to be analysed as diminished expression of a primary mode. That is, after all, what Plato suggests in his account of knowledge and belief and of the metaphysical basis for their distinction. It is also what Aristotle suggests in his identification of intellection with primary being and in his claim that embodied thinking must be able to access intellect.

Plotinus is, I believe, intent upon drawing out the consequences of the assumption that knowledge is a real feature of the world. He accepts the futility of assuming this and at the same time of trying to make knowledge a type of belief. If knowledge is not a type of belief, it is not a propositional attitude distinct from belief in the way that one propositional attitude is distinct from another. To say that the highest type of cognition is non-propositional does not go far enough. One must add the more severe doctrine that knowledge is a way of being in the world, not an encounter with the world *ab extra*.[10] And again, Plotinus is here not aiming to be an innovator, but rather a faithful expositor of the tradition he has received. Plotinus' pagan Neoplatonic successors Iamblichus and Proclus parted company with him at this point, at least to the extent that they denied that *our* intellects are undescended and eternally cognitively identical with all that is intelligible. His Christian successors had no difficulty in amalgamating the Demiurge, the Prime Unmoved Mover and the hypostasis

---

[10] Plotinus cites approvingly in seven different places Parmenides' words 'thinking and being are identical' (Fr. B3 DK).

Intellect into a single divine first principle. Within this Christian tradition, the *ne plus ultra* of cognition and its objects were easily identifiable with primary being.

Staying within the boundaries of philosophy and within the limits of this book, it seems worth considering whether the sort of naturalistic assumptions about knowledge that led ultimately to Neoplatonism still have any currency. In chapter 1, I contrasted this type of naturalism with the non-naturalistic criteriological approach to epistemology expressed in the Standard Analysis. In the concluding chapter, I would like to briefly compare ancient naturalism about knowledge and belief with some alternative naturalistic approaches found on the contemporary scene.

CHAPTER EIGHT

Varieties of naturalism

I NATURALISM REDIVIVUS

I have argued that the ancient philosophers generally treated knowledge and belief naturalistically. The non-naturalistic or criteriological approach of the Standard Analysis is aborted in Plato's *Theaetetus*, although the Standard Analysis itself lives on in its subsequent application to rational belief. If knowledge is a natural feature of human life like digestion or pregnancy, it would seem to be available for empirical scientific investigation. If that is so, ancient epistemological naturalism will find itself at a disadvantage, to put it mildly. For to admit the relevance of biology, neurophysiology, psychology and so on to the study of epistemology seems to ensure that ancient naturalism is doomed to melt into the deep background of historical curiosities. In this light, if one rejects a contemporary version of naturalised epistemology, the only plausible alternative would seem to be some non-naturalised approach, most appropriately rooted in logical or linguistic analysis and in the evaluative use of a certain class of terms and concepts. An analysis of how our words or concepts are used or even how they ought to be used need not have anything to fear from the deliverances of modern empirical science. By contrast, insofar as ancient epistemology is supposed to be dependent on ancient science, its subsequent obsolescence appears to be inevitable. I have in the preceding chapters tried to cast some doubt both on the supposition that ancient epistemological naturalism is susceptible to refutation by the claims of empirical science and on the perhaps more egregious error of supposing that ancient epistemology is not a form of naturalism. Thus, I hope to have at least established that the main alternatives to contemporary naturalised epistemology are two and not one. In this chapter, I want to briefly consider some of the elements of some versions of contemporary naturalised epistemology from the perspective of its ancient counterpart. My aim is to bring to the fore what I take to be most distinctive about the ancient approach and to consider to what extent contemporary naturalism can accommodate this.

The doyen of contemporary naturalism about knowledge is undoubtedly W. V. Quine who in 1969 published an essay titled 'Naturalized Epistemology'.[1] Since the appearance of that essay, philosophers have lined up in agreement or in disagreement with Quine's position and various versions of naturalism have flourished. The inspiration behind a naturalised approach to epistemology is that no branch of philosophy that deals with human inter-action with the world should fall outside the purview of modern science; hence, questions about knowledge and belief should be understood to be reduced to questions about the psychology and physiology of the acquisition of knowledge and belief.[2] Thus, normative or evaluative questions in epistemology are either to be left aside entirely or themselves brought within the ambit of science. In the latter event, talk in epistemology about such normative notions as good reasons or justification or warrant would be understood according to the healthy or normal operation of the organism just as talk of a 'good digestive system' would be.

As Quine constructs his argument, what he calls 'traditional' or 'old' epistemology is seized with the sceptical challenge to the justification of our beliefs about the world based principally upon our immediate sense-experience. Old epistemology is thus assumed to be exclusively focused on empirical knowledge. Naturalised epistemology, conceived of as a radically new alternative to attempts to meet this challenge, thus begins with the inadequacy of the Standard Analysis taken as the appropriate framework for doing the job. The inadequacy stems from the fact that this analysis seems to be untranslatable into the language of science and impervious to experimental confirmation. According to the adherent of naturalised epistemology, any sort of global scepticism is in principle misguided. Legitimate doubts about the deliverances of science must always be addressed within the sciences themselves according to their own standards of verification.

From the perspective of ancient epistemology, there are several striking assumptions in the contemporary versions of naturalism. The first is that, along with non-naturalism, they all simply assume that knowledge is a type of belief. The correct scientific analysis of how knowledge arises will be an analysis of the formation of our beliefs. Indeed, few naturalists acknowledge

---

[1] See W. V. Quine, *Ontological Relativity and Other Essays* (New York: Columbia University Press, 1969).

[2] Quine consistently sought to undermine the goal of a first philosophy prior to natural science. Wilfred Sellars nicely summarised this position and its implicit inversion of Protagoreanism in *Science, Perception and Reality* (London: Routledge & Kegan Paul, 1963): 'in the dimension of describing and explaining the world, science is the measure of all things, of what is that it is, and of what is not that it is not' (173). Here, the rejection of Protagorean relativism is in contrast to its rejection by Plato and Aristotle.

that there is a real distinction between knowledge and belief.[3] Second, whether the naturalist makes a distinction between knowledge and belief or not, knowledge is assumed to be representational, since it is the external sense world that is the object of knowledge claims. And third, it is assumed that the only possible basis for the autonomy of epistemology is a non-naturalistic one. On all three counts, the assumptions underlying the rejection of the Standard Analysis do not leave any conceptual space for ancient naturalism. The responses to scepticism in antiquity eschew these assumptions. The principal ancient 'dogmatists' I have discussed take the sceptic to challenge the possibility of knowledge and *therefore* the possibility of rational belief. Conversely, the defence of the possibility of rational belief depends upon the possibility of knowledge. In addition, not only do they distinguish the natural state of believing from the natural state of knowing; they tend to take knowing as prior to believing. So, knowing is included in the definition of believing, but not vice versa.

The contemporary naturalist's rejection of the relevance of the Standard Analysis to a scientific account of knowing and believing operates on one more far-reaching assumption, namely, that the procedure for the verification of the presence of knowledge or belief must in principle eliminate the primacy of the first person. I say 'in principle' because the first person might now generally in the infancy of neuroscience have a more ready access to her own mental states – just as with her bodily states – than any third person observer. In the ideal account of those states, her privileged access will drop out. This methodological desideratum is a cornerstone of a scientific approach to the world.

It is reasonable to suppose that this assumption is part of the explanation for the naturalist's elision of knowledge and belief. From the third person perspective, the way to verify the presence of knowledge or belief in someone will be behavioural, broadly conceived. It is, though, seemingly difficult or impossible to differentiate the behaviour of one who knows from the behaviour of one who believes, especially when it is also assumed that knowledge is a type of belief.

Again, from the perspective of ancient epistemology, the separation of knowledge and belief makes it theoretically possible to acknowledge that the third person account may be prior to the first person for belief without accepting that this is the case for knowledge. The Stoics were particularly enthusiastic about noticing the beliefs of ordinary fools the presence of which the fools themselves would deny. And who, after all, could gainsay

---

[3] A major exception is Timothy Williamson. See section 3 below.

the possibility of someone else being more insightful about what one believes than one is oneself? This, however, is not necessarily the case for knowledge. One way of expressing this is to say that A can only know that B knows p if A knows p. To express it thus is, however, to suppose that knowledge is propositional. It is also to raise complex and perhaps insoluble problems about differing paths to justification. For the ancient epistemologists, the more correct explanation for the absolute primacy of the first person in knowing rests upon the fact that knowledge is non-propositional and is constituted by a self-reflexive infallible mental state. Only A can be self-reflexively aware of the presence of the intelligible object in A. If B is a subject different from A, though B can have a belief about *what* A knows, B's knowledge of what A knows is never equivalent to some putative knowledge of B that A knows. Indeed, since knowledge is here taken to be non-propositional, there is no such thing as B knowing *that* A knows anything.

It is entirely understandable that the naturalist, faced with the claim that knowledge is non-propositional and an infallible mental state, would be inclined to view this approach as non-naturalistic or even super naturalistic, but nothing remotely like naturalism. It seems clear that the naturalism of ancient epistemology turns upon an understanding of nature more capacious that anything found today. For according to that ancient understanding, nature includes far more than what can be measured. A contemporary scientist or philosopher might in fact have little difficulty in acknowledging this. The real dispute is over whether the bits that cannot be measured are intelligible or not. If they are not intelligible, one is not likely to endorse the ancient conception of knowledge as a natural state and the primary mode of cognition. Contemporary naturalism wants to embrace knowledge and belief as intelligible ultimately in the same terms as other features of nature. The ancient approach resists the assimilation of knowledge to other processes and events in nature. On this approach, the understanding that the scientist seeks of nature is only possible if understanding is not itself a measurable feature of nature, that is, one for which the third person has primacy.

Criticisms of Quine and Quine-inspired naturalised epistemology frequently focus on the normativity missing in naturalism. One who knows is supposed to have achieved something that one who merely believes has not. The achievement is reflected in claiming that one has met the justificatory condition of the Standard Analysis. From the perspective of ancient naturalism, the normativity implicit in justification may be found in belief, but not in knowledge. Justification, insofar as it is interpersonal, involves giving reasons, even when these reasons include the causes for the belief. The giving and receiving of reasons is entirely propositional. There is, though, no evidential proposition that entails that someone know something non-propositionally, even if the evidence entails the proposition that someone knows something non-propositionally. Of course one might argue, like Plato in *Phaedo*, that unless one knew some things, one could not perform certain other cognitional acts. Even here, though, the justification is not on behalf of a claim to know occurrently.

Ordinary patterns of justification are intrinsically open to third person inspection. Indeed, B might be justified in believing that A is justified in believing that p, even though A does not believe this. If Socrates is justified in believing that someone is justified in believing that the equal sticks and stones are deficiently equal, that person might not believe that he is so justified. There is, however, no justification for the claim to know Equality. The putative justificatory *logos* one gives never entails that one knows even if it is the case that one who knows *can* give some sort of *logos*. Of course, if one were to give a *logos* that no one could find any fault with, that might be said to increase the justification for a belief that one knows. It is not, however, true on anyone's story – including that of the supporter of the Standard Analysis – that the *logos* itself is the knowledge. To say that one has knowledge when one is justified in believing true propositions is to acknowledge that the knowledge is other than of the propositions known.

When Plato claims that one who knows is able to give a *logos*, this is not, as we have seen, anything like a defining criterion of knowledge. On the contrary, knowledge would itself serve a justificatory role for beliefs regarding those things which are as they are owing to Forms. When the Stoics insist that knowledge is incontrovertible by *logos*, this is the obverse of the claim that there is no *logos* that turns a belief into knowledge. So, having a justification for what one knows is no part of knowing. Similarly, when Aristotle says that knowledge is 'with *logos*' (*Post. An.* 2.19.100b10), he does not mean that the knowledge *is* the *logos*.[4] The *logos* is clearly the expression of the knowledge, not constitutive of it. If we were to suppose that by providing a demonstration one could meet the necessary and sufficient condition for being justified in one's claim to know, anyone who could provide this demonstration would know. If 'provide' means to communicate the demonstration, anyone parroting the words without understanding would know. Instead of assuming that the knowing is the 'sum' of the

---

[4] As we have seen in chapter 4, knowledge is not for Aristotle the highest type of cognition. What is true here for knowledge is *a fortiori* true for that highest type.

provision of the demonstration *plus* something else, we should, I think, acknowledge that Aristotle has some reason to locate the knowing exclusively in the 'something else'. Doing this does not require that we disavow the obvious fact that one must represent what one knows with *logos*, even to oneself. The gap between the knowledge as a mental state and the representation of it is the main gap between ancient and modern naturalistic epistemology.

2 EPISTEMOLOGY AND NATURE

Hilary Kornblith's *Knowledge and its Place in Nature* (Oxford University Press, 2002) is an extended effort to refine Quinean-inspired naturalism in epistemology. This book aims to take account of thirty-five or so years of debate between naturalists and anti-naturalists. A brief consideration of its main conclusions will, I hope, serve to illuminate further some of the differences between ancient and modern naturalism.

The cornerstone of Kornblith's naturalised epistemology is the claim that knowledge is a natural kind like gold. In this regard, Kornblith sets his naturalism apart from that of Quine. As a natural kind, knowledge is available for scientific investigation, no less than gold or any other natural kind, particularly within the relatively new field of cognitive ethology. Kornblith's definition of knowledge as a natural kind is that it is 'reliably produced true belief ... instrumental in the production of behavior, successful in meeting biological needs and thereby implicated in the Darwinian explanation of the selective retention of traits' (62). With ancient naturalists, Kornblith argues that knowledge does not require a social context whatsoever. It is not essentially connected to the giving and receiving of reasons or to their necessary socially constructed linguistic and conceptual concomitants. Against ancient naturalism, however, Kornblith insists that the presence of knowledge in a natural creature does not require reflection just as the presence of a disease does not require awareness by the creature of its presence. In response to the non-naturalists' complaint that naturalism eschews the normative dimension of epistemology, Kornblith argues that normativity is addressed by reliabilism. For any animal which has a reliable means of acquiring beliefs is better able to cope with its environment than one which does not. Thus, the normative dimension of epistemology is, as with Quine, wholly pragmatic.

Since Kornblith bases his case on knowledge as a natural kind, he is it would seem obliged to supply reasons for thinking that knowledge is a natural kind different from belief. If he cannot do this, the way is open for the non-naturalist to claim that knowledge is nothing more than a belief that has met certain stipulated or imposed criteria. That is, there would be at most *one* natural kind, and that would be belief, not knowledge. Kornblith's reason for thinking that knowledge is a distinct natural kind is that any scientific account of sophisticated animal behaviour must see an animal's cognitive equipment as aimed at acquiring and processing information (61). If the acquiring and processing of information occurs in a reliable manner, it is knowledge. *That* is the natural kind. Unlike the relatively uncontroversial case of the natural kind gold, there is in the case of the putative natural kind knowledge no common ground between the modern and ancient naturalists on the basis of which there could even be a dispute over its correct account. Any case of knowledge that Kornblith would point to would be rejected by most if not all of the ancients, both because knowledge is not a type of belief and because the account of animal cognition must be radically different from the account of human cognition.

From the general perspective of modern science, it is easy enough to side with Kornblith against his ancient opponents. And yet, if we approach the search for a paradigmatic example of the natural kind knowledge beginning with our own human experience, the kind of arguments that we have seen the ancients providing preclude the assimilation of human knowledge to a type of animal behaviour for a singular *logical* reason: knowledge is irreducibly first person. There is no way of pointing to animal behaviour that uniquely evinces knowledge because there is no way of pointing to human behaviour that uniquely evinces knowledge (contra: Kornblith, 135). This may indeed seem to be a defect in the ancient account, but it can hardly be decisive if the issue is how to demarcate the natural kind knowledge. By appealing to cognitive ethology as providing the framework for an account of the natural kind knowledge, Kornblith, from the perspective of the ancient philosophers, both misses the natural kind in question and opens the door to sceptical arguments. If one wants to close that door decisively and put the study of epistemology on a scientific or quasi-scientific footing, perhaps the non-naturalist approach is preferable. On that approach, knowledge is not a natural kind at all, and we are once more on the threshold of the Standard Analysis and its attendant problems.

3 NATURALISM AND THE MENTAL

Timothy Williamson's *Knowledge and its Limits* (Oxford University Press, 2000) argues for a remarkably distinctive type of epistemological naturalism. I have no intention here of engaging in detail with this impressive book. I shall briefly discuss its main theses with the goal of illuminating the extent to which Williamson sides with ancient naturalism and the precise point at which they part company.

Williamson's naturalism is rooted in his claim that knowledge is a distinct mental state, incapable of analysis into any other mental state or into the typical terms of the Standard Analysis (184–90). It is a 'pure' mental state like belief or being in pain. Thus, knowledge is not a belief state in which some additional condition or conditions are met. Nevertheless, Williamson argues that if someone knows something, he also believes it. But since all knowledge is, as he puts it, 'factive', the reverse does not of course follow (21–3; 41–8).[5] If we are to suppose that if S knows p, S believes p, and further that if knowing is not to be analysed as a true belief that meets some additional condition, how are we to tell the difference (as mental states) between knowing and believing? Williamson answers that what one knows is the totality of what is evident to one. And by 'evidence' he seems to mean all that is empirically available to one or more potential knowers. It is knowing p that justifies S in believing p (185). The equation of knowledge with evidence thus 'suggests a very modest kind of foundationalism, on which all one's knowledge serves as the foundation for all one's justified beliefs' (185).

Since knowledge is what is evident to one, the way we tell if someone knows or if someone merely believes p is threefold. First, and most obviously, if it makes sense to ask for a justification for one's belief that p, and if one's justification is just that one knows p, we can conclude that one does not merely believe p. If one were to press a request for justification of what one claims to know (as opposed to what one merely believes), what in fact one would be doing is focusing on the belief that is entailed by the knowing, not the knowing itself. Second, the behaviour of one who knows is often different from the behaviour of one who merely believes. The former makes a contribution to the causal explanation of action that is distinct from the latter (60–4; 80). Thus, for example, people who persist in seeking an object despite repeated failures can best be understood as to be acting on the basis of knowing that the object is there to be found, unlike someone who merely believes that it is there. Third, only knowledge and not mere belief warrants assertion (253). The defeasibility of warrant depends entirely on the context within which assertions are made; what is evident to one at a certain time might not be evident at another.

---

[5] I pass over Williamson's argument that there is no substantial difference between facts and propositions. So, roughly, we can suppose in the usual way that Williamson maintains that knowledge is a propositional attitude.

What makes Williamson's foundationalism only a 'modest' variety and not the full-blown sort that spawned three hundred or so years of anti-naturalistic criteriology and the consequent naturalistic reaction to it is that knowledge is not an infallible mental state (191; 214). As Williamson puts it, knowledge is not 'luminous'. Neither are pain states nor appearances (94–5). Mistakes are always possible and always correctable. Williamson's general argument against luminous mental states is that when one is in a mental state, that is, when one is aware of being in a mental state, one is not necessarily in a position to know that one is in that state. One does not possess first-person authority for the claim to know. Thus, one can be in pain without being in a position to know that one is in pain (106). And one can know something, that is, be in a mental state of knowing, without knowing that one knows (114). The putative infallibility of knowing that Williamson rejects is taken by him to reside in the second-order cognition of the original mental state. Since this second-order condition ('I know that I am in pain', 'I know that I know p') necessarily involves the conceptualisation of the original mental state in a representation of it, it is always in principle possible to be mistaken about what is being represented. The possibility always exists because the original or first-order mental state can gradually change. More precisely, since the concepts we must apply to represent it are inevitably vague, our application of these is never totally unproblematic.

For Williamson, knowing that p justifies one in believing that p, though one never (or almost never, excluding trivial cases) knows infallibly. Knowledge is thus the foundation for rational or justified belief, but it is not the indubitable foundation that Descartes supposed it to be. Williamson can thus offer a radically new response to scepticism. We are not in fact justified in believing anything that we do not know or that does not logically follow from what we know. When the sceptic then says that this means that we are not justified in believing anything because we do not know anything, Williamson replies that, on the contrary, we know many, many things. The sceptic questions this because he maintains that it is extremely difficult or impossible to know, since one does not know unless one knows that one knows, that is, unless it is absolutely impossible that one is wrong. Williamson replies that though it makes no sense to say 'I know but I may be mistaken', this fact does not make knowledge infallible or luminous. Many non-naturalists have responded to the sceptic in a similar manner, insisting that knowledge is not an infallible mental state, one in which one knows that one knows. Williamson's innovation is found in his insistence that knowledge is a natural kind, in particular a (fallible) mental state. He thus appeals not to a stipulated sense of 'knowledge' which only defeats the sceptic by definition, but rather to a potentially much more powerful account of knowledge as a distinct mental state. If *that* is what knowledge is, the justified belief held by the sceptic to be impossible is no less real than other natural states, mental or otherwise.

Williamson profoundly agrees with the ancient epistemologists that the possibility of knowing is a condition for the defeat of the sceptic. He also agrees that this possibility must refer to a natural mental state if the defeat is not to be a completely hollow victory. The dispute between the ancient naturalists in epistemology and Williamson regards the character of this mental state; the one holds it to be infallible or luminous, and the other that it is not so. All parties agree that if S knows p, p is true, but they disagree as to whether S knows p if and only if S knows that S knows p. It might appear that this dispute flows from a prior dispute as to the possibility of empirical knowledge, with Plato, Aristotle and Plotinus denying this and Williamson, by contrast, affirming that all, or nearly all, our knowledge is in fact empirical. One might then conjecture that this is not quite right for the Stoics. They are after all congenial to empirical knowledge even if they do not think that this exhausts all that the sage knows. Their willingness to accept the principle that knowledge is 'incontrovertible by *logos*' is perhaps where they went wrong. That principle only makes sense if knowledge is the sort of thing that Plato and Aristotle thought it to be. On this interpretation, what the Stoics should have said with Williamson is that knowledge is a fallible natural mental state. As such it is not the preserve of the sage. Recognising knowledge to be a slightly more humble achievement than what their predecessors supposed it to be, the sceptic is defeated. The abandonment of even the possibility of the paradigmatic all-knowing sage seems a more than fair price to pay for this victory.

This is no doubt an attractive story. I doubt that it is one that will satisfy Plato and Aristotle and perhaps even the Stoics, too. It will certainly not satisfy those non-naturalists who maintain that a justified belief that p could only be knowledge or flow from knowledge if the justification entailed the truth of p. That is, knowing requires more than meeting the purely formal condition that if S knows p, p is true. It requires that S must know that S's belief is justified, or even on some formulations that S must know that he knows. Williamson and many non-naturalists agree that this condition cannot normally be met. They disagree in the appropriate inference to draw from this; the former, that knowledge is a distinct non-luminous mental state, the latter that knowledge can be stipulated to be attributable when certain justificatory conditions are met.

The ancient epistemologists share with the non-naturalists the supposition that if knowledge is not an infallible mental state, knowledge is not distinct from true justified belief. Indeed, they suppose that mental states are basically infallible or incorrigible, which if false, as Williamson's anti-luminosity argument would have it, might suggest that knowledge is not a mental state at all. Yet, the ancients share with the sceptics – and against the non-naturalists – the supposition that if knowledge is *not* a distinct, infallible mental state, justification is largely a bluff. With Williamson, they suppose that knowledge is a distinct mental state and that the possibility of knowledge is the prophylactic against scepticism. They also agree that knowledge alone justifies belief. Against Williamson, they insist that the distinct mental state that is knowledge is not to be found in our relation to the sensible world. Knowledge is no more of 'things that can be otherwise' than is vision of sounds. They make the bold claim that only things that *cannot* be otherwise are knowable because it is only these that we can cognise infallibly.

Williamson denies that if one knows, one knows that one knows. His denial stems in part from his argument that what one knows when one knows is a proposition. If the ancients insist on infallibility as a necessary condition for knowing, and gloss infallibility as 'knowing that one knows', they would seem to be inviting the objection that infallible propositional knowledge is impossible. We have already canvassed the reason for this, namely, that propositional 'content' does not determine the world to be one way or another. It is, I think, more accurate to represent the ancient position as maintaining that if the phrase 'knowing that one knows' has any use as an explanation of infallibility, the knowing here should not be supposed to be of propositions; rather, it is the self-reflexivity of a mental state, the being aware of the state one is in. The expressions of that state to which one might stand in some propositional attitude are attendant upon the state itself. It is important to realise that the question of whether or not embodied human beings are capable of achieving such a mental state is a separate one. The frequent negative answer to this question is, at least in the case of Plato, Aristotle and Plotinus, conjoined with another bold claim to the effect that if we were not capable of somehow achieving such a mental state, we would not be capable of other modes of higher cognition.

Williamson's case for the distinctiveness of the mental state of knowing rests importantly on his argument that we can often tell the difference between one who knows and one who merely believes by their behaviour. The other two properties of knowledge mentioned above – that only knowledge justifies belief and that only knowledge warrants assertion – seem either question-begging or to rest upon the previous property. Yet, as a number of critics have pointed out, the argument based on behaviour is a dubious one. It is also not too difficult to construct appropriate Pyrrhonian tropes in opposition to it. The plausibility of these tropes will depend on the extent to which we are convinced that 'being evident to me' does not entail knowing (as opposed to merely believing) unless being evident to me guarantees that I know. If it does not, one can easily imagine the state of one to whom p is evident, though p be false. And if that is possible, it is difficult to see how we could confidently discern the difference between the behaviour of the knower and the behaviour of the mere believer, indeed, of the believer who believes something false. Sometimes justified beliefs are false; but on Williamson's view, the only justified beliefs are those that amount to knowledge, which can never be false.

The comparison of the ancient view and the naturalism of Williamson and others is hampered by the fact that lying beneath their agreement that the defeat of scepticism depends on the possibility of there being a *ne plus ultra* of cognition other than mere belief is a profound disagreement. It is not just that Williamson has a more modest view of what that mode of cognition is capable of and what its objects are. The ancient view is that scepticism is not defeated unless we are capable of a mode of cognition far more exalted than anything Williamson is prepared to countenance. Williamson raises the stakes by insisting that the requisite mode of cognition is a natural state. This naturalism is far removed from that of Kornblith or Quine, neither of whom are focused on the sceptical challenge to justification. The ancient naturalists would point out, I suspect, that if knowledge were the modest and quotidian type of natural mental state that Williamson takes it to be, counterfactually, radical scepticism would not even be an intelligible or coherent position.

4 CONCLUDING REMARKS

I began this book by noting that any ancient form of epistemological naturalism is prima facie susceptible to being made irrelevant by scientific advances in the understanding of nature. Now, in the light of the details of my account, I would like to return briefly to my original question about the standing of the ancient approach to knowledge today, particularly in comparison with contemporary versions of naturalism.

A striking feature of the analysis of thinking in Plato, Aristotle and Plotinus is the immateriality or incorporeality of thought. If thinkers were not immaterial, they would be incapable of the self-reflexivity required for thinking. This self-reflexivity, thematised explicitly by Plotinus, is what, in my view, Plato was referring to when he spoke in *Theaetetus* of the 'having' of a 'piece of knowledge' as opposed to merely 'possessing it' and what Aristotle was referring to when he spoke of the actualisation of thinking by the identification of the thinker with the object thought. The basic argument that only an immaterial subject is capable of self-reflexive thinking is this. A material thing could not be both the identical subject of the content or object of thought and the subject that is aware of that content. The material part that instantiates the content could not be identical with another material part that 'cognises' the first. But self-reflexivity requires the identity of both subjects. That is, there must be only a conceptual distinction between the subject of the content and the subject of the awareness of the content. Unqualified or paradigmatic self-reflexivity is what the ancients generally took to be a state of knowing. Their doubts about the attainment of this state while embodied did not prevent them from maintaining that all embodied states of higher cognition depend on the subject being immaterial. Owing to embodiment and to the fact that the things we cognise while embodied are material or external to our intellects, embodied self-reflexivity is incomplete or imperfect. So, we would not be capable of embodied higher cognition if we were not the sorts of subjects capable of knowledge.

The point can be made in a slightly different manner. Whether we use the Platonic metaphors of seeing or the Aristotelian metaphor of touching for the identification of thinker with the intelligible object of thought, such an intelligible is not exhausted by its particular instantiation. There is a specificity in the universal, determinable, intelligible object that could not be identical with the specificity of a particular, determinate, material state. But if thinking were a material process or state, the presence of the intelligible in the intellect would be such a particular instantiation, that is, a particular, determinate material state. For example, we could not understand pure functions or logical relations if we were material subjects. But we can acquire such understanding. So, the subject of understanding is not material. If, by contrast, understanding or knowing is identical with following a rule implied by the content of the intelligible object, then anything capable of following that rule has understanding. Ancient epistemological naturalism insists on the distinction between following a rule and understanding a rule that is being followed. The achievement that is understanding or knowing is not open to arbitrary stipulation just as it is not reducible to a determinate material state.

It seems to me we do not have to assent to Plato's doctrine of recollection and the pre-existence of the soul or Aristotle's argument for an active or agent intellect or Plotinus' argument for an undescended intellect in order to appreciate the force of the above argument for the immateriality of thought. We can also acknowledge the as yet unsolved difficulty of explaining how immaterial thinkers are related to their bodies. But acknowledging this difficulty does not seem to me to compel rejection of the argument for the immateriality of thought.

I am not proposing ancient epistemology as the clear winner among the three contestants I have discussed in this book. I do think, however, that if we believe that a naturalistic account of knowledge has as serious chance of being right, we should not out of deference to empirical science assume that this naturalism must be something like one of the versions discussed in this chapter. Nor, if we believe that contemporary naturalism has insurmountable problems, should we assume out of the same deference that the only alternative is some version of what I have called the criteriological approach. The ancient account of knowledge and belief rests upon certain putative features of human cognition, like its immateriality, that could not in principle be explained by empirical science. Contemporary epistemology can only be enriched by keeping its ancient counterpart in the discussion.

Further reading

This essay has two purposes: (1) to offer the interested reader some suggestions for further reading in the topics dealt with in this book and (2) to indicate the works of other scholars who disagree (sometimes emphatically) with my interpretations. It is far from my intention to leave the reader with the impression that I have not here said controversial things. Space has prevented me from engaging directly with those whose carefully crafted interpretations differ from mine. I note the evident fact that a modern day Pyrrhonist could construct a pretty trope from the disagreements among scholars in ancient philosophy. I shall limit my references to works in English, though much excellent work in French, German and Italian exists. For a full bibliography of material largely in English up to 1990 on the subjects covered in chapters 2 to 6 see Stephen Everson (ed.), *Companions to Ancient Thought I. Epistemology* (Cambridge University Press, 1990).

Chapter 1. There is not a great deal of material dealing directly with ancient epistemological naturalism, especially in contrast to contemporary naturalism and non-naturalism. A good starting point for appreciating the ancient Greek philosophical concept of nature in relation to problems about knowledge and belief is James Lesher's essay, 'Early Interest in Knowledge', in A. A. Long (ed.), *The Cambridge Companion to Early Greek Philosophy* (Cambridge University Press, 1999), 225–49. The volume as well contains many useful articles on aspects of epistemology in the Presocratic philosophers. See also Michael Frede and Gisela Striker (eds.), *Rationality in Greek Thought* (Oxford: Clarendon Press, 1996), especially the introduction by Frede, which collects a number of essays on one of the core ideas underlying the debates of epistemology in antiquity. On the Standard Analysis and its discontents, an extremely helpful though now somewhat dated monograph is Robert K. Shope's *The Analysis of Knowing* (Princeton University Press, 1983). A somewhat more wide-ranging treatment of the Standard Analysis and various alternatives to it is provided by Michael Williams in *Problems of Knowledge. A Critical Introduction to Epistemology* (Oxford University Press, 2001). A sadly neglected monograph by Panayot Butchvarov, *The Concept of Knowledge* (Evanston, IL: Northwestern University Press, 1970), offers a sophisticated and penetrating critique of the Standard Analysis, and more generally issues surrounding the nature of knowledge. A seminal critique of both a criteriological approach to knowledge and, incidentally to ancient naturalism is Richard Rorty's *Philosophy and the Mirror of Nature* (Princeton University Press, 1979).

Chapter 2. See the essay by Edward Hussey, in Everson, *Companions to Ancient Thought I*, (above), 'The Beginning of Epistemology: From Homer to Philolaus', 11–38, for a good introduction to epistemology in the period. On Xenophanes' epistemology see James Lesher's *Xenophanes of Colophon. Fragments: A Text and Translation with a Commentary* (Toronto/Buffalo/London: University of Toronto Press, 1992), which includes a good bibliography of the scholarship on Xenophanes; and his 'Early Interest in Knowledge' in A. A. Long (ed.), *The Cambridge Companion to Early Greek Philosophy* (Cambridge University Press, 1999), 225–49. Two other volumes in the Toronto series are similarly useful. See C. C. W. Taylor, *The Atomists: Leucippus and Democritus. Fragments: A Text and Translation with a Commentary* (Toronto/Buffalo/London: University of Toronto Press, 1999) and David Gallop, *Parmenides of Elea. Fragments: A Text and Translation with an Introduction* (Toronto/London/Buffalo: University of Toronto Press, 1984). Mi-Kyoung Lee's *Epistemology After Protagoras. Responses to Relativism in Plato, Aristotle, and Democritus* (Oxford University Press, 2005) is an excellent treatment of epistemological issues uniting Presocratics and their successors. For analyses of Protagoras' argument that 'man is the measure of all things' see Myles Burnyeat's 'Protagoras and Self-refutation in Later Greek Philosophy', *Philosophical Review* 85 (1976), 44–69; and Gail Fine's 'Protagorean Relativisms', *Proceedings of the Boston Area Colloquium on Ancient Philosophy* 19, ed. J. Cleary and W. Wians (Lanham, MD: University Press of America, 1996), 211–43; and her reply to Burnyeat, 'Relativism and Self-Refutation: Plato, Protagoras, and Burnyeat', in Jyl Gentzler (ed.), *Method in Ancient Philosophy* (Oxford: Clarendon Press, 1998), 138–63. Of the enormous literature on Parmenides, for a good discussion of the epistemological implications of his argument see Patricia Curd, *The Legacy of Parmenides* (Princeton University Press, 1998); reprinted with a new introduction (Las Vegas: Parmenides Press, 2004). Mention here should be made of a topic not dealt with in this book, but well treated by Voula Tsouna in *The Epistemology of the Cyrenaic School* (Cambridge University Press, 1998), on the Socratic school which offered a form of scepticism flowing from their ethical hedonism.

Chapter 3. Most of the countless books on Plato's philosophy touch at least in part on his epistemology or various aspects of it. On the epistemological origins of Platonic epistemology in the so-called Socratic elenchus, see an influential paper by Peter Geach, 'Plato's *Euthyphro*: An Analysis and Commentary,' *Monist* 50 (1966), 369–82. Geach claimed that it was a fallacy to maintain that knowledge of a Form was prior to the recognition of its putative instances. See also along these lines Russell Dancy, *Plato's Introduction of Forms* (Cambridge University Press, 2004), 35–64; and David Wolfsdorf, 'The Socratic Fallacy and the Epistemological Priority of Definitional Knowledge', *Apeiron* 37 (2004), 35–67. An older book with which I disagree though from which I have learned a great deal is by Jon Moline, *Plato's Theory of Understanding* (Madison, WI: The University of Wisconsin Press, 1981). Another recent work of note is by Dominic Scott, *Recollection and Experience. Plato's Theory of Learning and its Successors* (Cambridge University Press, 1995). I have discussed at length the position developed in this book in Lloyd Gerson, *Knowing Persons. A Study in Plato* (Oxford University Press, 2003), especially chs. 4

and 5. Gail Fine, 'Knowledge and Belief in Plato's *Republic* V', *Archiv für Geschichte der Philosophie* 60 (1978), 121–39, reprinted in Gail Fine (ed.), *Plato I. Metaphysics and Epistemology* (Oxford University Press, 1999), in 'Knowledge and Belief in *Republic* V–VII', in Everson, *Companions to Ancient Thought I*, 85–115, in 'Knowledge and True Belief in the *Meno*', *Oxford Studies in Ancient Philosophy* 27 (2004), 41–81 and in a number of other papers has defended about as well as can be the position which is diametrically opposed to the one I defend here, namely, that for Plato the objects of knowledge and belief are different. This volume also contains a number of other helpful essays on knowledge and belief in Plato. Myles Burnyeat in his monograph-length introduction to *The Theaetetus of Plato* (Indianapolis: Hackett Publishing Co., 1990), argues in a nuanced fashion that at least in this dialogue Plato seems to be moving towards the position that Fine maintains Plato holds in *Republic*. Allan Silverman's *The Dialectic of Essence* (Princeton University Press, 2002) is focused on metaphysical considerations in Plato's dialogues, thereby illuminating much that concerns his account of knowledge. See Richard Sorabji, 'Myths About Non-Propositional Thought', in *Language and Logos. Studies in Ancient Greek Philosophy Presented to G. E. L. Owen* (Cambridge University Press, 1982), 295–314, for an influential argument against one position taken in the present work. On mathematical developments within Plato's philosophy two books by Kenneth Sayre are particularly helpful: *Plato's Later Ontology. A Riddle Resolved* (Princeton University Press, 1983); and *Metaphysics and Method in Plato's Statesman* (New York: Cambridge University Press, 2006). A seminal article by Mitchell Miller in support of Aristotle's testimony regarding Plato's (unwritten) mathematical philosophy is "Unwritten Teachings" in the "*Parmenides*", *Review of Metaphysics* 48 (1995), 591–633.

Wilfred Sellars's 'Empiricism and the Philosophy of Mind', in *Science, Perception and Reality* (Routledge & Kegan Paul, 1963), 127–96, is where the 'myth of the given' is first discussed and criticised.

Chapter 4. A collection of papers on Aristotle's *Posterior Analytics* by Enrico Berti (ed.), *Aristotle on Science: The Posterior Analytics. Proceedings of the Eighth Symposium Aristotelicum* (Padua/New York: Editrice Antenori, 1980), contains a number of superb papers, many of which focus on knowledge in that work. Of special note is Myles Burnyeat's 'Aristotle on Understanding Knowledge,' 97–139. See the reply by James Lesher, 'On Aristotelian *Epistēmē* as Understanding', *Ancient Philosophy* 221 (2001), 45–55. See also Aryeh Kosman's 'Understanding, Explanation, and Insight in Aristotle's *Posterior Analytics*', in E. N. Lee, A. P. D. Mourelatos and R. M. Rorty (eds.), *Exegesis and Argument: Studies in Greek Philosophy Presented to Gregory Vlastos* (New York: Humanities Press, 1973), 374–92. Michael Wedin in his *Mind and Imagination in Aristotle* (New Haven: Yale University Press, 1988) acutely argues for what I take to be a reductivist position about knowledge in Aristotle, one which would set him sharply apart from Plato. See Martha Nussbaum and Amélie Rorty (eds.), *Essays on Aristotle's De Anima*, (Oxford: Clarendon Press, 1992) for a good collection of essays both on epistemological matters and on other psychological issues in that work. C. D. C. Reeve's *Substantial Knowledge. Aristotle's Metaphysics* (Indianapolis: Hackett Publishing

Co., 2000), especially chs. 2 and 3, contains a good discussion of Aristotelian epistemology generally. For a recent nuanced defence of the view that the intellect in *De Anima* chapter five is in fact identical with the Unmoved Mover, see Victor Caston, 'Aristotle's Two Intellects: A Modest Proposal', *Phronesis* 44 (1999), 199–227.

Chapter 5. In recent years there has been a remarkable increase in scholarship on the material dealt with in this chapter and the next. The best place to begin is with A. A. Long and D. N. Sedley, *The Hellenistic Philosophers* (2 vols., Cambridge University Press, 1987), with volume I containing translations of the principal sources with a philosophical commentary and volume II containing the Greek and Latin texts. There are in volume I helpful chapters on Epicurean, Stoic and sceptical epistemology. Another major resource is Keimpe Algra, Jonathan Barnes, Jaap Mansfeld and Malcolm Schofield (eds.), *The Cambridge History of Hellenistic Philosophy* (Cambridge University Press, 1999). This volume contains substantial essays on Epicurean, Stoic and Academic epistemology. Also see Malcolm Schofield, Myles Burnyeat and Jonathan Barnes (eds.), *Doubt and Dogmatism. Studies in Hellenistic Epistemology* (Oxford: Clarendon Press, 1980). Also see Gisela Striker's *Essays on Hellenistic Epistemology and Ethics* (Cambridge University Press, 1996). A useful study on a crucial topic in Hellenistic epistemology is James Allen's *Inference From Signs. Ancient Debates About the Nature of Evidence* (Oxford: Clarendon Press, 2001). On Epicurean epistemology in particular see Stephen Everson's 'Epicurus on the Truth of the Senses', in Everson, *Companions to Ancient Thought I*, 161–83; C. C. W. Taylor's 'All Perceptions are True', in Schofield, Burnyeat and Barnes, *Doubt and Dogmatism*, 105–24; and Elizabeth Asmis's *Epicurus' Scientific Method* (Ithaca: Cornell University Press, 1984). On Stoic epistemology see Julia Annas's 'Stoic Epistemology', in Everson, *Companions to Ancient Thought I*, 184–203; R. J. Hankinson's 'Stoic Epistemology', in Brad Inwood (ed.), *The Cambridge Companion to the Stoics* (Cambridge Univeristy Press, 2003), 59–84; B. Reed, 'The Stoics' Account of the Cognitive Impression', *Oxford Studies in Ancient Philosophy* 23 (Oxford University Press, 2002), 147–80; Casey Perin, 'Stoic Epistemology and the Limits of Externalism', *Ancient Philosophy* 25 (2005), 383–401.

Chapter 6. Not surprisingly, ancient scepticism – as found in the Academy and in its Pyrrhonist versions – is the topic in ancient epistemology that resonates most frequently with contemporary philosophers. In addition to the collections mentioned above, see Richard Bett, *Pyrrho. His Antecedents and his Legacy* (Oxford University Press, 2000); Myles Burnyeat (ed.), *The Skeptical Tradition* (Berkeley/Los Angeles/London: University of California Press, 1983); Jonathan Barnes, *The Toils of Scepticism* (Cambridge University Press, 1990); Christopher Hookway, *Scepticism* (London: Routledge, 1990); Benson Mates, *The Skeptic Way* (Oxford University Press, 1996), which has a substantial philosophical introduction to a translation of Sextus' *Outlines of Pyrrhonism*; Alan Bailey, *Sextus Empiricus and Pyrrhonean Scepticism* (Oxford University Press, 2002). Peter Unger, *Ignorance. A Case for Scepticism* (Oxford: Clarendon Press, 1975) argues without reference to the ancient positions for scepticism about knowledge which, like the Pyrrhonists, entails scepticism about the possibility of rational belief as well.

A good starting-point for considering contemporary responses to scepticism is Steven Luper-Foy (ed.), *The Possibility of Knowledge. Nozick and his Critic* (Totawa, NJ: Rowman and Littlefield, 1987), a collection of wide-ranging essays primarily focused on Robert Nozick's attempted refutation of scepticism. Also, see Barry Stroud's *The Significance of Philosophical Scepticism* (Oxford University Press, 1984); Keith DeRose, 'Solving the Skeptical Puzzle', *The Philosophical Review* 104 (1995), 1–52; R. J. Fogelin, *Pyrrhonian Reflections on Knowledge and Justification* (New York: Oxford University Press, 1994). See also Julia Annas, 'Plato the Sceptic', in *Oxford Studies in Ancient Philosophy*, supp. (Oxford University Press, 1992), 43–72, which takes up the question of the justification for the Academic claim that scepticism is in harmony with Plato's teaching. On later Academics see Richard Bett, 'Carneades' Pithanon: A Reappraisal of its Role and Status', *Oxford Studies in Ancient Philosophy* 7 (Oxford University Press, 1989), 59–94; Charles Brittain, *Philo of Larissa: The Last of the Academic Sceptics* (Oxford University Press, 2001) and Brad Inwood and Jaap Mansfeld (eds.), *Assent and Agreement: Studies in Cicero's Academic Books* (New York/Leiden: Brill, 1997). Most recently, Charles Brittain has produced a new translation of Cicero's *On Academic Scepticism* (Indianapolis: Hackett Publishing Co., 2006) with an extensive and useful introduction treating of the Academic–Stoic debates.

Chapter 8. Plotinus' epistemology is not easily treated apart from his larger philosophical position, especially his metaphysics. An essay by Eyjólfur Emilsson, 'Cognition and its Objects', in Lloyd Gerson (ed.), *The Cambridge Companion to Plotinus* (Cambridge University Press, 1996), 217–49 is a good place to start. Also see his *Plotinus on Sense-Perception: A Philosophical Study* (Cambridge University Press, 1988). Also in *The Cambridge Companion* is Sara Rappe's 'Self-Knowledge and Subjectivity in the *Enneads*', 250–74, which takes up the theme of self-consciousness in Plotinus' epistemology. Of some value is H. Oosthout's *Modes of Knowledge and the Transcendental: An Introduction to Plotinus Ennead 5.3* (Amsterdam/Philadelphia: B. R. Grüner, 1991). A wider-ranging book on various facets of Plotinus' epistemology is Gary Gertler's *Plotinus. The Experience of Unity* (New York/Berne/Frankfurt: Peter Lang, 1988). Two valuable articles by Richard Wallis are '*Nous* as Experience', in R. B. Harris (ed.) *The Significance of Neoplatonism* (Albany: SUNY Press, 1976), 121–54; and 'Scepticism and Neoplatonism', in W. Haase and H. Temporini (eds.), *Aufstieg und Niedergang der Römische Welt*, 36.1 (Berlin/New York: Walter De Gruyter, 1989), 911–54. See also A. C. Lloyd, *The Anatomy of Neoplatonism* (Oxford: Clarendon Press, 1990), ch. 6; and Lloyd Gerson, *Plotinus. Arguments of the Philosophers* (London: Routledge, 1994), ch. 7. A valuable collection of essays on Neoplatonism generally that includes many discussions of epistemological matters is John Cleary (ed.), *The Perennial Tradition of Neoplatonism* (Leuven: University Press, 1997). Another collection on Plotinus with a number of articles that address themes in this chapter is Lloyd Gerson (ed.), *Plotinus, American Catholic Philosophical Quarterly* 71 (1997).

Chapter 9. A useful collection of essays on Quine's epistemology is Robert Barrett and Robert Gibson (eds.), *Perspectives on Quine* (Oxford: Blackwell, 1990). Hilary Kornblith edited a collection *Naturalizing Epistemology* (Cambridge,

MA: MIT Press, 1987) that includes seminal essays on the pros and cons of naturalism. His book *Knowledge and its Place in Nature* (Oxford University Press, 2002) elaborates on earlier work. An influential argument against naturalism in epistemology is by Jaegwon Kim, 'What is "Naturalized Epistemology?"', *Philosophical Perspectives* 2, Epistemology (1988), 381–405. See also Hilary Putnam's 'Why Reason Can't be Naturalized', in H. Putnam, *Realism and Reason: Philosophical Papers, III* (Cambridge University Press, 1983), 229–47; Philip Kitcher, 'The Naturalists Return', *The Philosophical Review* 101 (1992), 53–114; Richard Fumerton 'Skepticism and Naturalistic Epistemology', *Midwest Studies in Philosophy* 19 (1994), 321–40; Jeffrey Tile's 'The Dogma of Kornblith's Naturalism', *Synthese* 120 (1999), 311–24; José Bermúdez's 'Knowledge, Naturalism, and Cognitive Ethology: Kornblith's *Knowledge and its Place in Nature*', *Philosophical Studies* 127 (2006), 299–316. In addition to Timothy Williamson's *Knowledge and its Limits* (Oxford University Press, 2000) see his 'Scepticism and Evidence', *Philosophy and Phenomenological Research* 60 (2000), 613–28. A review critical of Williamson's naturalism is E. J. Lowe's, 'Is Knowing a State of Mind?', *International Journal of Philosophical Studies* 10 (2002), 483–503. See also the critical reviews by Frank Jackson in *Australasian Journal of Philosophy* 80 (2002), 516–21; and Richard Foley in *Mind* 111 (2002), 718–26. On a contemporary defence of the immateriality of thought see James F. Ross, 'Immaterial Aspects of Thought', *The Journal of Philosophy* 89 (1992), 136–50.

Index of main texts of ancient authors cited

General index